STATE
AND
CONFLICT
IN THE
MIDDLE
EAST

STATE
AND
CONFLICT
IN THE
MIDDLE
EAST

EMERGENCE OF
THE POSTCOLONIAL STATE

Gabriel Ben-Dor

Library of Congress Cataloging in Publication Data

Ben-Dor, Gabriel.
 State and conflict in the Middle East.

 Includes index.
  1. Near East—Politics and government—1945-
2. Jewish-Arab relations. 3. State, The. I. Title.
DS63.1.B46 1983   320.1'0956   82-24616
ISBN 0-03-063559-4

Published in 1983 by Praeger Publishers
CBS Educational and Professional Publishing
a Division of CBS Inc.
521 Fifth Avenue, New York, New York, 10175 U.S.A.

© 1983 by Praeger Publishers

3456789   052   987654321

Printed in the United States of America
on acid-free paper

The modern state power is merely a committee which manages the common business of the bourgeoisie.

Karl Marx

The State presupposes a public power of coercion separated from the aggregate body of its members.

Friedrich Engels

The Lord has entrusted the well-being of the state to five or six people. These should govern the fate of the state.

Ali Pasha (1815-1871)

Stateness may well be a quality developing in societies with a tradition of politically articulated class dissensus, while consensual societies do not in fact require or develop a state.

J. Peter Nettl

Such is the dialectic of the political that the state seeks and must seek to foster the growth of a nation, indeed it must posit its potential coming into being.

Carl. J. Friedrich

We live in a society that has not yet taken form. It is still fluid and agitated and has not yet settled down or taken a stabilised shape.

Gamal Abdel Nasser (1955)

Political science starts with a state and examines how it affects society, while political sociology starts with a society and examines how it affects the state.

Reinhard Bendix and **Seymour Martin Lipset**

The great majority of our nation is not yet Jewish, but human dust, bereft of a single language, without tradition, without roots, without a bond to national life, without the customs of an independent society. We must mend the rents of the Diaspora and form a united nation.

David Ben-Gurion (1948)

An idea that has dominated the political consciousness of modern Arabs is nearing its end, if it is not already a thing of the past. It is the myth of pan-Arabism.... At the height of its power, pan-Arabism could make regimes look small and petty.... What this meant was that states were without sufficient legitimacy.... Now, however, *raison d'état*, once an alien and illegitimate doctrine, is gaining ground. Slowly and grimly, with a great deal of anguish and of outright violence, a "normal" state system is becoming a fact of life.

Fouad Ajami (1977)

The sovereign has a right to govern until another and stronger one shall oust him from power and rule in his stead. The latter will rule by the same title and will have to be acknowledged on the same grounds; for a government, however objectionable, is better than none at all, and between two evils we must choose the lesser.

The **qadi Ibn Jama'a of Damascus** (d.1333)

It is thus clear that the caliphate at first existed without the power-state. Then, the characteristic traits of the caliphate became mixed up and confused. Finally, when its group feeling had separated from the group feeling of the caliphate, the power-state came to exist alone.

Ibn Khaldun (1332-1406)

Preface

This book is written in the genre of "soft" social science; that is, categories, concepts, and logical constructs developed in modern social science are utilized to analyze political problems without, however, following the approach of the more quantitative behavioral sciences by anchoring the argument or analysis in "hard" empirical data. For one thing, such data relevant to the questions here discussed are by and large simply unavailable, due both to the prevailing sociopolitical conditions in most Middle East countries and to the methodological orientation of most social scientists conducting such research. Also, the macro concepts that constitute the backbone of the theoretical argument put forth here do not lend themselves easily to the acquisition of hard data. Yet, a real dilemma exists: the questions discussed in this book seem to cry out for serious discussion and analysis, while concomitant, accurate methods and data are, broadly speaking, out of reach at the moment. I have consciously decided, therefore, to write at a very high level of generalization, not only in the hope that readers will nevertheless find the argument interesting, stimulating, and useful, but also because I am fully confident that the future Middle East, researched by a more sophisticated social science, will present a picture essentially congruent with that depicted in this book.

In the terms identified by Bendix and Lipset, this is a work in political science rather than political sociology. That is, it focuses on the state and its effects on society, rather than the other way around. This is due only partially to my disciplinary background and more to my conviction that it is indeed the state as a generic phenomenon that is the dominating factor in Middle East society and politics today. It is not that I find the state more important than society; rather it is that I find in the real world of the Middle East a concrete situation in which at this stage the overwhelming power of the state shapes the development of society. This argument, of course, will be elucidated in great detail in what follows, and it will have to stand or fall on its own scholarly merits. I feel compelled, however, to emphasize one point at the outset: I neither admire nor worship state power. Quite the contrary, I tend to distrust and even fear it. The values I believe in—creativity, love, fellowship, the free pursuit of individual interests—can be best realized on the personal or communal level; yet these activities are surely unrealizable in the violent disorder accompanying the birth pangs of a "normal" state system. One's values, therefore, ought not to preclude paying attention to the enormous importance of the most comprehensive system by which people organize their lives and the tremendous changes involved in the evolution of that system.

My thinking on the Middle East state included elements and orientations from both comparative politics and international relations. The generic phenomenon of the state helps explain, I believe, the most important domestic and regional conflicts in the area. Moreover, one of the main points argued here is the tremendous importance of the interdependence of these two types of conflicts, linked through the explanatory variable of the state—all this against the historical background of a concrete stage in the political development of the countries. In some ways, therefore, this book cuts across some conventional (and perhaps somewhat artificial) disciplinary lines of international relations, comparative politics, and political history. It will no doubt be criticized on these grounds by experts from each of these fields, but this is a risk I have consciously decided to take.

Originally, I had planned to write a shorter book. I intended to present a concise thesis: a pointed, emphatic argument, with a minimum of footnotes and quotations. Regarding the latter, I wished to avoid the appearance of seeking to impress the reader with endless streams of notes presenting evidence of erudition, and I feared that numerous quotations in a volume of the wide scope and high level of generalization attempted here would detract from the book's readability. I wanted only to acknowledge proper intellectual debts, document certain critical and/or controversial events, direct the reader to further texts on key points where appropriate, and give a fair and balanced picture of the critical and methodological schools and problems relevant to the main thesis. As the study proceeded, however, it became obvious that achieving these aims was incompatible with a short book, for even a minimum involved numerous citations and references. Consequently, the final product is much more heavily documented than I had at first envisaged.

While I have abandoned brevity in order to avoid a cryptic presentation, I have nevertheless sought to make a balanced rather than an exhaustive presentation. Thus, not every point has been documented or footnoted, and the reader must still trust my word that I have indeed read the enormous quantity of pertinent books, articles, and documents that could not be even mentioned, much less quoted, if reasonable limitations of space were not to be ignored. While aware that extensive use of citations tends to break up the text, I decided that the theoretical nature of the present work made it necessary to quote directly and to refer to an extensive body of literature in the footnotes in order to indicate the sources of my ideas, to allow the reader to further pursue points of interest, and to give a modest picture of "the state of the field."

This reorientation drastically altered my attitude to quotations. Thus, in the opening theoretical and historical chapters, the reader may be struck by the frequent and occasionally lengthy direct quotes, often from secondary sources. There are two main reasons for this. First, the principal objective of the book is to generate more explanatory insights, via the use of one key theoretical concept, into phenomena in Middle East politics that are essentially known and have been authoritatively studied by others. Since the ambition is not merely to describe new facts but to reinterpret and to elucidate known phenomena, there is little point in affecting excessive originality when it comes to basic assessments. The reliance on authoritative works by others is obvious, necessary, and natural, and the proper way to acknowledge this is to let the authorities speak for themselves. This applies both to the theoretical background against which my own thesis is set and to the empirical situation in Middle East politics, which the thesis seeks to clarify. Second, my belief in extensive scholarly dialogues as the proper way for the advancement of theoretical social science necessitates the avoidance of contrived originality at all costs in favor of directly relating to pertinent works by predecessors and contemporaries whenever possible. Again, this is best done by letting the particular scholars speak for themselves (whether for purposes of illustration, background, reinforcement, or even controversy). This, in turn, means direct quotation, rather than paraphrasing, in order to reduce the risks of distortion and/or misunderstanding and, particularly where short quotes are concerned, to lessen the adulteration often concomitant with citing out of context. By citing the sometimes lengthy original formulations, these dangers have, I hope, been minimized. While there must inevitably be some loss of "flow," I am confident that in wending their hard but rewarding way through the initial thicket of quotations to my own ideas, serious readers will enrich their knowledge of the complex state of the field both in the study of Middle East politics and in the study of the state in contemporary political science. The complexity of the subject does not make for easy research; presenting this research does not make for easy reading; but I am confident that for the interested reader the effort will be worthwhile.

Transliteration of names, terms, and concepts from Middle East languages to English always presents a problem. I have decided to present frequently used words as they normally appear in the press and literature of the English-speaking countries; less common terms have been transliterated simply in accordance with common sense. For the purposes of this book I see little merit in pedantic, strict transliterations variously used in specialized journals. In direct quotations, however, the original spelling and punctuation have been preserved.

Since most of the substantive chapters of the book address themselves to specific questions involving the Arab states and Israel, these countries receive the lion's share of attention. In the chapter dealing with Islamic stateness, Iran and Turkey naturally occupy a more pivotal place in the analysis. In the opening and concluding chapters the analysis refers to the Middle East as I understand it, namely, the Arab countries, Israel, Iran, and Turkey.

Acknowledgments

Much of what is said in this book is the product of years of thinking on this and related subjects. I began to consider seriously these ideas in the mid- and late 1970s and held numerous discussions about them with friends and colleagues in the Department of Political Science and Middle Eastern History, as well as the Jewish-Arab Center, at the University of Haifa. I gave several papers on related topics and received most useful feedback in conferences variously organized by the Leonard Davis Institute of International Relations at the Hebrew University of Jerusalem; the Shiloach Center for Middle Eastern and African Studies and the "Peace Project" at Tel-Aviv University; the Annual Paterson Conference organized by the Jerusalem Institute for Federal Studies and the Department of Political Studies at Bar-Ilan University; the Study Group on Israel politics at the Lehrman Institute in New York; the Conference on Hierarchy and Stratification organized by the Joint Committee on Near Eastern Studies of the Social Science Research Council and the American Learned Societies in Mount Kisco, New York; the School for Advanced International Studies at the University of Miami; and the Office of Arms Control at the University of Illinois (supported by the Rockefeller Foundation). Several of these institutions supported my efforts with travel and research grants, for which I am very grateful.

The manuscript was written while I was Visiting Professor of Political Science and International Affairs at Carleton University in Ottawa (1979–81), under the auspices of the Canada-Israel Foundation for Academic Exchanges. I would like to express to the Paterson Center for International Programs my appreciation of support in research. Particular gratitude is due to Jon Persson of the Richardson Institute, Lancaster University, for assisting, with a diligence and dedication far beyond the call of duty, in researching, organizing, and editing the material in this book. My thanks, also, to his wife Linda, who has cheerfully and competently overcome the difficulties of transferring a lengthy handwritten—and at times, I am assured, indecipherable—manuscript into a neat and presentable typescript. At this stage, of course, it is customary to absolve everyone from blame related to errors and omissions; therefore, in the context of my earlier comments relating to my intellectual indebtedness to others, I take, for better or worse, the customary full and sole responsibility for the contents and views herein expressed.

I would like to express my thanks to my wife and children, who patiently endured the painful process of producing this volume. I wish to dedicate the book to the memory of two gracious ladies, both of whom regrettably passed away during the preparation of this manuscript: my mother-in-law, Rachel Tetenboim, who heroically struggled to raise a healthy and happy family against great odds in harsh circumstances; and my aunt, Gisella Goldberger, without whose courage and resolve I would not have survived the first year of my life during the dark days of the Holocaust in the Nazi inferno of Europe.

I completed the manuscript in the summer of 1981. I do not believe in updating scholarly books. Political science is not journalism: the book must stand or fall on the merits of the analysis and not on being <u>au courant</u> with newspaper headlines.

The manuscript was thoroughly revised and edited in the summer of 1982—but only to make it more coherent, compact, and readable. I would like to thank Lydia Gareh, who typed the revised version, for a prompt, efficient, and competent job. And I would like to express my profound gratitude to Helen Silman for her patient, cheerful, responsible, and thoroughly competent role in editing the book. She was not only an editor but also a true intellectual partner in developing the final version, of which she was then the first reader. Nothing else would have been more symbolic of her tremendous contribution.

Finally, this is a book by an Israeli scholar on Middle East politics. I have never believed that a person has to be black to have empathy for blacks, has to be a woman to write about women's problems. This is a book about problems common to Israelis, Arabs, Turks, Persians, and many others. What is needed for the writing of such a book is proper training, intellectual honesty, devotion, skill, and a lot of diligent study. These have little to do with a scholar's national origins: none of us should feel obligated to deny (or apologize for) who and what one is. A more stable and peaceful Middle East may or may not be around the corner; scholars of all origins, however, should enter a genuine dialogue about where we are in Middle East politics today and where we go from here. The only pretension of this book is to make a modest contribution to such a dialogue.

Contents

STATE
AND
CONFLICT
IN THE
MIDDLE
EAST

the persistence of the state as a functional unit. The ensuing intellectual debate has, inter alia, exposed a particular difficulty: that of relating the European experience of state formation to the political experiences in developing countries in the postcolonial era. Attempts to construct a new theory have partially foundered on the intractable problem of definition whenever the state is perceived as a generic phenomenon. If, however, the state is treated as a variable phenomenon, [6] then a more flexible theory emerges, which greatly assists a sensible comparison between European states' evolution and the more recent arrivals to the scene, the Third World states. When such a comparison is possible, forecasting developments in these seemingly inherently unstable states has a sounder theoretical base.

Among the contributors to the special issue of Daedalus, George Armstrong Kelly attempts the most ambitious definition—even characterization—of the state. [7]

> At its core, the state is a juridical ensemble that enables men—especially strangers—to live together in relative peace, intelligible concord, and with reasonable expectations of one another's performances. This necessarily implies coercion and punishment, but it implies much more. . . .
> In brief, the normative state has pacification, adjudication, and guidance functions. Its purpose is not to fulfill instantly the wants and needs of its citizenry (however organised in tribes, "estates", groups, or parties) but rather best to express the values that are its own in a lawful way. This entails, historically and globally, that the parliamentary or democratic regime is not the only legitimate form of state, although it denies the legitimacy of countless regimes (modern states would seem to have to be constitutional, i.e., with the distinguishing features of guarantism, pluralism, and the division of powers). It implies that the state requires the capacity of wisdom, arbitration, and authority. Wisdom is a function of the talent and integrity of the state's agents, the propriety of its institutions, and the gathered strength of its political traditions. Arbitration depends on a sensitive balancing of values, rights, and interests by the appropriate parts of the state machinery (especially judicial and administrative). Authority, whose failure in the modern world was so eloquently dissected by Hannah Arendt, [8] "depends on an acquiescence in certain forms and uses

of power; but it does not inhere totally in persons or even in role-playing persons as a general rule. It is an intersubjective sensing of patterns of conformity built on social and public confidence."[9] The task of state-building and state-maintenance is to act so as to approach these conditions. Conversely, it will be the task of citizens to contribute to the enterprise by debating their interests and values in order to cultivate a common viewpoint, by judgment and surveillance of the state's agents, by adaptation to consensual rules and procedures, by forming reservoirs of new capacities, and by practicing a reciprocity of respect. A state's dignity is articulated through its agents and magistrates; its legitimacy is confirmed or consented to by its citizens, that is, all those who hold rights within it and receive its protection.[10]

Appropriately, Kelly ends on this note: "If it should be asked 'Who needs a theory of citizenship?' my answer would be 'The state'. But first there must be a theory of the state to inform the citizen."[11]

It appears that the closest thing to such a theory of the state at our disposal from neoclassicist or revisionist sources is a brilliant effort by the late British political sociologist J. P. Nettl in a very important article worthy of greater attention.[12] It definitely seems that most social scientists attempting to look at the analytical and empirical relationships between states and nationalism, and those who try to treat the question of the state not as a given but as a variable phenomenon, draw significantly on Nettl's conceptualization in one way or another, as the Tilly volume demonstrates.[13] Nettl's approach, definition, and criteria deserve, therefore, detailed and serious scrutiny.

The first and in many ways the most important thing to note in this context is that Nettl does not treat the state as a given generic phenomenon; its importance does not lie in its being the ubiquitous unit of analysis (as was assumed in an earlier age), sure to be found in the real world of politics. Quite to the contrary, its importance lies in the analyst's ability to ask significant, researchable questions about its existence (and degree thereof) in any given, particular case: "This argument suggests that the concept of the state is and ought to be treated as a variable in social science, as a reflection of the varying empirical reality with which social science concerns itself."[14] In other words, a rigid assumption that states exist and are terribly important in every country/society creates a situation in which "the concept of state is at risk. . . . But if it can be made into an operating variable that points up significant

differences and discontinuities between societies, making possible
systematically qualitative or even quantitative distinctions, there
may be a case for bringing it back in."[15]

Nettl rightly goes on to suggest that several definitional and
conceptual problems have to be addressed in order to engender the
possibility of rigorous comparative analysis, for which, of course,
reasonably well-defined dimensions of variance are needed. First,
then, comes the definition of the state, which in itself encompasses
several different dimensions. What is the state, according to Nettl?

> 1. In the first place, it is a collectivity that summates
> a set of functions and structures in order to generalize
> their applicability. . . . The difficulty of relating state
> and sovereignty as a primary identification is not so
> much that the relationship is, in socio-political terms,
> inapplicable as that it is insufficient, both in the sense
> that it is too narrow by leaving out spatial and social
> dimensions and that it is too broad in that it fails to
> "prepare" the concept for the right level at which it re-
> lates to other relevant concepts. . . . The overall con-
> ceptual identification of state with law, with bureaucracy,
> or with government merely reimposes an artificial (and
> to a large extent self-defining) notion of state by grouping
> structures that are better particularized and that are part
> of the state in some empirical situations but not in many
> others where some or all of these structures exist and
> function without any valid notion or phenomenon of state
> at all. In fact, as we shall see, they may substitute for
> the state in certain cases altogether. . . .
>
> 2. In the second place, and following from the sum-
> mating aspect, the state represents a unit in the field of
> international relations. . . . Here the state is the basic,
> irreducible unit, equivalent to the individual person in a
> society. It is nowadays fashionable to refer to "national
> actors" in this role rather than states, but this is mainly
> to provide a sensible contrast to international and supra-
> national units that analysts hopefully see emerging as
> part of a more ordered international system—an analyti-
> cal convenience rather than a genuine erosion of the
> state. . . . For almost all intents and purposes the
> state acts for the society internationally. . . . In
> short, the state is the gatekeeper between intrasocietal
> and extrasocietal flows of action.
>
> 3. Third, the state represents an autonomous col-
> lectivity as well as a summating concept of high societal

generality. It is thus in a functional sense a distinct sector or arena of society. [This] . . . emphasizes what is in fact a limitation upon sovereignty; every association tends toward maximization of autonomy, and once we accept a pluralistic view of society, the greater autonomy of the state vis-à-vis other associations or collectivities becomes an empirical question for each individual case. . . .

4. Fourth, the state is essentially a sociocultural phenomenon. This follows from the liberation of the concept from exclusive association with particular structures, and from the emphasis on autonomy. It is also strongly suggested by empirical evidence. . . . What is being argued here is that the identification of state with nation—indeed, the more general recognition of the state as a significant factor in political and social life—depends not only on empirical problems relating to the activity and structure of a particular state but on the existence of a cultural disposition to allot recognition to the conceptual existence of a state at all. This disposition can be isolated in various ways. One is historical: Is there a historical tradition in any particular society for the existence, primacy, autonomy, and sovereignty of a state? Another is intellectual: Do the political ideas and theories of the society past or present incorporate a notion of state, and what role do they assign to it? Yet another approach is cultural: To what extent have individuals generalized the concept and cognition of state in their perceptions and actions, and to what extent are such cognitions salient? This last is perhaps the most important of the approaches, since it appears to be the only one that makes possible any kind of systematic ordering in what must otherwise seem to be a random proliferation of quantitatively as well as qualitatively distinct phenomena captured by the all too general notion of state.[16]

These are, according to Nettl, the "variable qualities of statehood or 'stateness.'"[17] Nettl goes on to demonstrate the utility of these variables of stateness by making observations on the nature of the state in various Western societies along the four dimensions identified, and along historical, intellectual, and cultural lines. Perhaps the most intriguing usage Nettl makes of the concepts of stateness in its cultural dimension is in the European context.

The way to approach this problem is simply to inquire to what extent notions of state have become incorporated in the thinking and actions of individual citizens in different societies. In Italy and France, the state is instantly recognizable as an area of autonomous action, parallel to other spheres of economy, religion, family, and so on. In Germany, too, there is some of this autonomy, though as we have seen, it is, as in France, strongly linked to notions of supremacy and superordination. In England, it would be on the whole difficult to find an agreed definition at all, while in the United States, the word has a precise but totally different meaning in contradistinction to its European meaning—namely, the residual area of regional government and territory. Insofar as there is any salient notion of autonomy in the area of central government, there it is sometimes characterized by the term "United States": "Governor resists United States intervention. . . ." It would not be overly difficult to quantify the relative cultural impact of notions of state on individuals by asking specific questions cross-nationally. In all probability we would find that responses that specify "state" in certain countries would specify quite different terms and structures in others. This raises a problem of functional substitution. . . .

There is of course no need to rely only on a positive orientation toward the state as evidence of a high degree of stateness. The salient negative attitudes toward the state, as in Italy, and the whole antipathy of etatisme in countries like Belgium, and formerly in France among the business community, are both evidence of a high level of stateness in the individual cognition within these societies. As already pointed out, the saliency of state is positively correlated with tendencies to well-structured dissociation and is thus a distinct factor of both integration and disintegration, whereas societies that do not have a strongly developed concept of state have to manage their problems of integration and control in more informal, socially consensual ways. Where they succeed in diffusing a high degree of internalized norms, the articulation of dissent accordingly finds it harder to structure itself effectively. Stateness as a sociocultural phenomenon accordingly operates as a variable in the context of formal or informal mechanisms of both non-native control and its complement, normative dissent.[18]

In the wake of a lengthy analysis Nettl goes on to develop the notion of stateness, or the saliency of the state, by examining the functions the state performs and by analyzing the way these functions are performed in societies in the absence of the state. There are five such functions:[19] (1) the process of administration; (2) the institutionalization of sovereignty;[20] (3) sectoral autonomy; (4) law enforcement; (5) social goal attainment and representation.

Here again, in the elaboration of the functions, Nettl makes a number of unorthodox observations. In the discussion of sectoral autonomy, for example, he states:

> Autonomy and sovereignty in this respect appear as polar opposites; as we have already pointed out, the deeply anchored acceptance of governmental sovereignty, together with the deferential class structure of society, inhibits as well as compensates for the absence of any concept of state autonomy. . . . , [that] stateness may well be a quality developing in societies with a tradition of politically articulated class dissensus, while consensual societies do not in fact require or develop a state, [and] this suggests that the state may, in sociological terms, be the integrative phenomenon of socio-political dissensus typical for a certain period of historical development—quite the contrary of the more frequent and traditional notion of the state as the epitome of national or societal consensus.[21]

Yet again, a provocative comparative analysis follows the discussion of law enforcement. "Thus to a considerable extent we may regard the problem of functional equivalence in the following terms: continental Europe—state; Britain—political parties; the United States—the law."[22] And more stimulating ideas are generated in the discussion of the last function, social goal attainment: "It may well be argued that even in countries with a high level of stateness the state does not necessarily act as the structural quintessence of the political system and therefore does not necessarily fulfil either goal-setting or goal-attainment functions."[23]

> The absence of a potentially inhibiting tradition of stateness may make the development of functional political prerequisites for goal-attainment easier and more flexible. . . . This analysis therefore suggests that the variable development of stateness in different societies is a crucial factor in specifying the nature of those societies' politics. . . . But if the area in

question is already filled with a set of state norms or
even state morality, this norm-creating function of
politics is necessarily inhibited; all that can be left
is the articulation of interests. This is necessarily
the lower "level" of politics. [24]

As the above account has indicated, the scope and depth of
Nettl's conceptual framework are impressive. There are, however,
three major problems with his formulation.

First, even though the present author admits to being far from
a specialist on European politics or political history, Nettl seems to
vastly overstate his case in differentiating between the continental
European state, on the one hand, and the Anglo-American/Soviet
types, on the other. This, of course, is not a fatal flaw, for it was
merely intended to show the potential for generalizations inherent in
the conceptual framework. One need not accept lock, stock, and
barrel what Nettl has to say on parties and states in Western countries in order to recognize the rich possibilities of his basic approach.

Second and much more serious are the difficulties of definition
and methodology. The state—and therefore, stateness—is defined in
four different dimensions and performs five different functions. Do
all four dimensions of the definition of stateness necessarily go together? Is any one of them intrinsically more important than the
others? What is the "stateness score" of a country that is very high
on two dimensions and very low on others? Is such a case logically
and empirically possible? All these questions are of immense practical value and importance; yet they are unasked, much less answered.

In this context, immense methodological difficulties arise as the
possibility of research on the macro level is entertained. Recall that
most of Nettl's own generalizations were formulated in response to
his three basic approaches, which are really questions: "Is there a
historical tradition in any particular society for the existence, primacy, autonomy, and sovereignty of a state?"[25] This question is in
principle answerable by sound historical scholarship, although, obviously, historians will disagree on almost any given case due to the
lack of specific criteria.

The next question for Nettl is "intellectual: Do the political
ideas and theories of the society past or present incorporate a notion
of state, and what role do they assign it?"[26] Again, there is no reason why intellectual historians and political theorists should be unable to answer this question and, again, there is no particular reason
why they should be able to agree on answers any more than on a host
of similar problems that have been in the forefront of their research
from time immemorial.

Finally, writes Nettl,

Yet another approach is cultural: To what extent have
individuals generalized the concept and cognition of state
in their perceptions and actions, and to what extent are
such cognitions salient? This last is perhaps the most
important of the approaches, since it appears to be the
only one that makes possible any kind of systematic ordering in what must otherwise seem to be a random proliferation of quantitatively as well as qualitatively distinct phenomena captured by the all too general notion of
state.[27]

Indeed, this is a crucial question. Also, it appears to be the
most answerable of the three by the methods of contemporary social
science (say, the kind of survey research employed in the study of
political culture and political socialization).[28] There is already a
voluminous literature on the methodological and conceptual difficulties involved. Beyond all that, in the particular part of the world
discussed in this book, field research of this type is simply not
feasible in most countries.[29] Thus, it is necessary to fall back on
inferences from actual behavior, crude textual analyses of speeches
and pronouncements, and other questionable and not particularly reliable methods. It is in this sense, inter alia, that a book concerned
with stateness must remain on the level of soft social science.
     Yet Nettl did not offer a full-fledged paradigm[30] for the study
of the state. Rather, he posited a conceptual variable in the literal
sense of the term, intended to be a step in initiating research perhaps culminating in an eventual paradigm. Thus, the crude methodology involved perhaps should be considered an "infantile disease,"
curable if a community of scholars undertakes serious research
along the lines suggested in the original, potentially rich formulation. The methodological price is worth paying if only because
Nettl—at least on the burning question of the state—seems closer
than most others to the prescription that "the academic study of politics is typically responsive to the pressing problems of the day."[31]
His approach has at least the potential to address itself to relevant,
important, and yet reasonably researchable questions, as prescribed
in Joseph LaPalombara's well-known lament on the state of the art.[32]
If this means a soft social science in the initial stages, so be it.
     The third major problem in Nettl's analysis is one that is most
directly relevant to the subject matter of this book: bluntly put, it is
that most of what he has to say on the state in developing countries
is by and large inadequate, incorrect, or both.[33] That his analysis
should be so flawed, leading him to overly pessimistic conclusions

as to the potential for state building in what he calls the Third
World, [34] is really curious, as several perceptive analysts have
persuasively argued that serious research conclusively points to
the centrality of the state precisely in the so-called non-Western
part of the world. Thus, for example, Bedeski's study of China
leads him to conclude:

> In general, it appears that there are two major views
> of the sovereign state in the world today. The Western
> countries, which have developed within the framework
> of the nation-state for centuries, passed through vari-
> ous stages of nationalism, and have experienced the ex-
> cesses of state apotheosis in two world wars; the non-
> Western countries, on the other hand, and especially
> China, are now struggling to achieve what they per-
> ceive as the complete autonomy and unity of established
> states. The condition of sovereignty remains a fragile
> ideal more than a routine fact of national existence for
> them. [35]

Bedeski goes on to speak of the

> much slower process of state building in Europe, the
> historical birthplace of the modern sovereign state.
> Perhaps centuries of wars, reformulations of ideals,
> and rearrangements of political institutions are being
> compressed into a few decades for China. If so, we
> are witnessing in the space of a generation or two, not
> so much a crisis of modernization, but rather a self-
> conscious adaptation to a world organized around sov-
> ereign nation-states. If we are discouraged by the
> violence and apparent unpredictability of this process,
> we should remind ourselves of the long genesis of the
> Western state and the tribulations involved in develop-
> ing the original models. [36]

In an even more general theoretical vein, Hedley Bull has
elaborated the following argument:

> Nor is there much evidence of any threat to the state
> as an institution in the attempts—sometimes success-
> ful, sometimes not—of nationalist separatist groups to
> bring about the disintegration of existing states, as in
> Nigeria, Pakistan, Yugoslavia, Canada, the United
> Kingdom, or Iraq, to name only a few. For if we ask

what have been the goals of the separatist Biafrans, East Bengalis, Croats, Quebecois, Scots, or Kurds, the answer is that they have been trying to create new states. While the regional integrationists seek to reduce the number of states in the world, and the nationalist separatists seek to increase it, both are as committed as the defendants of existing states to the continuation of the state as an institution. It might be thought that a serious challenge to the position of the states lies in the tendency of Socialist and Third World states to accord rights and duties in international law to nations that are not states; and that, in particular, national liberation movements—most notably, the Palestine Liberation Organization—have achieved a degree of recognition in the United Nations and elsewhere that in some ways sounds the death knell of the state, or at all events brings to an end its claims to a privileged position among political groups in the world today. But again, what we have to notice is that the thinking both of the national liberation groups and of the states that lend support to them is confined within statist logic. What national liberation movements seek to do is to capture control of existing states (as in the case of the PLO or the FLN in Algeria), to create new states (as in Eritrea or Nagaland), or to change the boundaries of states (as in Ireland). In seeking recognition of their claims in international society, the starting point of their argument is the principle that nations ought to be states, and the strongest card they have to play is that they represent nations that seek to be states.[37]

It would be an unfair exaggeration to claim that this forceful line of argument escapes Nettl altogether. He does pay attention to the problem of stateness in developing countries, but much of what he says appears (today, at least) as a somewhat overly pessimistic afterthought. This is most conspicuous in the following statement:

The very instability of governments in developing countries suggests that the competition for norms is very strong. A state could therefore develop only if a politically supported regime remains in power for a considerable time and is able to transpose its own norms across the high threshold of time and internalization of legitimacy into a situation of stateness, within which interests can eventually be articulated and institutional-

ized by cleavage structures. All the current evidence
from the third world is to the contrary; the political
area of normlessness is large and evident, and hence
the possibility of developing states of the European type
in today's new nations seems remote.[38]

Nettl's subsequent analysis of the party-nation-state triangle
in the developing countries appears to me to be completely incorrect as a generalization, or is at least subject to so many major
exceptions as to be substantially (and demonstrably) false:

It is worth noting that the notion of state has not, in
fact, taken root in today's developing countries. Insofar as a deliberate search for adequate political models
from the experience of developed countries has taken
place, it has led to the adoption of, and emphasis on,
parties. Leaving aside the general question of the relevance of the European political experience for developing
countries, the evidence suggests that where a state-party
dichotomy exists, the emphasis is more strongly on
party. Even in the so-called no-party states, run largely by the military or at least subject to ultimate military control, there has been little attempt to manufac-
ture a concept of the dominant state. Rather, the emphasis has been on nation—what might be described as the
national-constitutional structure. In this regard, British experience seems to predominate over that of Europe—
perhaps partly because of the preponderance of the British colonial experience. Even the high point of the
French rationalist tradition among French-speaking
Africans can hardly be said to have picked on the state
as the quintessential form of the desirable European experience; indeed, the wave of left-wing and French-
inspired political thought in Africa, which has anyhow
ebbed before the hard facts of traditional social structure and political instability in the developing world,
tended visibly to move at a level of abstraction beyond
that of "mere" political institutions and concerned itself with the philosophical orientations of French
thought rather than the concrete form of French experience.[39]

Nettl goes as far as categorically stating that "the tradition
and ideas of the European state do not figure substantially in the
ideas, programs and concrete developments of today's third world."[40]
Nettl attributes this partly to the implosion-explosion dichotomy:

Apart from the question of deliberate borrowing which
has played quite an important part in the development
of socio-political ideas and their application in developing countries, there are probably good reasons why no
idea of state is likely to develop from the increasingly
unique and particular political experience of these countries. As they develop their own autonomous traditions
in coping with their particular problems, which in turn
are very unlike those of historical Europe, it seems improbable that any adequate concept of state will appear.
The European experience of stateness was essentially
the product of a particularization or narrowing of sovereignty into ethnically homogeneous or at least ethnically defined areas. The transformation of post-
medieval sovereignty into stateness and nationality has,
with some exceptions such as Austria and Russia, generally resulted in an overall shrinking of significant
territoriality and in all cases in a narrowing of potential references—the almost boundless European hori-
zons available to those few who broke out of the paro-
chialism of isolated geographical communities up to
the end of the eighteenth century gave way to the specificity of national references shared by all. The process can be described as an _implosion_—with all the increasing intensity implied by that word. Only the Soviet
Union has been a deviant case, in that the Soviet state is
essentially the product of a supranational territory, and
Soviet citizenship runs counter to ethnic communalism.
But, as has been argued above, the Soviet state does
not have the full connotations of the European traditions,
and many of its functions are vested in the single Com
munist party.

Developing countries, on the other hand, have in
common the extension of central authority across ethnic boundaries and particular, hitherto "sovereign" communities. The colonial experience was not in itself productive of nationhood, except in a dissociative or anti-
pathetic sense of opposition to foreign domination. The
real incorporation into new units of the arbitrary areas
carved up by colonial powers followed and did not precede the attainment of independence. The process here
was one of _explosion_, in which the concentration of
power resulting from antipathy to colonial rule, structure successfully either through political independence
parties or disciplined military-political insurrection-
ary organizations, was then applied to the new "inherited"

territory—the <u>nation trouvée</u>. The metaphor accurate-
ly directs attention to the opposing notions of inward
concentration and outward extension and hence scatter-
ing of energy. Obviously the opposite movement of energy in the two experiences is hardly likely to give rise
to the same phenomenon of state. [41]

This generalization seems questionable. Indeed, Nettl is obviously aware of the immense importance of the international system
in creating, recognizing, and legitimizing states in the Third World,
not to mention the immense resources a state apparatus can now
muster in developing countries. Yet he seems to dismiss this enormously important factor too easily:

There remains only the one constant—the invariant development of stateness for each national actor in the
international field. New and developing nations have
sought self-definition, integration, and even domestic
viability by emphasizing their international role and—
they hope—status. But this hardly suggests evidence
of the development of the European types of states we
have been discussing. If anything, the contrary is true:
while the European tradition is one of stateness both in-
trasocietally and extrasocietally and of the relationship
between these two aspects, the development of a purely
or even mainly extrasocietal form of state, which constitutes and defines itself primarily through its foreign
relations, is likely to give rise to something very different from the received European tradition. For instance, <u>personalismo</u> regimes at home, such as Cuba
or Egypt, are mediated in interesting ways by the intervention of stateness and its apparatus—including
regional pacts or blocs, and United Nations delega-
tions—in the international field. [42]

This entire line of argument is far from convincing, because
if there is one point on which Marxist scholars are right, it is that
it was precisely in the field of state apparatus that the colonial
powers left an "overdeveloped" infrastructure behind. The building
of a new nation or society, the reshaping of a society along different
ideological lines, or even the institutionalization of a single party,
are extraordinarily difficult and inordinately lengthy processes. In
comparison, the mastering of "state technology" by a trained power
elite is a more manageable task, as a logical and empirical analysis
readily demonstrates.

Yet Tilly, who deals with these very questions, does not substantially differ with Nettl. Tilly starts from the complexity of the questions related to state building, and says:

> Our only hope of contributing to their resolution lies in
> the possibility that the particular variables we have
> chosen to scrutinize—the variations in the extractive,
> repressive, control activities of governments—operate
> in a regular way, and that we have caught some of the
> regularity in our formulations.[43]

Needless to say, these very activities are the ones in which most Third World countries (certainly those in the Middle East) have made the greatest steps toward learning astutely from the Western experience. Indeed, some of the related regularities appear to be taken almost exactly from the Middle East today:

> Extreme stateness, of course, neither guarantees politi-
> cal stability nor assures power in the international arena.
> One might guess that an increase in stateness does ordi-
> narily increase a government's command of the mobile
> resources within its subject population, does increase
> its capacity to free resources which are embedded in
> traditional networks of obligation, and thereby augments
> the government's power to apply resources to objec-
> tives at a national or international scale. But if the
> European experience is a guide, the short-run cost is
> an increase in the likelihood of resistance and revolt.
> Hence, a close historical connection among increases
> in stateness, expansion of armed forces, rises in taxa-
> tion, and popular rebellion.[44]

Of course, Tilly is entirely justified in pointing out the international context for the expansion of the contemporary state,[45] which includes "the crystallization of a _system_ of states acknowledging, and to some extent guaranteeing, each other's existence"[46] as well as the global expansion of what Immanuel Wallerstein calls the "European world-economy."[47] Tilly is also justified in pointing to the "high cost of state-building,"[48] again eerily reminiscent of so many Middle Eastern (and other developing) countries. He repeats the oft-asserted claim that "war shaped and reshaped the European state system,"[49] yet for the penultimate section of his major introductory essay he chooses the title "Why Europe Will Not Occur Again."[50] He states there: "Our ability to infer the probable events and sequences in contemporary states from an informed reading of

European history is close to nil. The profundity of all these changes might make worthless any inference whatsoever from European experience to today's world."[51] This categorical argument is of such enormous importance that its reasoning should be quoted in full:

> The European state-building experiences will not repeat themselves in new states. The connections of the new states to the rest of the world have changed too much. The statesmen of the contemporary world find themselves faced with alternative models of statebuilding, not to mention eager promoters of those models. The manager of a contemporary state may well be ineffective and/or wrong, but he is likely to assume the necessity of promoting an efficient and submissive civil service, a general and uniform system of taxation, a well-trained native military force, and a high level of industrial production. In Europe of the fifteenth or sixteenth century the available models were fewer, different, less well-defined and less obviously appropriate for the objectives of the powerful.
>
> Moreover, the European state-makers and a few non-European collaborators, through war, conquest and alliance, eventually fashioned a worldwide system of states. As the nineteenth and twentieth centuries have worn on, the newcomers to the system have had less choice of the positions they would occupy in it, even down to the exact territories they would control. Among other things, that prior existence of a state system has fundamentally altered the role of the military forces in the smaller states, since their strength or weakness no longer makes the major difference in the territory controlled by the state or in its relations with other states.
>
> Again the resources on which today's statemakers draw and the forces against which they struggle are deeply different from those of the early European experience. All the builders of European states occupied themselves, one way or another, in wrestling their wherewithal from largely self-sustaining agrarian populations. They could not borrow military might, technical expertise, or development funds from neighbouring states. They could not assume the existence of a world market for any of their products, or the readiness of their producers to respond to a world market if it existed. They could not dispossess foreign capitalists

(unless one wants to press the analogy of the Catholic
Church with Kennecott Copper). . . . Finally, the
managers of contemporary states have undertaken different tasks from their predecessors: building a certain kind of economic system, creating specific facilities like research institutes, steel mills, airports, or
holiday resorts; maintaining some minimum of public
welfare; increasing the supply of scientists; and others.
The new tasks flow in part from the available models of
state-building, in part from the logic of the international system, in part from pressures within each individual country. [52]

This author agrees with Tilly and Nettl (and numerous others)
that in general there are grave limitations to using European models, experiences, and analogies in analyzing the contemporary
political experience: however, they push the argument much too
far. The present author thoroughly disagrees with them on a key
point: even if the European experience with social ideology, nationalism, and similar cultural-behavioral phenomena is not necessarily applicable to developing countries, the structural[53] experience
of European state building is applicable (and in fact has been widely
applied) at least in the case of most Middle East countries. This
structural experience, in turn, in time produces several important
behavioral consequences. The importance of this argument cannot
be overstated; it will be discussed, analyzed, and demonstrated in
detail in subsequent chapters.

Prior to this, however, yet another dimension of the stateness[54] about which Nettl spoke must be identified. It is an idea of
a form of "state logic." To describe this, the Machiavellian term
raison d'état will be used—of course, in a somewhat different context and thus meaning. As Bedeski explains,

At the level of the state, the will to concentrate public
power into a single sovereign entity grew into raison
d'état when statecraft became conscious of itself and
when its practitioners subordinated all other considerations to its ends (an imperative which may be the ances-
tor of present notions of "national security"). But before the state assumed its modern form, and before
Machiavelli could dissolve the medieval links between
secular statecraft and religious beliefs, an institutional
setting had to be prepared which denied the particulari-
ties of feudalism and the universality of Christian loyalties. The modern state emerged from late feudal

Europe out of the conflicts between national monarchs
and the papacy, and among the monarchs themselves.
The idea of sovereignty developed as new centralized
legal institutions undermined the feudal autonomy of
estates, municipalities, and ecclesiastical orders.[55]

This dissolution of the "medieval links between secular statecraft and religious beliefs" created disturbing ethical connotations.
It seemed that the universal morality applicable to all human activity would be excluded from statecraft, which would thus have a justification all its own—one that would be derived from the interests
of the state (meaning mostly its rulers) and would overwhelm any
other moral or ethical constraint or consideration. Raison d'état,
as projected by Machiavelli, came to be regarded as a terrifying
logic of the immorality of naked power, disguised under the thin
veneer of "state interest." Ernst Cassirer, in a well-known work,[56]
complains bitterly about this "depraved condition," in which the
political world after Machiavelli "lost its connection not only with
religion or metaphysics but also with all the other forms of man's
ethical and cultural life."[57]

Today, it is recognized that Machiavelli neither created nor
even necessarily advocated this "depraved condition," but merely
identified it as a reality and attempted to utilize historical generalizations in the study of establishing political order and stability.
This led to his laying down maxims of statecraft to the effect that
states must be established or reformed by a powerful individual,
that statecraft is inseparable from the military arts,[58] and the like.

Yet Cassirer's depraved condition is a very real danger.
Total orientation to power creates fascist states. Comprehensive
attempts of the state to penetrate every social subsystem may create totalitarian states. This century is all too full of such cases
and examples. Still, these are clear instances of a reductio ad
absurdum of the logic of stateness at the expense of every alternative consideration. It is argued here that this is only one, indeed a
pervertly extreme, way of interpreting raison d'état. Also, it is
one that is generally a more viable alternative in industrialized
societies, where the resources for building such states are more
likely to be found.[59]

The logic of stateness, however, can and should be interpreted
in other, less extreme ways. (Of course, every political logic, if
pushed to its "pure," extreme form can, and usually does, become
a perverted, dangerous ideology.) An alternative conception of
raison d'état would be that of a filter through which interests related to social, national, or particularistic ideologies and interests
are sifted, refined, aggregated, and perhaps moderated. The state

is embedded in political communities larger than itself, and in most cases it also controls a territory populated by political communities smaller than itself. A reasonable working relationship with both levels must be worked out and maintained if political order is to endure. This is even more so in the developing countries in the era of the revolution in expanding communications and participation.[60] As Alexis de Tocqueville observed, "Among the laws that rule human societies, there is one which seems to be more precise and clear than all others. If men are to remain civilized or to become so, the art of associating together must grow and improve in the same ratio in which the equality of conditions is increased."[61]

The art of associating together can be (and has been) interpreted in a variety of ways. To this author, it seems that in the real world of politics in the developing countries today a political elite conditioned to look at conflict through the eyes of state responsibility (that is, interacting in an orderly fashion both with other states and at the same time with smaller political units within the state) might come closest to this ideal. Obviously, conflict in politics, as Rousseau observed long ago, will never go away: "If there were no different interests, the common interest would be barely felt, as it would encounter no obstacle; all would go on of its own accord, and politics would cease to be an art."[62] This art is not likely to become superfluous. The different interests are very persistent indeed. The common interest, however, for better or worse, is increasingly articulated by states. The very stateness of a country and particularly its political elites[63] create the basic condition for a conception of common interest (with other states as well as the various sectors of society) in the first place. A state elite is less likely to pursue either clear cut social or national ideologies; the resulting vagueness, while it may be reprehensible to a great many ideologues, is an important step in the containment and reduction of conflict to manageable proportions. As Lord Acton argued,

> Few discoveries are more irritating than those which expose the pedigree of ideas. Sharp definitions and unsparing analysis would displace the veil beneath which society dissembles its divisions, would make political disputes too violent for compromise and political alliances too precarious for use, and would embitter politics with all the passions of social and religious strife.[64]

Stateness is a crucial layer in Lord Acton's social veil. Furthermore, political elites are likely to perceive others to a significant extent in their own image.[65] One can relate in a reasonable way to other states, and to other groups and forces in society as reasonable partners or allies, only to the extent that one indeed possesses a sense of stateness beyond a critical minimal threshold. Peace and stability in a region of states, just as prosperity and legitimacy in a unit in such a region, are attainable under the present circumstances only as the (structural) building of the state and the (behavioral) evolution of stateness in attitudes progress. In totalitarian or fascist Europe just before mid-century, the exaggerated strength of the state caused untold human misery; in the Middle East today, the chaos and vacuum (which politics can never tolerate) in countries with low stateness, such as Lebanon, seem to cause more devastation than any other factor. To paraphrase Lord Acton, one may say that if absolute power (of states) tends to corrupt absolutely, so does absolute weakness (of states)—in a different, but nevertheless devastating way.

And yet, it seems no exaggeration to claim that the state has not received anything commensurate with the attention it deserves in the amorphously defined, indeed slippery, field of Middle East studies.[66] Of course, the problems of political turmoil, the lack of stability, the difficulty of acquiring legitimacy, and the general quest for a post-Ottoman political order have all been repeatedly emphasized, but often in ways that underestimate or ignore the dimension of stateness. A few examples should demonstrate this vividly.

For many standard and unquestionably competent and informative textbooks, the starting point is the more or less conventional perspective of comparative politics on modernization and development. Thus, in a fine general survey, James A. Bill and Carl Leiden argue that

> the dialectical relationship that prevails between the intertwined processes of modernization and political development is a central issue in the contemporary Middle East. Modernization acts as a catalytic process, stimulating demands that must be confronted by the various political systems. At the same time, the political elites must make most of the key decisions that promote and shape patterns of modernization. The circular and reciprocal interaction between these two dynamic processes is riddled with uncertainty. Many of the fundamental problems that now confront the Middle Eastern peoples emanate from this situation.[67]

Yet the starting point for examining these fundamental problems for Bill and Leiden is not the state, but rather, religion:

Politics are often inextricably intertwined with religion. It would be difficult to discuss the political dynamics of modern Spain or Ulster without paying attention either to the role of some institutionalized church or to the religious beliefs and practices of the inhabitants. This is certainly true of the Middle East. The great revealed religions all came into being there. Middle Eastern history is rich in religious wars and conquests. The storm center of the area today, Israel, was founded on the right of a religious people to return to ancestral pastures. It is not an exaggeration to say that no understanding of the complex political patterns of the area can be attempted without giving prior attention to its religious characteristics. [68]

The question of state, then, receives attention in the framework of Islamic political thought, all under the heading of religion! But surely the state is a more logical starting point. Would it not make more sense to treat it as the dependent variable, so to speak, and examine the impact of religion on it? (if indeed Islam and Judaism can be properly labeled religions in this context—numerous scholars have argued this is not the case).

Other textbooks start from what Halpern calls "incoherence." Bruce Borthwick, for example, holds that

in all political systems, but particularly in the Middle East, no component is static. The culture that is a part of the warp and woof of the society, the structures through which authoritative decisions are made, the groups that participate in politics, the leaders who make decisions, and the policies that they institute are in a continuing state of flux. [69]

In the 1980s, however, it is increasingly obvious that the centrality of the role of the state can no longer be ignored; hence Borthwick, while not articulating a theory of the state, does stress what many earlier textbooks underemphasized:

The state adopts one or another of the various forms of socialism, Marxism, or modern Islam.

Governments make basic decisions, not in the issuance of one decree, the enactment of one law, the institution of a new regulation, but in the stream of decrees, laws, and regulations that emanate from them over a significant period of time involving matters such as: Is the state to be officially designated as socialist, democratic, Islamic, or something else? Shall it have a one-party or multi-party system, or shall it function without political parties? Shall the state support and defend religion, be neutral towards it, or militantly combat it? What shall be the role of the private and public sectors in the economy, and which shall the government favor? What shall be the form of taxation and who shall be heavily taxed? What type of weapons shall the country buy, whom shall it be prepared to fight against, and with whom shall it ally itself?

Decisions on questions such as these affect one or another group adversely or favourably. The military officer corps may receive higher salaries and fringe benefits and may get new weapon systems with which to work. State funds may be used to support mosques and religious schools, thereby enhancing the status and influence of the clergy. State capital may be poured into industry rather than agriculture, to the benefit of engineers, technicians, and workers, and the detriment of peasants and farmers. In each case one group has benefited and another has lost out.

Policy decisions also affect the structures of the society. An old constitution is abolished and a new one instituted; the bureaucracy is reorganized; a modification or change is made in the legal system. And the culture is altered, for policies determine what the official ideology of the state is to be. That ideology is then pronounced over the state radio and television, taught in the schools and indoctrinated into the soldiers. [70]

One may choose to quarrel with the particular items on this agenda as far as ideologies and policies are concerned, but at least they are discussed in the salient perspective of the state. Perhaps this is a signal for a change in the trends for textbooks in the 1980s.

Unquestionably, one of the more influential textbooks of the 1970s was Michael C. Hudson's Arab Politics: The Search for Legitimacy. [71] What is relevant here is its theoretical orientation, which, as the subtitle indicates, is almost classically Weberian, with the addition of the Deutschian model of social mobilization. [72] Much like the other authors, Hudson presents a terrifying picture of political disorder in the region, and depicts many of the associated problems in a sophisticated way. When it comes to focusing the discussion on a key variable, however, he deals almost exclusively with the problem of legitimacy, exacerbated by rapid social mobilization. This, in turn, is related to nationalist and socialist ideologies. The entire approach is so characteristic of what is perhaps the most dominant school in the study of Middle East politics that the heart of the argument deserves to be quoted in some detail:

> The central problem of government in the Arab world today is political legitimacy. The shortage of this indispensable political resource largely accounts for the volatile nature of Arab politics and the autocratic, unstable character of all the present Arab governments. If one were called upon to describe the contemporary style of politics in the Arab world—a region that stretches from Morocco to Kuwait, organized into eighteen sovereign states (excluding Mauritania and Somalia, which recently joined the Arab League) embracing some 125 million people—the adjectives that immediately spring to mind include mercurial, hyperbolic, irrational, mysterious, uncertain, even dangerous. Arab politics today are not just unstable, although instability remains a prominent feature, they are also unpredictable to participants and observers alike. Fed by rumor, misinformation and lack of information, the Arab political process is cloaked in obscurity and Arab politicians are beset by insecurity and fear of the unknown. If their behavior appears at times quixotic or even paranoid, the irrationality lies less within themselves than in their situation. Whether in power or in the opposition, Arab politicians must operate in a political environment in which the legitimacy of rulers, regimes, and the institutions of the states themselves is sporadic and, at best, scarce. Under these conditions seemingly irrational behavior, such as assassinations, coups d'etat, and official repression, may in fact derive from rational calculations. The consequences of such behavior, which itself stems from the low legitimacy accorded to political processes and institutions, contribute further to the prevailing popular cynicism about politics. These consequences, so dysfunctional for political development by almost any definition, are all the more damaging when juxtaposed against the revolutionary and nationalist values that are today so widely and intensely held by the Arab people. These values include liberation of the entire national homeland by regaining Palestine and throwing off indirect forms of

external influence; fulfillment of Arab national identity through integration, if not fusion, of the numerous sovereignties; and the establishment of democratic political structures through which social justice and equality can be achieved. Such are the staples of virtually all political platforms in the Arab states, regardless of regime orientation; and such appeals have amply proved their political salience from one end of the Arab world to the other, as evidenced by the wave of independence and revolutionary movement throughout the region since World War I. So widespread are these appeals that every Arab politician of consequence has felt compelled to endorse and exploit them; and today, as we shall see, even the ideologically conservative monarchies have become fervent advocates of Arabism, democracy, and social justice. But such vast, if not utopian, ideals, held by so many with almost sacred fervor, contrast strikingly with the grim realities of political life. This incongruence cannot but complicate the task of building a legitimate order. Indeed, one observes from conversations with politicians and government officials across the Arab world a sense of frustration. They find themselves caught between ideology and political-administrative realities. They discover apathy, indifference, and corruption within their own bureaucracies and among the constituencies to be served. One also observes a widespread negative attitude, even fear, toward government among ordinary people. Even census taking in countries such as Sa'udi Arabia, Yemen, the United Arab Emirates, and of course, Lebanon is regarded with suspicion. Such attitudes cannot be satisfactorily explained simply as the superstitions of "traditional" people but rather appear to be rationally derived from unhappy prior experience with "the authorities."[73]

All this comes back to a well-known Weberian thesis:

Without legitimacy, argued Max Weber, a ruler, regime, or governmental system is hard-pressed to attain the conflict-management capability essential for long-run stability and good government. While the stability of an order may be maintained for a time through fear or expediency or custom, the optimal or most harmonious relationship between the ruler and the ruled is that in which the ruled accept the rightness of the ruler's superior power.[74]

It is important to recall, however, that Weber's own discussion of legitimacy took place by and large with implicit or explicit reference to the state. (How can one attain durable legitimacy without a stable state? The question can be put this way at least as well as the other way around!)

Even more important is the way Hudson links the diverse variables he works with. He refers to conditions of political disorder such as assassinations, coups d'état and official repression, and correctly argues that the consequences of such behavior contribute further to the prevailing popular cynicism about politics.

The problem described here is not necessarily that of political development. Nor is it necessarily true that low legitimacy breeds dysfunctional acts, that these breed cynicism, or that these are exacerbated when seen against the background of the aforementioned "revolutionary and nationalist values." Rather, it is much more logical to argue that it is just not possible, in the short run, to build the type of state structure that is likely to inspire legitimacy, when revolutionary and nationalist values overwhelm state elites with competing transcendental-messianic claims and ideals, and/or when basic questions such as the fulfillment of Arab national identity through integration, if not fusion, of the numerous sovereignties remain unsettled, even though they relate to the very existence of the present states in the region. It is not that lack of legitimacy breeds cynicism reinforced by excessive ideological competition: rather, it is the debilitating weakness of the state (which is not capable of sifting, filtering, mediating, and aggregating radical ideological perspectives) that breeds confusion, disorder, and cynicism. Cynicism may have to do less with strong states that repress ideological forces and much more with weak states that seem (to Hudson) incapable of containing them. The first problem is that of building states (otherwise what is it that seeks legitimacy?) and stateness (for otherwise legitimacy may be diffused between so many centers as to cause only more instability). In this sense, Hudson's diagnosis may be partially correct, but by failing to focus his variables around the key—the state—he seems to miss something of enormous importance.

As has been seen, Hudson points out that "vast, if not utopian, ideals, held by so many with almost sacred fervor, contrast strikingly with the grim realities of political life" and that people "find themselves caught between ideology and political-administrative realities." This is certainly true. The political-administrative reality that Hudson depicts is a state incapable of dealing with the forces of ideology (at least in the 1960s). It is not clear, however, that any political-administrative machinery would be capable of accommodating so many ideological demands. Stability requires a simultaneous strengthening of political-administrative capabilities at the center,[75] and the weakening of ideological forces capable of challenging that center—in other words, enhancing the state. When Hudson observes that the rational widespread suspicion of census taking is derived from an unhappy prior experience, what he is describing is a low level of stateness, or a negative attitude to the state, or both. The Weberian framework of legitimacy for analyzing this question is clearly far less adequate than Nettl's "The State as a Conceptual Variable," however imperfect in its present formulation.

Furthermore, Hudson's identification of the political agenda of the Arab world, even if correct for the 1970s, may have changed substantially by the early 1980s, shifting toward less ideological and more pragmatic, state-oriented questions. Partial disillusionment with the gap between reality and ideology does not necessarily breed cynicism: it may breed a certain newly found sobriety. Some of the little relevant empirical research available does, in fact, point partly in this direction.[76]

Moreover, while Hudson—and therefore Weber—are obviously right in claiming that "the stability of an order may be maintained for a time through fear or expediency or custom,"[77] this question (of the persistence of regimes and states over time, by force if necessary, against a background of an international sanctification of the status quo and immense practical resources available to rulers) has many complexities, subtleties, and nuances that need further exploration and elaboration. In what follows, it will be necessary to delve deeply into these.

Middle East politics is in constant flux, its agenda subject to incessant change. Perhaps the most salient features of the evolving agenda of the 1980s are to be found in the essay by Bernard Lewis, certainly one of the best-known authorities in the study of Middle East history, entitled "Loyalties to Community, Nation and State."[78] Lewis points, inter alia, to this very phenomenon of the endurance of the state in the Middle East (Lewis is exceedingly careful to make the necessary distinctions between state, nation, country, and religious community) from its very origins in Islam:

> A remarkable feature of the modern age and of the
> changes that modernization has brought to Islam has
> been the strengthening not the weakening, of the state
> as a focus of activity. One reason for this is an important internal development. In the traditional Islamic
> society, the power of the state was in both theory and
> practice limited. There is a common tendency to think
> of Islamic political tradition as conducive to despotic,
> even capricious rule, and this view may appear to

receive some support from recent events. It is based,
however, on a misreading of Islamic history and law.
The traditional Islamic state may be autocratic; it is
not despotic. The power of the sovereign is limited by
a number of factors, some legal, some social. It is
limited in principle by the holy law, which, being of
divine origin, precedes the state. The state and the
sovereign are subject to the law and are in a sense
created and authorized by the law and not, as in Western systems, the other way around. In addition to this
theoretical restraint, there were also practical restraints.
In traditional Islamic societies, there were many well-
entrenched interests and intermediate powers that imposed effective limits on the ability of the state to control its subjects. With the process of modernization in
the Islamic world, these intermediate powers have one
by one been weakened or abolished, leaving the state
with a far greater degree of autocratic control over its
subjects than it ever enjoyed in traditional Islamic
societies. And whereas the limiting powers have
dwindled or disappeared, the state itself now has at its
disposal the whole modern apparatus of surveillance
and repression. The result is that modern states in the
Islamic world, even those claiming to be progressive
and democratic, are—in their domestic affairs at least—
vastly stronger than the so-called tyrannies of the past. [79]

This is a very important point, to which the next chapter (which
addresses itself more specifically to questions of this nature) will
return. For the time being, Lewis's historical analysis is most useful in supplying an explanatory counterpoint to Hudson's Weberian
approach to the endurance of the states in the region:

This may help us to understand another somewhat surprising phenomenon of the recent and current Middle
Eastern world—the extraordinary persistence of states
once created. Before the First World War, there were
in effect only two—or, we might say, two-and-a-half—
states in the Middle East. The two were the surviving
monarchies of Turkey and Iran, both conceived not as
nation-states in the modern Western sense, but as universal Muslim empires. Both sovereigns, the Sultan
of Turkey and the Shah of Iran, saw themselves and
projected themselves as universal sovereigns of Islam
to whom all Muslims owed allegiance, and it was only

in comparatively recent times that they began to adopt
territorial and national designations in their protocol
and official usage. The half is Egypt, which, although
under external suzerainty or domination, first Ottoman
then British, nevertheless retained a very large measure of autonomy in its internal affairs. There was an
Egyptian government, an Egyptian administration running Egypt, under fairly remote Ottoman or somewhat
less remote British control. In this sense, Egypt has
functioned as a political entity for a very long time,
even if not as an independent state. Apart from these,
some smaller groups managed to maintain a precarious
independence in remote mountain or desert areas, while
recognizing the nominal suzerainty of one or other of
these states. The rest of the Middle East had had no
experience of separate statehood or of the exercise of
political sovereignty for a very long time. The nations
who lived there had merged their identities in the larger
communal and dynastic loyalties; the countries in which
they lived were no more than imperial provinces; their
very names and boundaries were subject to frequent
change, and—with the exception of Egypt—they had little
historical or even geographical significance.

As a result of two world wars and of the extension and withdrawal of European imperial power, a
whole series of new states were set up, with frontiers
and even identities largely devised by colonial administration and imperial diplomacy. Some of these rested
on genuine historical entities; some were entirely artificial. Nevertheless, in spite of the very strong ideological urge toward unification arising from pan-
Arabism, not a single one of these Arab states has disappeared. On the contrary, they have shown—even the
most improbable of them—an extraordinary capacity for
survival and for self-preservation, often in very ad-
verse circumstances. There have been many attempts
to unite or even associate two or more Arab states; no
such attempt has so far lasted for very long. In earlier
days the failure of attempts at Arab unity could be and
was attributed to outside influence. The record of more
recent times illustrates that whatever the role of the
outside interference in the past, it is no longer a sufficient explanation. The barriers to greater Arab unity
arise within the Arab world and the failure of the merg-
ers testifies to the remarkable persistence and growing
power of the state itself as a political factor.[80]

This lucid and convincing analysis leads to an image that indeed appears much closer to capturing the reality of the present Middle East scene than does the mainstream of the earlier "conventional" literature. This should suffice to justify a detailed application of the notion of stateness to some key aspects of Middle East politics, in the hope that such application will yield useful theoretical and analytical insights. It is obvious that in the Middle East it is states that make war and peace; it is states against which people rebel and revolt; it is states that allocate resources. Thus, more than any other single factor, it is the state that permeates those phenomena that are of interest to the political scientist. Important though these considerations are in their own right, what perhaps ought to be of paramount interest at this stage is the extent to which one can utilize the variable, stateness, to learn something about considerations of explanatory and/or predictive value that may otherwise have been missed.

While there are considerable problems pertaining to the complexity of the definition and methodological difficulties of application, the depth and originality of Nettl's formulation promise to break so much new ground that it is safe to say it has thus far been unduly neglected. Notwithstanding its lack of development and its flaws, there is ample evidence that no better definition of the state is available. Therefore, in the substance of this book, Nettl's definitions of state and stateness will be followed, along the lines of his four dimensions and five functions in the context of his historical, intellectual, and cultural approaches. Since Nettl's own formulation was neither vigorous nor fully worked out, the usage here, of necessity, will be somewhat loose, and will be far less systematic than the ideal prescriptions of social science require. Yet, it appears that the dialectics of social science are such that only by applying original formulations, however imperfectly expressed, to the analysis of problems in the real world can progress be made toward a more sophisticated methodology. In what follows, an effort along these lines will be made in four issue areas: the Islamic state, the Jewish state, the Arab-Israeli conflict, and relations between the Arab states.

NOTES

1. Robert E. Bedeski, "The Evolution of the Modern State in China: Nationalist and Communist Continuities," World Politics 27 (July 1975): 542.

2. Charles Tilly, ed., The Formation of National States in Europe (Princeton, N.J.: Princeton University Press, 1975).

3. <u>Daedalus</u> 108 (Fall 1979). Contributions of especial relevance are Richard Haas, "The Primacy of the State . . . or Revising the Revisionists"; Hedley Bull, "The State's Positive Role in World Affairs"; Michael Howard, "War and the Nation-State."

4. The general relevant literature is so voluminous that not even a representative fraction can be cited here. See the annotated multilingual bibliography in Tilly, <u>Formation of National States</u>; the bibliographical references in J. P. Nettl, "The State as a Conceptual Variable," <u>World Politics</u> 20 (July 1968): 559-92; and the numerous bibliographical footnotes in <u>Daedalus</u> 108 (1979). On the decline of the state in modern political science see Alexander Passerin d'Entrêves, <u>The Notion of the State</u> (London: Oxford University Press, 1967). For a few important earlier works, consult Ernst Cassirer, <u>The Myth of the State</u> (Garden City, N.Y.: Doubleday, 1955); Heinz Lubasz, ed., <u>The Development of the Modern State</u> (New York: Macmillan, 1964); Frederick M. Watkins, <u>The State as a Concept of Political Science</u> (New York: Harper, 1934); Harold J. Laski, <u>The State in Theory and Practice</u> (New York: Viking Press, 1935); Robert M. MacIver, <u>The Modern State</u> (London: Clarendon Press, 1926); Carl J. Friedrich, <u>Man and His Government</u> (New York: McGraw-Hill, 1963). For the transnational perspective see Joseph Nye and Robert Koehane, <u>Transnational Relations and World Politics</u> (Cambridge, Mass.: Harvard University Press, 1972). For recent approaches, see Michael Donelan, <u>The Reason of States</u> (London: Allen and Unwin, 1978), and Gianfranco Poggi, <u>The Development of the Modern State</u> (Stanford, Cal.: Stanford University Press, 1978).

5. See as examples of the functionalist approach Chalmers Johnson, <u>Revolutionary Change</u> (Boston: Little, Brown, 1966); Gabriel A. Almond and G. Bingham Powell, Jr., <u>Comparative Politics: System, Process and Policy</u>, 2d ed. (Boston: Little, Brown, 1978). As examples of the Marxist approach, see Hamza Alavi, "The State in Post-Colonial Societies—Pakistan and Bangladesh," <u>New Left Review</u> 74 (July-August 1972): 59-81; Nicos Poulantzas, <u>Political Power and Social Classes</u> (London: Schocken, 1973); Leo Panitch, "The Role and Nature of the Canadian State," in <u>The Canadian State: Political Economy and Political Power</u>, ed. Leo Panitch (Toronto and Buffalo: University of Toronto Press, 1977); Ralph Miliband, "Poulantzas and the Capitalist State," <u>New Left Review</u> 82 (November-December 1973); idem, <u>The State in Capitalist Society</u> (London: Weidenfeld and Nicolson, 1969); idem, "The Capitalist State; Reply to Nicos Poulantzas," <u>New Left Review</u> 95 (January-February 1970); E. Ladau, "The Specificity of the Political: The Poulantzas-Miliband Debate," <u>Economy and Society</u> 4 (February 1975): 87-110; Poulantzas, "The Capitalist State: A Reply to Miliband

and Ladau," New Left Review 95 (January–February 1976): 63–83; and the articles by Poulantzas and Miliband on "The Problem of the Capitalist State," in Ideology in Social Science, ed. R. Blackburn (London: Fontana, 1972).

6. Nettl in his "The State as a Conceptual Variable" has developed such a theory, which is discussed at length hereafter.

7. George Armstrong Kelly, "Who Needs a Theory of Citizenship?" in Daedalus 108 (Fall 1979): 21–27.

8. Hannah Arendt, "What Is Authority?" in Between Past and Future (New York: Viking Press, 1954), pp. 91–141.

9. George Armstrong Kelly, "Politics, Violence and Human Nature," NOMOS 17: Human Nature in Politics (New York: New York University Press, 1977), p. 132.

10. Kelly, "Who Needs a Theory of Citizenship?" pp. 23–24.

11. Ibid., p. 35.

12. Nettl, "The State as a Conceptual Variable," pp. 559–92.

13. Tilly, The Formation of National States.

14. Nettl, "The State as a Conceptual Variable," p. 562.

15. Ibid.

16. Ibid., pp. 562–66.

17. Ibid., p. 566.

18. Ibid., pp. 577–78. Italics in the original.

19. Ibid., pp. 579–89.

20. Ibid., pp. 580–81. Here again Nettl makes some highly provocative and controversial statements on the relationship between state and party: for example, "Where no state exists, however, parties carry a much larger functional weight" (p. 581), and "It can be argued that precisely the absence of a state also prevents the political articulation of social cleavage." (ibid.).

21. Ibid., pp. 583–84.

22. Ibid., p. 586.

23. Ibid., pp. 586–87.

24. Ibid., p. 588.

25. Ibid., p. 566.

26. Ibid.

27. Ibid.

28. The prototype of this is to be found in Gabriel A. Almond and Sidney Verba, The Civic Culture (Princeton, N.J.: Princeton University Press, 1963). On this see also Gabriel Ben-Dor, "Political Culture and Political Corruption: Some Attitudinal Dimensions," International Review of History and Political Science (forthcoming).

29. This is analyzed in G. Ben-Dor, "Political Culture Approach to Middle East Politics," International Journal of Middle East Studies 8 (January 1976): 43–63.

66. For an earlier assessment, see Manfred Halpern, "Middle Eastern Studies: A Review of the State of the Field with a Few Examples," World Politics 15 (October 1962): 108–22; for a recent assessment see Bernard Lewis, "The State of Middle Eastern Studies," American Scholar 48 (3) (Summer 1979): 365–81. Cf. the controversial Edward Said, Orientalism (New York: Pantheon, 1978.

67. James A. Bill and Carl Leiden, The Middle East: Politics and Power (Boston: Allyn and Bacon, 1974), p. 22. This formulation draws heavily on the deservedly influential work by Manfred Halpern, The Politics of Social Change in the Middle East and North Africa (Princeton, N.J.: Princeton University Press, 1963) and later studies by Halpern further evolving the ideas there presented.

68. Bill and Leiden, The Middle East: Politics and Power, p. 25.

69. Bruce Borthwick, Comparative Politics of the Middle East: An Introduction (Englewood Cliffs, N.J.: Prentice-Hall, 1980), p. 13.

70. Ibid., pp. 12–13.

71. Michael C. Hudson, Arab Politics: The Search for Legitimacy (New Haven, Conn. and London: Yale University Press, 1977).

72. Best articulated in Karl W. Deutsch, "Social Mobilization and Political Development," American Political Science Review 55 (September 1961): 493–514.

73. Hudson, Arab Politics, pp. 2–3.

74. Ibid., p. 1. The references are to Max Weber, The Theory of Social and Economic Organization (New York: Oxford University Press, 1947), pp. 124–26; Reinhard Bendix, Max Weber (New York: Doubleday, 1960), pp. 294–95.

75. Cf. Daniel Lerner, "Some Comments on Center-Periphery Relations," in Comparing Nations, ed. Richard L. Merrit and Stein Rokkan (New Haven, Conn.: Yale University Press, 1966) following Edward Shils's famous formulation of center and periphery, as presented in "Center and Periphery," in The Logic of Personal Knowledge: Essays Presented to M. Polanyi (London, 1961), pp. 117–30.

76. See the results of the special research project on Arab unity of the Center for the Research of Arab Unity (C.R.A.U.) located in Amman and Beirut, reported in the March–May 1980 editions of Al-Mustaqbal al-Arabi (Beirut).

77. Hudson, Arab Politics, p. 1.

78. Bernard Lewis, "Loyalties to Community, Nation and State," in Middle East Perspectives: The Next Twenty Years, ed. George S. Wise and Charles Issawi (Princeton, N.J.: Darwin, 1981).

79. Ibid., pp. 15–16.

80. Ibid., pp. 16–17.

2
Stateness and
the Return of Islam

When one speaks about the return of Islam, a distinction must be made between serious scholarly analysis on the one hand, and a fleeting intellectual (perhaps even pseudointellectual) fad, on the other. Unfortunately, the tumultuous revolution in Iran and its obviously powerful impact have given rise to a voluminous semi-popular literature,[1] much of which is not only worthless from a scientific point of view,[2] but is also literally behind the times, as the following instructive example should suffice to demonstrate.

"The return of Islam" was a phrase coined by Bernard Lewis in a famous article of that title published in January 1976.[3] The present author firmly believes that Islam never did go away, and is convinced that any profound reading of the above article will reveal that Lewis himself is also of this opinion. The Iranian revolution, however, some three years later, implanted the term and its connotations in the media and in the minds of scores of more or less reputable analysts, and the early 1980s have witnessed a veritable flood of verbiage along such lines. Lewis himself (whose article apparently has been more influential and inspiring than any other piece of writing on the subject), in a scientific colloquium held at the Shiloach Center for Middle Eastern and African Studies at Tel-Aviv University on June 25, 1980, ventured to say that "the Islamic resurgence has reached its peak, and that from now onwards it will probably decline rather than ascend."[4] He attributed this mainly to two things: the threat posed by radical Islam to incumbent Moslem governments, and a growing realization that the sense of collective Moslem power was ill founded, as the failure by Moslem states to take effective action against the Soviet invasion of Afghanistan had demonstrated.

The substance of this particular argument need not be of concern at the moment, but the conspicuous fact is that at the precise time the return-of-Islam movement in the literature was

approaching fever pitch, the originator of the concept was already
prophesying the decline rather than the further ascendance of the
tide. Obviously, then, a much more profound analysis of this
Islamic wave is required, at least insofar as its relationship to the
state is concerned.

It is beyond the scope of this study to attempt an exhaustive
survey of Islamic political thought,[5] and only one dimension will be
considered: the state (and stateness) in theory and practice.
Nevertheless, to begin with the crucial statement that has by now
(fortunately) become commonplace is unavoidable:

> Islam is the community of Allah. He is the living truth
> to which it owes its life. He is the center and the goal
> of its spiritual experience. But he is also the mundane
> head of his community which he not only rules but
> governs. He is the reason for the state's existence,
> he is the principle of unity, the Staatsgedanks, which
> both upholds and justifies the continuance of the
> commonwealth. . . . What is more, it places the
> life of the community in its entirety, as well as the
> private lives of the individual members, under his
> direct legislative and supervisory power.[6]

Thus, Islam is a civilization embracing all spheres of human
activity; as such it is much more than a religion, as the term is
commonly understood in the West. The failure of Western observers and analysts to grasp this essential truth, when confronted
with this conception of religion in the Middle East, has caused
much confusion, as has been forcefully articulated by Lewis:

> If, then, we are to understand anything at all about what
> is happening in the Muslim world at the present time
> and what has happened in the past, there are two essen-
> tial points which need to be grasped. One is the uni-
> versality of religion as a factor in the lives of the
> Muslim peoples, and the other is its centrality.
> "Render unto Caesar the things which are
> Caesar's; and unto God the things which are God's."
> That is, of course, Christian doctrine and practice.
> It is totally alien to Islam. The three major Middle
> Eastern religions are significantly different in their
> relations with the state and their attitudes to political
> power. Judaism was associated with the state and
> was then disentangled from it; its new encounter with
> the state at the present time raises problems which

are still unresolved. Christianity, during the first formative centuries of its existence, was separate from
and indeed antagonistic to the state with which it only
later became involved. Islam from the lifetime of its
founder <u>was</u> the state, and the identity of religion and
government is indelibly stamped on the memories and
awareness of the faithful from their own sacred writings, history, and experience. . . . Islam was associated with power from the very beginning, from the
first formative years of the Prophet and his immediate
successors. This association between religion and
power, community and polity, can already be seen in
the Qur'an itself and in the other early religious texts
on which Muslims base their beliefs. One consequence
is that in Islam religion is not, as it is in Christendom,
one sector or segment of life, regulating some matters
while others are excluded, it is concerned with the
whole of life—not a limited but a total jurisdiction. In
such a society the very idea of the separation of church
and state is meaningless, since there are no two entities to be separated.[7]

Islam, then, made a comprehensive effort to restructure the
lives of a huge community so as to conform with the commandments
emanating from God. This was an immensely ambitious task,
made increasingly difficult by the large number of centrifugal
sociopolitical forces in a vast geographic area, with relatively low
technological levels of transportation and communication. The
ensuing practical difficulties, coupled with the increasingly obvious
gap between the required ideal rule, on the one hand, and the very
imperfect reality of much weakness and corruption, on the other,
created several cruel dilemmas and fears. Chief among them,
perhaps, was the fear of anarchy—or, better put, the disintegration of the community of the faithful—which would render any other
consideration irrelevant. It has been argued elsewhere[8] that this
fear had tremendously important consequences for the actual structure of the Islamic state in the Middle East. The argument stems
from the following basic assertion:

Traditional Islamic society was characterized, among
others, by the overwhelming strength of ubiquitous
ascriptive, particularistic groups; by the wide preva-
lence of fluid conflict (mostly, but not exclusively
among the afore-mentioned groups) and thus also
sophisticated techniques and mechanisms of conflict

management; by a low level of differentiation (thus as
Halpern and others argue, it is clearly correct to assert that power led to wealth far more often than wealth
led to power); and by a generally low level of institutionalization, all this in a "convergence" society. . . .[9]
Within this complex framework, the maintenance of the
political and social order which enabled conflict to continue concurrently with the submission to the existence
of a very thin, but very authentic ideological super-
structure within which the search for the perfect manifestation of (and submission to) the will of God could
continue was an immense task, but also a supreme
necessity which often led to compromise, realism and
the preference of a broad consensus over ideological
purity and rigidity. The fear of disorder and disintegration was very real, external pressures were
great; diversity was immense; and breakdown was all
too real a possibility. Thus, uncommonly pragmatic
efforts were necessary to build and maintain a political
center capable of holding the fragile structure together.[10]

Some scholars, von Grunebaum for one,[11] derive from such
a state of affairs a theory of the genesis of "cynicism" and "failure"
in Islamic politics. An alternative conception, however, may be
equally plausible, for those Islamic scholars cited in support of
the cynicism thesis argue a particular logic of stateness. It is a
logic of the state as the necessary framework (indeed, the only
framework) within which the values of the community have a chance
to be realized. One interpretation is that of cynicism and hopeless
tyranny; but, in a way, these statements reflect a very modern need
for the existence of some viable political order, however imperfect
in its manifestation. This is not a Machiavellian raison d'état,
but something quite different: the state does not have a logic all its
own, for it does not exist as a political creature generating its own
values and raison d'etre. Quite the contrary: an imperfect state
may be intolerable if judged by its own (that is, state-oriented, and
hence political) standards; but it must not, and cannot, be judged
by these standards, for its existence is necessary and justified—
the protection of a community dedicated to certain ideals. Without
a state, however imperfect, the community is likely to disintegrate
altogether, and without a community of believers, the ideals of
Islam are lost. Hence, the imperfection of the state is tolerable:
what matters is not what the state does, but what the community does
in terms of responding to the commandments of God. That is not
very cynical. Compare this line of reasoning, for instance to "the

old Oriental maxim that a ruler can have no powers without soldiers, no soldiers without money, no money without the well-being of his subjects, and no popular well-being without justice."[12]

A respected Turkish historian fuses this maxim (which is indeed much closer to cynicism) and some of what von Grunebaum described in medieval Islam, to the structure that later evolved in the Ottoman Empire:

> Ottoman social policy conformed closely to the traditional view that for the sake of social peace and order the state should keep each man in his appropriate social position. Ottoman society was divided into two major classes. The first one, called askeri, literally the military, included those to whom the Sultan had designated religious or executive power, through an imperial diploma, namely officers of the court and the army, civil servants and ulema. The second included the reaya comprising all Muslim and non-Muslim subjects who paid taxes but had no part in the government. It was a fundamental rule of the Empire to exclude its subjects from the privileges of the "military." Only those among them who were actual fighters on the frontiers and those who had entered the ulema class after a regular course of study . . . could obtain the Sultan's diploma and thus become members of the military class.[13]

If this analytical description is correct, much of the original Islamic logic was transformed. While the fundamental distinction between Muslims and others endured, the original raison d'être of the Islamic political structure was less clearly emphasized, while a type of raison d'état emerged relating to the Empire as such. The stress here is simply on "social peace and order in the state," and less on what the state is supposed to do by way of enabling the Islamic community to function as believers in values, ideas, and commandments.[14] Yet, even amid this growing cynicism, the Islamic community endured as the ultimate justification. Much has been written on the despotism and tyranny involved in the cynicism thesis, as well as on the centrality of military power to the Islamic state.[15] Yet, somewhat different arguments have also been made:

> Loyalties were accorded, on the one hand, to kinship groups, neighborhoods or guilds, and, on the other, to Islam and the Shari'a, but not to the state as such. As for the changing balance of power between caliph and sultan, the philosophers and theologians had by that

time produced the necessary rationales. Al-Mawardi
declared that the caliph's duties were the defense of
religion and the administration of state but that he
could hold office even if under arrest and could right-
fully delegate some of his governing powers to others.
Al-Ghazzali proposed a cooperative relationship between caliph and sultan: the sultan would designate
the caliph and the caliph would accept and legitimize
the secular role of the sultan. In terms of the rightful
basis of government these distinctions were and still
are important, but in terms of actual political behavior they were academic almost from the time they
were proposed. Since the middle of the tenth century,
when Baghdad fell under the Umayyid kings, the
caliphate had been reduced to the merest appendage
of royal authority. Caliphs were jailed, humiliated,
and exiled. Furthermore, by the thirteenth century
local dynasts on both extremes of the Dar al-Islam
were claiming the title for themselves. As the
Ottoman Turks burst into predominance, defeating
the Egyptian Mamluks early in the sixteenth century,
Sultan Selim I imprisoned the nominal Abbasid caliph
and appropriated the functions of the caliphate into
the office of sultan. There they remained until
1923-24 when the proclamation of the Turkish Republic led to the abolition of both offices.

Although the Ottoman state was always dominated by wordly as opposed to religious rule—a
condition evident in the absolute superiority of the
sultan's office compared to that of caliph—it is a
fact nonetheless that under the Ottoman system, especially in the sixteenth and seventeenth centuries,
the law of Islam reached its most elaborate and
effective form. Under the administration of the
Chief Mufti of Constantinople, the Shaykh al-Islam,
the Shari'a was applied throughout the empire through
a system of competent and independent judges—qadis;
and it covered not only the domain of personal status
but also commercial and civil law. However brutal,
despotic, and unstable the politics of the sultanate
may have been, the system remained to most of its
subjects the domain of Islam. Even in its last days
it is significant that the great majority of its Arab-
Muslim subjects refused to take up the standard of
the Arab revolt.[16]

The continuity from medieval Islam to the Ottoman period is unmistakable when related to the fundamental Islamic frame of reference.[17] This shared ethos of Islam, along with certain structural features of the Islamic establishment, requires a cautious examination of the claims of tyranny:

> Rulers and the ruled shared basic values; most rulers did not impose alien norms on their subjects, and so tyranny, in the sense of "wrong rule," was the exception. If authoritarian political culture implies acceptance of any authority, just as long as it is the strongest, then it is misleading to assert that Islam was a prime contributor to the authoritarian political cultures of the Arab world. Furthermore, as we have seen, the unorthodox dissenting movements in Islam militated against the dogmatic and scholasticist influence of the establishment ulama.[18]

The real problem, according to this view, was not that of tyranny, but that of succession, the orderly transition of power: the true test of political stability. On this point, it is more or less agreed that

> the Quran, the hadith (Quranic commentaries) and ijma (rule of consensus) were not explicit about the succession. . . . the Arabic term for caliphate—khalafa—does not appear. There was thus no divine guidance as to whether it should be by heredity, election, or designation. The only point that does seem clear is that the successor was to be a guide to the divine law for ordinary men, as Ibn Khaldun later put it; that is, the executor of the shari'a as interpreted through the consensus of the ulama.[19]

Indeed, the relationship between succession and stateness is very close, as an etymological examination reveals. The Arabic term currently used for state is dawla. Under this heading in the authoritative Encyclopaedia of Islam[20] one finds the following:

> 1) An Arabic word signifying the period of an individual's rule or power but also often employed in the meaning of "dynasty". . . . 3) From its original meaning, dawla developed quite a few specialized connotations. . . . In modern times, an adjectival formation dawli or duwali—from dawla or its pl. duwal, in

> the meaning of "nation" state government dynasty—
> has become accepted in Arabic as the current term for
> "international . . ."

This terminological evolution of individual rule and dynasty to state
is of utmost significance, and it leads back to an examination of the
concept of the state proper in Islamic political thought.

Clearly, the concept of state understood by Muhammad was
that of theocracy. [21] This had to be developed against the tradition
of the sayyid:

> The only type of ruler the Arab had known in his own
> country had been the sayyid, the chieftain of a tribe (or
> possibly leader of an agglomeration of tribes). The
> sayyid held this office thanks to his personal prestige,
> which in part was due to his noble lineage, but which
> mostly sprang from his qualities as a leader, his
> generosity, and his ability to deal with people. The
> sayyid had no power to enforce his bidding. Some-
> times he became guilty of arrogance, but as a rule
> his prerogatives did not infringe on the essential equal-
> ity of all members of the tribe. He was freely acces-
> sible. No ceremonial protected him and his position.
> His heir would succeed him only if his capabilities
> recommended him, but socially the descendant of a
> reverenced leader had a considerable advantage. . . .
> [Initially,] the princes of the Umayyad dynasty
> (661-750) tried to maintain the mores and mannerisms
> of the sayyid, although intrinsically their position as
> rulers of an enormous empire, as successors, caliphs,
> of the Prophet, and as "Princes of the Believers"
> (amir al-mu'minin) had completely outgrown frame and
> scope of the ancient ideal. . . . [However,] the acces-
> sion of the 'Abbasids, made possible largely through
> the support of Persian Muslims, brought to the fore the
> humanly less attractive but politically more adequate
> concept of kingship to which the Iranians had been ac-
> customed from their native rulers. [22]

This created a new type of ruler: "the prince, isolated from the
uniform herd of his subjects, consecrated by divine designation for
his office, legitimized by his descent from a long line of kings,
guarded by an elaborate etiquette devised to guard his person from
defiling contact with the lowly crowd and to overawe the slaves over
whom he had been set by the Lord of the Worlds."[23]

Thus, "since everything was God's, including the political process, there was no need to explore the rights of secular leaders. Yet, in a pragmatic way, Muslim rulers still had to confront most of the same problems that secular rulers in the West did."[24] And, in fact, notwithstanding some Western popular misconceptions, medieval Islam did produce several important and sophisticated theories of politics and the state. A detailed and lucid examination of these is to be found in Rosenthal's work.[25] He starts from the following state of affairs:

> Siyāsa, government, is determined by the Shari'a and, according to the Muslim jurists, falls to the caliph or imām. But whilst the Islamic, that is the religious and political, character of the state is assumed as a matter of course by all Muslim writers, jurists, historians, philosophers and moralists, the meaning and content of siyāsa undergo significant changes in the course of Islamic history and under the impact of the decreasing coherence of the Abbasid caliphate. The imāma, though presupposed, gives way to the mulk, literally "kingdom," in the thought and reflections of writers on morals and politics. They are interested in the actual state and principally in its effective ruler.[26]

The resulting literature is of different types and significance. The least important type is that of the "guidebooks for princes" variety.[27] Although their very practicality on the technical level of politics suggests that their authors must have had at least a patrimonial notion of stateness (for the moral Islamic dimension in them is very weak), they remain on the level of "governmental technology."

A very different kind of logic is to be found in the writings of the fourteenth-century thinker Ibn al-Tiqtaqa. Although the theocratic Islamic caliphate remains the ideal, in his own work he is principally concerned with the mulk as a state now in existence, which, as such, must be studied as a unit of analysis in its own right, having a specific concept of its own.

> Ibn al-Tiqtaqa is the first to think of the state as an entity in its own right, yet not independent of the ruler, who at that period of Islamic history was still an essential part of the state. The state exists as an object of study, and a ruler is judged only by the performance of his duties in relation to its best interests.[28]

The notion of stateness is already present here in an astonishingly modern form, and this alone should suffice to provide a check against hasty generalizations about dichotomies between Western and Islamic political thought, at least in the medieval period. Add to this the impact of a heritage of Greek philosophy on medieval Islamic thought, and the inescapable reality of the political realm.

The outstanding contribution to Islamic political thought was made by Ibn Khaldun, "perhaps the last of the giants of the Arab-Islamic tradition . . . , the fourteenth-century Tunisian scholar, traveler, jurist and diplomat, whose 'Introduction' (al-Muqaddima) to the study of history is acclaimed as a masterly sociological study of political power and authority."29 Indeed, his "writings convey an uncanny sense of modernity to the twentieth-century reader."30

Practically the first thing that comes to mind on an informed reading of Ibn Khaldun's work is the affinity of his ideas to those of Machiavelli. Notwithstanding some notable differences, a detailed comparative study leads Rosenthal to conclude that

> it is their insight into human nature and their realization of the importance of force and power, supported by indispensable authority, which links the Muslim historian of human civilization to the man of the Renaissance, who had studied the history of Rome and of Christian Italy.31

While Machiavelli was himself a political activist and reformer, Ibn Khaldun's ambitions were more "properly intellectual." Even so, both thinkers "share an impartial empiricism. . . . But Ibn Khaldun inquires into the origin and development of the state in order to find and formulate an underlying law."32 They share some fascinating insights as to the relationships between religion, law, military power, and the viability of the state, a most salient theme in the history of the Islamic state:

> In one respect both men came to practically identical conclusions quite independently. Both stress the importance of religion for the state and the connection between religion and power. In his Discorsi Machiavelli says: "If we read Roman history attentively we will always find how much religion contributed to obedience in the army, to courage among the people, to the preservation of morality and to shaming the wicked. . . . As the worship of God is the cause for the greatness of republics, so is its neglect the cause of their ruin. . . ." Religion consolidates the state. Ibn Khaldun stated that

religion without 'Asabīya is unable to impress people, impose its law on them and secure their obedience. Only authority backed by effective power can bring success, in religious matters no less than in political affairs. Machiavelli says: "Only he should set out to conquer who has also ability and force. . . ." In the sixth chapter of his Principe he speaks of the difficulty of preserving newly won power and says: ". . . but when he must rely on himself and can use coercion, he rarely runs a risk. It is for this reason that all armed prophets have been victorious, and all unarmed ones have perished." This agrees with the quotation from the earlier chapter: "The religious call (da'wa) is not complete without 'Asabīya," to which this further passage may be added: "The situation of the prophets was the same when they called men to God with the help of clans and groups, and they were fortified by God. . . ."

Machiavelli also resembles Ibn Khaldun in his evaluation of religion in relation to the state when he claims (Discorsi II, 2) that Christianity makes man humble and submissive. From the passage quoted above it is clear that Ibn Khaldun exempts pure Islam from such a charge, at any rate when the khilāfa corresponded in reality to its theory as laid down in the Shari'a. It is true this formulation happened long after the khilāfa had been transformed into the mulk, and for this reason Ibn Khaldun avers that once the Shar' had become a science to be studied at a time when religion has lost its impetus, the deference of the students towards their teachers resulted in a decline in manliness and self-reliance. But while he safeguards Islam as a religion and the khilāfa as the ideal state he would agree with Machiavelli as far as the mulk is concerned, that is, the mulk which is based on a mixed government, and whose law contains both the ordinances of the Shari'a, and political statutes promulgated by the autocratic ruler.

Machiavelli is at one with him in stressing that the fear of God which religion inspires in man makes him obedient to orders and laws, reliable in keeping an oath or a promise, and easy to rule. In his view, religion is also conducive to the formation of a good army; indeed, he summed up those things which preserve the state in the words: "Religion, laws and army."[33]

Yet another critical point on which a comparison of the two systems of thought is very much in order is the conception of raison d'état:

> We have seen that in the power-state (mulk), in contrast to the khilāfa in the strict sense under the first four caliphs, the interest of the state is the overriding consideration. The ruler is responsible for the state, its safety, good order and welfare. To discharge his responsibilities he must have sufficient power. Machiavelli's attitude to the state is basically the same: the interests of the state are paramount. But Machiavelli would go much further than Ibn Khaldun, who held to Muslim ethics, was prepared to go. [34]

Thus, there is a definite logic of raison d'état in Ibn Khaldun's thought, as is evidenced by his unprecedentedly profound treatment of the mulk, the prevailing nonideal "kingdom." In his study, Rosenthal shows unusual insight and judgment in translating mulk as "power-state" in his analysis of Ibn Khaldun's political thought. Ibn Khaldun's philosophy of the power-state does not, however, lead to Cassirer's depraved condition in which politics becomes disconnected from moral systems. [35] The raison d'état of the mulk is not so dismal, since the state and its logic have not lost their connection with Muslim ethics, and in his opinion they ought never to do so.

Wherein lies Ibn Khaldun's distinctive contribution to the study of the state of Islam? It is of immense scope, and thus deserves a detailed examination, in which Rosenthal's succinct and lucid analysis will be closely followed.

Ibn Khaldun was a prototype of the realistic but humanistic social scientist.

> His realistic approach to man in the state made him recognize the will to power and domination as the principal driving force; but he was convinced that the higher aspirations of rational man could only develop in a society efficiently organized in an effective political organization, and only the state could provide it. Hence his interest in politics springs from his Islamic heritage, with its stress on the "community of the faithful," the umma or jamā'a of orthodox Islam. Together with his impartial observation, this living heritage enabled him to deduce a general law which he applied to the whole of human civilization.

It is true that his concept of universal civilization
is derived exclusively from a dispassionate study of the
Islamic empire of his day, with its variety of political
entities and cultural levels. But this does not seriously
affect his generalizations, nor impair the validity of
most of them in the realm of human culture and civilization. It is no exaggeration to say that Ibn Khaldun's
"new science of history" represents a medieval witness
to the premature birth of modern scientific inquiry into
the human group, transcending the bounds of Islam, and
it is no coincidence that he speaks of insāniya, humanitas,
of the citizens of the state, a concept which we usually
associate with the Renaissance and the humanism of the
West. [36]

Ibn Khaldun adopts an Aristotelian approach in arguing that
"the state as such is the natural result of human life which requires
association (ijtima) and organization."[37] He distinguishes between
different types of states, such as the ideal Islamic theocracy, government based on man-established laws of reason, and an ideal
Platonic state of philosophers. But the driving force behind the
state is power, dominion, rule (mulk), which is intrinsic to human
nature, and it even precedes the state as a structure.[38]

Ibn Khaldun was a fervent believer in the cyclical explanation
for the rise and fall of states, and indeed outlined five specific
phases a state goes through. This cycle is closely associated with
its ruling dynasty. "The dynasty has a natural term of life like an
individual."[39] As a realist, his emphasis was not so much on the
normative utopia of an ideal theocracy, but on the existing power-
state:

It is clear from Ibn Khaldun's statement that we are
dealing not with a state based on the Shari'a, but an
autocracy dependent on a mercenary army for the maintenance of power. It is in this power-state that the political and economic egotism of the ruler and his asso-
ciates leads to abuses much more easily and frequently
than in the state based on the moral law founded in
revelation.

Ibn Khaldun, far from moralizing, does not criticize moral offences and shortcomings as an open flout-
ing of moral precepts, or as a sin deserving divine
punishment; he sets them in relation to the state,
registers their political significance and implications
and dispassionately states their disastrous effect on
good government and public welfare. [40]

The main concern in this system of thought is public welfare
and the interest of the state. Ibn Khaldun was realistic enough to
observe and accept the transformation from the caliphate, dominated by law revealed by religion, to the mulk (power-state), even
if it is still an Islamic mulk. The interplay of religion and politics
in general, and Islam and state in particular, never ceased to
fascinate Ibn Khaldun's fertile mind:

> His own contribution to political thought consists in two
> important findings. They are the result of the blending,
> in his searching mind, of empiricism and traditionalism,
> and they are: (a) that the khilāfa has survived in the mulk
> of the Islamic empire, and (b) that religion, if not the
> determining factor as it is in the khilāfa, still remains
> an important factor in the mulk. He applies his own
> experience in Islam to society and civilization in gen-
> eral. He thus combines a primarily theological with a
> power-political concept of the state, without in any way
> abandoning the accepted Muslim position, since the
> spiritual and the temporal power are united in the caliph
> or imām. This does not mean, however, that there is
> simply a difference of degree: religion being either the
> sovereign ruling factor, a primus inter pares, or only
> one factor among many, though a very important one.
> For Ibn Khaldun maintains again and again that domina-
> tion is as necessary as the will to power and domination
> is natural, and that power can be gained and dominion
> established without the call of religion, so long as
> 'Asabiya unites a large enough group of like-minded en-
> thusiasts to supply the man aspiring to political leader-
> ship with sufficient backing. But he would not be a
> Muslim if he did not stress the support, often decisive,
> which religion lends to the 'Asābiya, transforming a
> driving force originally based on descent or common
> material interests into an irresistible spiritual in-
> fluence reinforced by the energy and striking power of
> a closely knit group of activists. This applies in par-
> ticular to Islam in its period of expansion and consoli-
> dation into a world power.
> Ibn Khaldun has correctly deduced that a weaken-
> ing of the religious élan must strengthen the temporal
> component of the khilafa and inevitably lead to its trans-
> formation into absolute monarchy in the form of the
> mulk. [41]

Not surprisingly, "The observer of the state as it is has drawn the conclusion from this knowledge that the transformation of the khilāfa into the mulk is natural and inevitable."[42] The importance of Ibn Khaldun's effort to develop a comprehensive theory of the state (and of what would perhaps be called stateness today), stems primarily from his recognition of the "inevitable correlation between the political situation and the standard of living, the state of civilization of rulers and ruled."[43]

Of course, this examination of the philosophical heritage culminating with Ibn Khaldun does not, and cannot, settle historical issues, nor does it have the necessary behavioral connotation. If, however, it is accepted that "medieval Islamic political theory is more contemporary for the Muslim world than medieval Christian theory is for the West,"[44] it should decisively settle the question whether Islamic culture has an intellectual heritage of stateness.

Furthermore, there is no persuasive reason to argue that the oft-quoted "Islamic wave" is directed against the state, or that it constitutes a serious threat to it. As has been shown, the state and Islam are not contradictory in either logical or empirical terms. Their coexistence is déjà vu. So, also, is the ubiquitous tension between Islamic universalism on the one hand and state (and lower-level) particularism on the other. Ibn Khaldun dreamed of the caliphate, but lived in, served, studied, and analyzed the mulk, as have multitudes of lesser men ever since. While it is unquestionable that Muslims—and thus Muslim states—generally feel a strong affinity with one another religiously, culturally, and politically,[45] this is a far cry from a challenge to their continued existence as autonomous entities: all Muslim, to be sure—all sharing a rich, attractive heritage, perhaps cooperating within a variety of frameworks—but separate, all the same.

> Summit conferences like the one held in Lahore in 1974 and institutions like the Islamic Economic Conference appeal to those who wish to speak of the resurrection of Islam without shaking the power of the state. No one wants to unite Saudi Arabia and Bangladesh, Indonesia and the United Arab Emirates.[46]

Much has been said about pan-Islamic sentiments posing a threat to fragile states of all kinds, but this author agrees with Ajami that

> the only challenge that Islamic sentiment might pose would come from far below the world of state elites, where a militant, popular kind of Islam may reject—

as it does in Iran, and to a lesser extent in Egypt—
the world view and preferences of state elites. [47]

Some of this misunderstanding is perhaps due to the complex
triangular relationship between Islam (and the Islamic community,
or ummah), the nation (and in particular the Arab nation, qawm)
and the particular homeland (watan), [48] where present states are
territorially situated. This confusing trinity has had a particularly
debilitating effect on the Arab countries, where the pan-state appeal
of Arab nationalism dominated the political scene until the 1960s,
and much of its rhetoric continues to dominate attitudes to this very
day. [49] This appeal, indeed, created intolerable tensions when
allegiance to the state was "tacit, even surreptitious" while Arab
unity was "the sole publicly acceptable objective of statesmen and
ideologues alike."[50] This condition is discussed later.

But what is the role of Islam in all this? A lucid historical
perspective on the evolution of this trinity is offered by Elie
Kedourie,[51] who traces the emergence and manipulation of pan-
Islamic sentiments in the later stages of the Ottoman Empire and
then shows the curious theoretical tension between Islam and the
Arab nationalist movement in the latter's formative stages (in
which, as is well known to any historian of the Middle East, the
Western powers in general, and Britain in particular, played a
visibly active role).

> This overriding feeling of Islamic solidarity somehow
> came increasingly to be depreciated and indeed forgotten
> during and after the First World War. Such oblivion, as
> has been said, suited the Allies. But there was more to
> it than a deliberate playing down of dangerous beliefs
> and attitudes. British officials in particular genuinely
> thought that Arab nationalism was opposed to, and would
> thus weaken, what they called Pan-Islamism. This was
> not the least reason for encouraging the Sharif's rebel-
> lion and spreading the gospel of a future independent
> Arab state. The notion that Arabism and Islam were
> opposites was spread by Arab nationalists. These, at
> the outset, were mostly officers who had deserted from
> the Ottoman army. Their training and education had
> Westernized them more or less profoundly; they were
> accustomed—like their young Turk fellow-officers—to
> the categories of contemporary European political dis-
> course, and had adopted Western political ideas—first
> and foremost that of nationalism. In nationalism, as is
> well-known, the primordial value is the nation, and not,

say class or religion. The Arab nationalists therefore
sincerely proclaimed that their aim was to establish an
Arab nation-state in which, Muslims, Christians and
Jews would enjoy equal citizenship. These nationalists
were also aware that their Western patrons and pro-
tectors looked with fear and aversion on Islam as a
political force, and they emphasized therefore all the
more the opposition between Arabism and Islam.[52]

However sincere, a nationalist movement cannot, of course,
remain for long purely on the intellectual level. In a way, the real
test of its sincerity is met only by its appeal to the masses and by
the way the masses are made to understand its message. By then,
the "opposition between Arabism and Islam" is transformed almost
to its exact opposite.

It was between the wars that the theory of Arab nationalism was endowed with a body of theoretical literature,
and began to make real headway in the schools and col-
leges from whence the official classes—whether civilian
or military—were recruited. As propounded then by its
most influential theoretician, Sati al-Husri, the doctrine
of Arab nationalism clearly differentiated between loyalty
to Arabism and loyalty to Islam, and it was in no doubt
that the former ought to have the primacy over the latter. But this aspect of the doctrine did not occasion a
great debate. The younger generations who were becoming enthusiastic Arab nationalists did not feel that there
was anything in the circumstances of the Arab world which
required a confrontation between Arabism and Islam:
the struggle for Arab independence and unity—a struggle
directed against European-Christian powers and against
Zionism—was in no way weakened or harmed by Islam,
or any Islamic figures or institutions. One can even
go further and say that Islam actually gave great strength
to Arab nationalism. This is because the Arab world is
overwhelmingly Muslim, and Arab nationalist leaders,
Muslims almost to a man, naturally attracted to themselves the powerful feelings of and solidarity towards
their leaders which Islam has instilled in its followers.
Whether these nationalist leaders practised their religion or were indifferent to it did not affect the issue.
And the situation was the same all over the Arab world:
in Iraq and the Levant as well as in the Maghrib.

On the level of practical politics, then, not only
was there no opposition between Islam and Arabism,
there was actually cooperation. But this cooperation
was not formulated or incorporated in the doctrine of
Arab nationalism until after the Second World War.
This development may be seen as a dialectical one,
arising out of the very doctrine of Arab nationalism as
originally formulated. The doctrine insisted, as has been
seen, on the primacy of Arabism, on there being a historic Arab nation, now dismembered and subject to alien
rule, but entitled—and destined—to full independence and
unity. It was therefore necessary for the doctrine to
seek out and describe the lineaments of this nation; the
doctrine, in other words, had to rely heavily—as other
nationalist doctrines have commonly done—on a historical mode of argument. But to define the Arab nation in terms of its history is—sooner rather than
later—to come upon the fact that Islam originated among
the Arabs, was revealed in Arabic to an Arab Prophet.
Great significance must be attached to this tremendous
fact. The ideologies of Arabism drew in the main two
consequences which, in spite of their difference of emphasis, yet produced a new theoretical amalgam in
which Islam and Arabism became inseparable.[53]

Thus, the Islamic dimension of universalism was fused, as
it were, with the vast appeal of Arab nationalism. This created
enormous ideological tensions at a different stage of state building
in the Arab countries.

The "national aspirations and popular expectations"[54] aroused
by Arab states' elites included a variety of tenets derived from
pan-Arabism (chiefly the ideal of Arab unity) as well as various
forms of Arab socialism, promising solidarity, class cooperation,
progress, economic development, and social justice.[55] This
created a potent appeal indeed: "The mixture of socialism, Arabism and Islam is a powerful one."[56] But it is also a confused,
ambivalent, and ambiguous mixture. While erudite intellectuals
may actually enjoy sorting out its elements and the links among
them, at the popular level the entire mixture clearly stands or falls
with Islam: "The appeal to Islam will find a wide response among
the traditionally-minded masses. The 'socialism' which has somehow been yoked together with Islam and Arabism will not elicit
from them the same response."[57]

Indeed not. Thus, a fantastic paradox came into being: one
that is important to the understanding of the Middle East today.

Nationalism gained a total and overwhelming triumph, but in so doing it expanded the circles of the masses who participate in politics, and in the dialogue with them the ideological barrenness of nationalism became increasingly—and embarrassingly—clear. The contrived ideological artifacts attracting secular Muslim (as well as many Christian) intellectuals rang hollow in the ears of the masses:

> As the nationalist movement has become genuinely popular, so it has become less national and more religious—in other words, less Arab and more Islamic. In moments of crisis—and these have been many in recent decades—it is the instinctive communal loyalty that outweighs all others.[58]

Moreover, the prominence of many radical Christian intellectuals and politicians in the forefront of the Arab nationalist movement came increasingly to be resented. This prominence was quite natural in the beginning, due to well-known ideological and sociological factors:

> When the idea of Arabism as a common nationality was first launched in the late 19th and early 20th centuries, Arabic-speaking Christians played a prominent part in the movement. It was natural that they should be attracted by a national rather than a religious identity, since in the one they could claim the equal citizenship to which they could never aspire in the other. According to this view, the Arabs were a nation divided into various religions, in which Christians and even at times Jews might hope to share in the common Arabism along with the Muslim majority. . . .
> As Christians, they were more open to Western ideas and identified themselves more readily in national terms. The superior education to which they had access enabled them to play a leading part in both intellectual and commercial life. Christians, especially Lebanese Christians, had a disproportionately important role in the foundation and development of the newspaper and magazine press in Egypt and in other Arab countries, and Christian names figure very prominently among the outstanding novelists, poets, and publicists in the earlier stages of modern Arabic literature. Even in the nationalist movements, many of the leaders and spokesmen were members of Christian minorities. This

prominence in cultural and political life was paralleled
by a rapid advance of the Christian minorities in material wealth. [59]

As is well known, however, once the ancien régime is de-
molished, the revolution often begins to devour its own sons. The
Arab nationalist revolution has been no exception, a fact that has
served to make many Christian Arabs cling to their revolutionary
ideals (and organization) even more tenaciously:

> In recent decades, this prominence has ceased to be
> tolerable. Partly through measures of nationalization
> adopted by socialist governments, partly through other
> more direct means, the economic power of the Chris-
> tian communities has been reduced in one country after
> another and is now being challenged in its last strong-
> hold, the Lebanon. Christian predominance in intellec-
> tual life has long since been ended, and a new generation
> of writers has arisen, the overwhelming majority of
> whom are Muslims. There are still Christian politicians
> and ideologists, but their role is much circumscribed in
> a society increasingly conscious of its Muslim identity,
> background, and aspirations. Among the various or-
> ganizations making up the Palestine Liberation Organiza-
> tion, the Fatah is overwhelmingly though not exclusively
> Muslim. On the other hand, many of the extremist or-
> ganizations tend to be Christian, for in the radical ex-
> tremism which they profess Christians still hope to
> find the acceptance and equality which eluded them in
> nationalism. [60]

Clearly, a radical nationalist seeking to communicate with the
masses of his country (and those of other countries!) and to find
some widespread appeal could not ignore the enormous potential of
popular Islam. So, Gamal Abdel Nasser, after a visit to Mecca,
remembered his growing awareness "of the potential achievements
cooperation among all these millions can accomplish—cooperation
naturally not going beyond their loyalty to their original countries,
but which will ensure for them and their brethren-in-Islam unlimited power."[61]

As Lewis soberly comments, however: "Attempts at international pan-Islamism have produced limited results."[62] Looking for
deeper reasons for the persistent weakness of "official pan-
Islamism," he observes that

in the first century and a half of the Caliphate, Islam
was indeed one single world state. But at that early
date, it ceased to be so, and was never reunited again.
Thus, while the political experience of Muslims, the
shared memories of the past which they cherish, condition them to a sense of common social and cultural
identity, they do not bring them any tradition of a single
Islamic state, but rather one of political pluralism combined with socio-cultural unity.[63]

In other (theoretical) words, then, there is indeed a tradition
of stateness in Islam, but it is not that of one Islamic superstate,
but that of many Islamic states. To the extent that legacies of
stateness point to the future, they point to the persistence of a
reality known already to Ibn Khaldun: a yearning for an all-Islamic
caliphate coming to terms with many Islamic mulks, so to speak.
The Islamic state, as has been seen, is dialectically related
to nationalism. Nationalism has won ideologically. In so doing, it
involved the masses, who demanded increasing emphasis on its
Islamic component; as revolutionary regimes searched for "practical ideologies"[64] to respond to the expectations raised by the
nationalist revolution, they increasingly found their baggage empty
and thus fell back on traditional Islamic rhetoric. In the Arab case,
the triumph of nationalism has been so overwhelming as to practically cause its failure, for its own impractical but dangerous
ideals had to be replaced by the safer universal Islamic slogans.
Ajami rather pointedly says:

> Muslim universalism is a safer doctrine than the geo-
> graphically more limited but politically more trouble-
> some idea of pan-Arabism; the 148 Muslim countries
> and 700 million Muslims is a safe and distant symbol,
> giving a semblance of "super-legitimacy" without pos-
> ing a threat to reason of state.[65]

As to the domestic problems involved in the rise of militant, popular Islam, it is, "at least in the Arab context . . . a different problem from the disruptive doctrine of pan-Arabism, for it is a challenge contained within the boundaries of the state."[66]
Ajami believes, probably rightly, that the increasing saliency
of Islam also has to do with realities of regional politics.

> This shift in belief corresponds to concrete changes in
> the distribution of power in the Arab system. Power

has shifted to the state (Saudi Arabia) that has long been
a foe of pan-Arabism and has traditionally seen itself
as a guardian of the turath, the heritage, or Islam, to
be more precise. [69]

There is even some empirical evidence indicating a strong
association between rising sentiments of Islamic identity and loyalty
to the state: not at the expense of each other, but both gaining at
the expense of nationalism:

A social scientist at Kuwait University has supplied us
with important evidence substantiating the demise of
pan-Arabism and suggesting the shape of things to come.
Taking a sample of students from practically all Arab
countries, he administered a questionnaire to nearly 500
undergraduates at Kuwait University with the aim of ascer-
taining their views on pan-Arabism, family, state and
religion. What he found was a remarkable assertion of
Islamic sentiment and of patriotism associated with
particular Arab states—in other words, the vacuum
left behind as a result of the demise of pan-Arabism is
being filled by religious belief on one level and by loyalty to the state on another. His data led him to conclude that the discussions of "one Arab nation" and
"Arab brotherhood" are myths and exhausted slogans. [68]

This "remarkable" assertion of Islamic sentiment and of patriotism
associated with particular (Arab) states would certainly have been
no surprise to Ibn Khaldun!

So, Islam has not "returned" against the Arab state in the
Arab countries; rather, to a certain extent it has virtually allied
itself with the state against nationalism. Such a development, if
pushed close to its logical culmination, may (and should) create
states with raison d'état of their own, tempered and checked by an
Islamic ethic, one in which affinity with other Islamic countries
and solidarity with other Arab countries will continue to be important permanent considerations. But raison d'état itself will be
derived neither from Islam nor the Arab nation, but from the
Egyptian, Syrian, Iraqi, and other states. To the extent that the
elites and peoples in these states continue to identify themselves as
Muslims and Arabs, state interests will continue to give a high
priority to matters Muslim and Arab; but the states will belong to
neither Islam nor Arabdom. Islamic and Arab ideals will be
filtered, sifted, refined, and interpreted by the prism of raison
d'état. "Egypt first" does not necessarily mean an Egypt divorced

from other Islamic and Arab countries, as many Israeli and other observers mistakenly assume, but rather an Egypt that determines its own identity, one in which Islamic and Arab themes have an important place. The Egyptian state will, however, continue to be an instrument of the Egyptian people, and their instrument alone, its obligations being to Egyptians only.[69] Because Egyptians by and large happen to be Muslim and Arab, these themes will continue to play an important role, but their relative weight in Egypt's national priorities will depend on momentary constellations of forces in Egyptian society and politics. It is not that Arabdom and Islam will continue to be ubiquitous "givens" to which the Egyptian state must adapt itself; rather, it is the Egyptian state and its interests that will be ubiquitous, with the fortunes of Islam and Arabdom in Egypt ebbing and flowing.[70] "Whether Egypt makes peace or war is primarily its own affair" will become a trivial statement, whereas until a short time ago it was virtually tantamount to treason. And yet, by now, "whether Sadat's diplomacy stands or falls, it will do so on its own merit, judged in terms of what it will or will not do for Egypt; charges of treason, or tribunals against Sadat by Iraq or Libya, will be to no avail."[71] The logic of the (real) mulk has triumphed over the logic of the (ideal, but only imaginary) caliphate.

It can be (and has been) argued that the Egyptian case is unique, perhaps comparable among the Islamic countries of the Middle East only to Turkey, not only in its strength of statehood but even in the resemblance to a Western-type nation-state:

> A parallel process of evolution may be seen in Egypt, which alone among the Arabic-speaking countries has a long history of separate political identity. In the transition toward modern-style nationhood, the Egyptians are in some respects better placed, in some respects worse placed, than the Turks. They did not possess the Turkish advantage of long-standing sovereignty, although it should be noted that they enjoyed a large measure of autonomy and that the Egyptian political entity is by far the oldest in the region after those of Turkey and Iran. To compensate, the Egyptians have a much stronger sense of continuity with the past. . . . Pan-Islamic and pan-Arab ideologies and political forces have a more recent and more powerful role in Egypt than their equivalents in Turkey. It would be rash to prophesy that their role has come to an end. For the moment, however, Egypt seems to be set on the path toward a modern nation-state. Although the course of

events in the two countries has been very different,
there are nevertheless striking similarities between
Turkey and Egypt. In both, the quest for modern nationhood has been linked with a turning toward the
West—with an attempt to seek closer relations with the
Western world and to adopt more and more of the
Western way of life in social, economic, and political
matters. Both countries—at the present time alone in
the world of Islam—have entered into diplomatic relations with Israel. Egypt's task is complicated by many
difficulties—by the heritage of Nasserism, the pull of
pan-Arabism, the crippling economic burdens that the
country and its people still have to bear. The resistance to modernization is stronger in Egypt than in
Turkey. But the sense of nationhood is stronger too,
and of Egypt, also one may say that in the absence of
interference or domination from outside, the most
probable future form of Egyptian corporate self-
awareness will be the pride of the Egyptians in their
nationhood and their patriotic love of Egypt.[72]

This may be an overstatement of the case. It is true that a
comparison of Egypt with most other major Arab countries clearly
shows the great advantages that the Egyptian military (and postmilitary)[73] regimes enjoyed in national, but also other (chiefly
administrative and sociological) terms, in their attempt to hold
and strengthen the machinery of the state.[74] The Egyptian attempt
to organize a network of 'trusted men" (ahl al-thiqa) dominating
the focuses of power was easier because such networks in Egypt
are less likely to be torn apart by sectarian and factional fratri-
cide. Even so, the ease with which Egypt was lured into the
temptation to become the leader of pan-Arabism, and the rapidity
with which disenchantment set in due to frustrations and the costs
of this role, render suspect arguments that make stability in Egypt
contingent on national identity. It seems more reasonable to see
in this process the continuity of the Egyptian state in confrontation
with a plethora of identities, eventually harnessing them to its own
increasingly pragmatic purposes.[75] Yet this pragmatism must be
in tune with the politically relevant sectors of the people and must
be acceptable to them; hence, a most instructive switch in Egyptian
terminology from "identity" to "authenticity." Note the following
lucid statement by a prominent Egyptian intellectual-diplomat,
Tahseen Basheer:

The new idea is the search for authenticity, what it
means to be Egyptian or Arab. What it means in my
relation with myself, with my community, with my
society, with the neighboring Arab states, and with
the world. The search for authenticity, the ability to
integrate within oneself and one's immediate and surrounding environment is the great burning desire that
is moving the people. With that search for authenticity,
all the ideologies of the 1920s and 1960s have been found
to be inadequate. We have not met the challenge. So
now we have a new language. The language that has
spread is the language of Islam. . . . If you want to
talk to the people and not simply to import models of
change that are alien to the majority, the models must
be translated into terms the people understand; thus,
the language of Islam has prevailed once again, in
every Arab country and not simply in Iran, as the
language that can evoke, on a massive scale, understanding by the people. The closer you go to that
vantage point, of Islam confronting the present tense
and the needs of the people, both now and tomorrow,
you see what the Muslim world must confront and
tackle. [76]

In this view, which seems entirely correct, the renewed emphasis on Islam in Egypt is simply the bankruptcy of the alternative
ideologies of the Egyptian state, namely Arab nationalism and Arab
socialism. Since the Egyptian state continues to pursue its own
interests, it must justify these in terms acceptable to its people—
which brings it back to Islam. Thus, Sadat denounced the Arab
leaders opposed to his policies; "the latest comedy in Arab solidarity has ended." But he also believed that his conduct would
eventually bring about the establishment of an "Islamic League"
that may help the Middle East "rise from the abyss of Arab policy
to the glory of Islam."[77] Basheer himself freely admits the difficulty in deriving real answers to pragmatic questions from the
Islamic perspective in Egypt; but this is exactly what needs to be
done.

The question then arises whether Islam represents an alternative ideology or a general frame of reference in terms of which
state interests are articulated. On this, Basheer argues in no uncertain terms:

> The Arabs, and Muslims in general, will take many
> years in which they will debate and re-debate what is
> a Muslim society in the twentieth and twenty-first
> century. . . . But the answer to this question is not
> simple. . . . Islam will continue to be a source of
> reference, but what it needs to be translated into work-
> ing policies and living ideologies in all aspects of
> human living is another question mark, and it is an-
> other nagging question mark at this moment. 78

If Islam is "a nagging question mark," in this view, the state is a
conspicuous exclamation mark:

> The fifth trend that I see is that the 1960s and 1970s
> witnessed the strength of the state. The state, what-
> ever kind of regime it was, an old monarchy like that
> in Morocco, new budding monarchies that existed and
> exist in Saudi Arabia and the Gulf, which are a new
> phenomenon—these shaykhdoms were not old monar-
> chies, but are new monarchies in a state of "becom-
> ing." States, through elitist parties like the Baath,
> the charisma of leaders like Nasser and Sadat, were
> able in the 1960s to perfect state power. And the
> state became the strongest dominant shadow over the
> lives of the individual and society. What we witnessed
> in Iran is a new phenomenon: the rise of the people,
> mostly unarmed, against a very strong state, a whole
> evolution of unfolding rejection of the social order,
> the political order, the economic order, and the search
> for something new. The new order might not stay for
> long. But the search is there, and it is a genuine search
> for community, different from the simple absolute power
> of the state. 79

The nagging question marks of Islam often arise, then, precisely at the point where the state is so strong that it is beyond
challenge. Popular, militant Islam does not challenge the state
machinery: it wants to use it in order to implement a set of policies
intended to create a social order (usually only vaguely defined) different from the one offered by the incumbents. In some ways, then,
yet again is witnessed the intriguing relationship between Islam and
the state; as it is likely to have created a sort of ideological vacuum
via the centrality of nationalism, it is the well-established state
that has already outgrown the stage (of searching for identity via
nationalism) that is most vulnerable to the Islamic wave. Once a

reasonably strong state is institutionalized solely on the basis of an established sense of identity, it is unable to supply answers to the policy-oriented questions of the day, insofar as those relate to priorities in distribution and social justice. Is, then, Egypt likely to be the next target of Islamic fundamentalism? Before attempting to answer this, it may be useful to first address the matter of political development in other parts of the Middle East. A perspective on the non-Egyptian Arab world has been offered by Lewis, [80] who observes that whereas the Arab claims to statehood have been satisfied, the attainment of nationhood remains tenuous. Certain Arab-state elites, in Lebanon, Syria, and Iraq, have conjured up links with ancient "ancestors" in an attempt to arouse a patriotic commitment in the hearts of their diverse citizens. Simultaneously, they continue to pay lip service to the aspirations of pan-Arabism. A reconciliation of these conflicting demands is contrived by claiming that such patriotism will strengthen the particular Arab state, thus qualifying it for leadership of the Arab world.

Lewis draws a picture of an Arab world suffering a time lag vis-à-vis Egypt. Statehood gained strength later than was the case in Egypt, and the bankruptcy of the pan-Arab version of nationalism is becoming apparent much later also. [81] This is also indicated by the Assyrian-Babylonian flirtation of the Iraqi regime, reminiscent of similar Pharaonic symbols being manipulated by the Egyptian elite, not to mention the parallel ill-fated efforts of the late Shah of Iran. [82] Is one then to conclude that perhaps there is a predictive logic in the sequence Iran—Egypt—"the rest of the Arab world"? [83]

Perhaps some clues can be gained from the tumultuous Iranian revolution. [84] As with every other major process of the type, this revolution and its Islamic transformation must be considered against the background of the target ancien régime, especially in comparison to those ancient regimes of the Arab countries:

> The position of Iran is very different. There are some
> twenty Arab states, and relations between them must
> inevitably be an important consideration for Arab poli-
> ticians. There is only one Turkish state, but the Turks
> can never entirely forget that they are the last indepen-
> dent segment of the great Turkic family of nations ex-
> tending from the Aegean to the China Sea, the more so
> since many Turkish refugees from these countries live
> among them. There is only one Iran and although there
> are Persian-speaking populations in Soviet Tajikistan
> and in Afghanistan, these are comparatively minor com-
> pared with the realms of Iran itself. And even Iran is
> far from unitary. Barely more than half of the population

of Iran speak Persian as their primary language, the
rest belonging to a variety of ethnic and linguistic and
sometimes even religious minorities. Since the destruction of the old Persian Empire by the Arab Muslim
conquerors in the seventh century, Iran has only excep-
tionally formed a single, unified realm. For almost a
thousand years, it was either part of some vaster empire
or subdivided into a number of small states. The modern empire of Iran dates from the sixteenth century,
when rulers of the Safavid dynasty for the first time
created a united Iranian realm bounded by the Ottoman
Empire in the west and by Central Asia and India in the
east. This has held loosely together since that time,
although often the authority of the central government
was very limited outside the capital and its immediate
environs. The Safavids were Shi'ites and were successful in imposing this form of Islam on what had
previously been a country of mixed denominations with
at least as many Sunnis as Shi'ites. Under the Safavids
and their successors, the Shi'i faith gave the Iranian
realm its distinctive character, marking it off from the
Sunni Turks, Central Asians, and Indians on all their
frontiers.

　　While retaining this Shi'ite character, the late
Shah tried to create a secular and territorial nation
based on the language, culture and homeland of Iran.
Like his predecessors in Egypt and Turkey, he laid
great stress on the ancient glories of his country and
tried to inculcate a sense of a continuing Iranian identity, independent of the Shi'ite or indeed of the Islamic
faith, and connecting the present-day people of Iran
with the ancient glories of Cyrus and Darius and with
the Parthian and Sasanian emperors. The core of the
Shah's propaganda was the idea of the monarchy as the
prime element of unity, stability and continuity in the
Iranian realm. The festivities amid the ruins of
Persepolis, the ancient Iranian capital, were directed
to this end. [85]

The Shah's efforts to create his own kind of "imperial nationalism" (perhaps a particularly dismal and unpopular functional
equivalent of Arab nationalism) completely failed, and gave way to
the onslaught of Islamic forces:

This policy has, for the time being at least, ended.
Political Islam, which has so far failed in Turkey and
has only limited effect in Egypt, has overwhelmingly
succeeded in Iran, where, if present trends continue,
the leadership in that country will create a new kind of
order based on Islamic rather than on Iranian or any
other kind of national or patriotic sentiment. In the
earlier stages of the Islamic revolution, the very idea
of nationality was rejected as un-Islamic or even anti-
Islamic. Should the Gulf be called the Persian Gulf or
the Arabian Gulf—a point about which there had been
long arguments? Neither, said an Ayatollah in Iran.
Let it be called the Gulf of Islam. The Ayatollah
Komeini went even further—there are no frontiers
in Islam, he said, or between Muslim peoples. Islam
is one.

This had indeed always been the theory. [86]

This theory did not, however, materialize under the Khomeini
regime any more than in previous instances. The terminological
disagreements relating to geographic entities such as the Gulf were
easy to resolve; not so the political disputes that had raged over
them from time immemorial. The Iranian-Iraqi war is particularly
instructive in this regard. It very much resembles the previous
rounds of conflict between revolutionary Iraq and Iran under the
Shah. Notwithstanding its terminological generosity, the Khomeini
regime failed to withdraw the Iranian forces from the three key
islands that dominate the mouth of the Straits of Hormuz: a significant nonevent that is a classic example of a case where "the dog
did not bark" (as Sir Arthur Conan Doyle's classic creation,
Sherlock Holmes, put it). The problem of the Shatt-el-Arab river
in relation to the boundary raised yet again the problem of the
region's colonial heritage of arbitrarily delineated borders. The
problem of Khuzistan involves ethnic irredentism, Arab nationalist
claims, and oil. The entire confrontation could have taken place
(which it did) as easily under the Shah as under Khomeini: plus ca
change, plus c'est la meme chose.

Where is the Islamic revolution in all this? Khomeini and
his people made much of the secular, "atheistic" orientation of the
socialist regime in Baghdad: they gained in return the support of
both Syria (itself a secular, socialist regime) and Islamic socialist Libya. Conservative Islamic regimes, like the one in Saudi
Arabia, seemed to prefer the other side. At the same time, Iraq

endeavored to project its efforts as an attempt to reconquer parts
of the lost Arab homeland, trying thus to endow its war with the
legitimacy of Arab nationalism. Such leading Arab nationalist powers as Libya and Syria, however, took Iran's side, whereas the
Iraqi case was supported by Jordan, a reactionary dynasty that for
many years was the whipping-boy of radical Arab nationalism; Saudi
Arabia, a bastion of conservative Islam and a traditional foe of radical Arab nationalism; and ultimately, Egypt, the current pariah of
radical Arab nationalism. If all this seems to make so little sense
as to call to mind the world of Alice in Wonderland, it is only because people have been conditioned for so long to think about Middle
East politics almost exclusively in ideological terms. Here there
is essentially a clash of two states pursuing their respective national interests, defined by raison d'état, with other states aligning
themselves on the issue according to their interests and raison
d'état. To be sure, all the usual colorful ideological mumbo jumbo
is being generously used, but this confounds, rather than clarifies,
the reality.

Inside Iran the struggle for the consolidation of power within
the revolutionary regime rages on.[87] In this respect, too, the Islamic terminology obfuscates rather than elucidates, which is of
little help to those seeking an explanation of territorial and other
power-oriented conflicts with Iran (although, when the time comes
for compromise and settlement, as it must, there may be mediation
by Islamic countries, legitimation by Islamic conferences, and the
like).[88] Similarly, Khomeini's concept of an Islamic republic is
far from clear, and the very idea of a republic, of course, is as
alien a Western concept as any. What has been happening in Iran is
a twin attempt to maximize the power of the clergy and to practice
strict Islamic jurisprudence; but this takes place in a "republic"
based in a state in the most traditional, literal sense of the term.
Moreover, increasingly it seems that a self-perpetuating process
takes place, whereby the closer a person is allowed by Khomeini to
the machinery of the state (Bazargan, Bani Sadr, Gotbzadeh), the
more he becomes alienated from the unstatelike logic of the clergy,
resulting in his eventual removal from power with Khomeini's sanc-
tion and blessing. There is a frightening pattern to these events.

It appears that, despite trying to come to terms with the Islamic ideology, this state faction of the revolution literally does not
know what to do when it controls the state apparatus. It may well
transpire that while the Islamic ideology is indeed more than acceptable to the masses and the elite alike, it may be no more capable of supplying answers to practical problems than were either the
imperial or radical versions of nationalism in Iran or the Arab
countries. If this should be so, there will be serious political consequences.[89]

Does the Khomeini version of "return to Islam"[90] really have an ideology? Yes, if one accepts Karl Mannheim's sceptical definition of ideologies as "more or less conscious disguises of the real nature of the situation";[91] no, if one regards ideology as "an explicit statement of political ends and means capable of inspiring and guiding action; a general theory applicable to the problems of the day";[92] maybe, if one follows the elaborate formulation of Clifford Geertz:

> Ideology is a response to a strain. . . . It is a loss of orientation that most directly gives rise to ideological activity, an inability, for lack of usable models, to comprehend the universe of civic rights and responsibilities in which one finds oneself located. . . . It is . . . the attempt of ideologies to render otherwise incomprehensible social situations meaningful. . . . Ideology . . . provides novel symbolic frames against which to match the myriad "unfamiliar somethings," that like a journey to a strange country, are produced by a transformation to political life. Whatever else ideologies may be . . . they are, most distinctively, maps of problematic social reality, and matrices for the collective conscience.[93]

In this latter formulation, ideology is "a cognitive map of the universe."[94] This Khomeini does indeed seem to possess. The response to stress is evident also—for instance, in the return to the traditional Shi'ite Muslim responsibility to rebel against injustice and to refrain from cooperating with "godless powers, tyrannical authorities and their judiciary agencies." Says Khomeini: "Whoever refers to them is seeking the judgement of the false god which God has ordered us to disavow."[95] This helps in a negative way, in that it concentrates energies against the ancien régime; but where is a theory of the state, once one captures it? The vague formula of the Islamic republic may indeed help in creating a collective conscience, but how does it help to make policy?

The situation is much the same as far as foreign policy is concerned; Khomeini's views about terminating cooperation with the United States or Israel are clear enough:

> They [the Shah's regime] purchase the Phantom aircraft so that the Israelis may be trained on them. Considering that Israel is in a state of war with the Moslems, then whoever helps and supports it is in turn in a state of war with the Moslems.[96]

This is all very lucid and logical, but what is a Bani Sadr (the president of the state of Iran) to do about a war with a Muslim neighbor? And what to do about Israel when Iran's interests coincide with those of the former, if only in regard to Iraq (which happens to be in a state of war with both of them)? And what to do about Phantoms that are used by Muslim powers against one another? And what to do about a major Muslim power such as Egypt that is no longer in a state of war with Israel? How to resolve the "hostage crisis" with the United States in the midst of war with Iraq?

While no ideological framework can be expected to specify concrete answers to problems of this magnitude, Khomeini's thought is enigmatic on almost all of them. And the fact remains that the elite in charge of the state machinery consistently opts for policies unacceptable to the holier-than-thou-style clergy, and consequently is periodically removed from power. The ensuing endemic disorder can hardly be encouraging to Khomeini-style revolutionaries elsewhere; quite the contrary, in this regard the meager achievements of the Islamic republic in Iran are decidedly counterproductive. Lewis—and many others—may well be right in asserting that "Khomeinism has shattered a myth of a pivotal element generating the revival of Islam—that Islamic values are superior to Western values, and that they can considerably improve the well-being of Muslim societies."[97] This latter the Khomeini regime has manifestly failed to demonstrate, nor is it likely to do any better in the future.

This is not to say that Khomeinism is already an entirely spent force: it is very important indeed as a negative channel of protest and rebellion. As P. J. Vatikiotis argues,

> It is important to realize that Islamic resurgence remains a protest movement in the main and still negative in character. Yet, even as a negative protest movement, it will clearly influence politics in the region, at least to the extent that the conditions of stasis tend to destabilize regimes. If the experience in Iran so far is any indication, this movement will not succeed in making Islam a workable principle for political organization or the sole basis of political power.[98] (Emphasis added)

Of course, this means merely that the Islamic basis of the Iranian state is shaky, and that more stable states should be able to overcome similar movements. Even so, many of them will have to contend with this problem, as was evident in the late 1970s:

> Khomeini's revolution had its echoes in neighboring countries with Shi'i communities—in the Persian Gulf

and, more significantly, Iraq. Muslim Brethren were engaged in a violent struggle with the <u>Baath</u> regime in Syria, co-existed with the Hashemite regime in Jordan in a comfortable symbiosis, and enjoyed a status of semi-legitimacy in Egypt, thus allowing them rapidly to augment their constituency. The movement manifested itself in various forms of Mahdism among the subversive groups in Saudi Arabia and in the politics of the Sudan. In Palestinian society, the upsurge of Islam found different expressions among Israeli Arabs, within Fath, and in the Palestinian diaspora. It would be wrong to regard all these diverse manifestations as identical in nature, but they do have a common denominator of which the conviction that Islamic beliefs, sentiments and aspirations should be channeled into radical political action forms a part. [99]

It would be unrealistic to expect an event of the magnitude of the Iranian revolution <u>not</u> to have a ripple effect, especially in view of the ubiquitous nature of popular militant Islam. Even so, the single most important statement one can make about Khomeinism is that—unlike Nasserism—it is <u>not</u> an exportable commodity; it can be contained by the state. So far, at least, its revolutionary manifestations have been contained in the Iranian state (in a diabolical struggle with it), and every other state has managed to contain it as well.

The clearest case of what Ajami calls "petro-Islam" can be seen in Turkey. True, the resurgence of Islam in Turkey is undoubtedly an authentic popular phenomenon reflecting the revolt of parts of the traditional rural periphery against a thoroughly Westernized urban center. [100] It is doubtful, however, that this particular form of Islam has had much impact on the essentially secular Turkish elite. Indeed, Lewis, one of the foremost authorities on Turkish history, flatly asserts:

In Turkey, identity has been defined very precisely in national or, rather, in patriotic terms. This was made clear in a clause adopted in the Republican People's Party program of 1935: "The fatherland is the sacred country within our present political boundaries, where the Turkish nation lives with its ancient and illustrious history, and with its glories still living in the depths of its soil." This formula, with its insistence on the present boundaries of the Turkish republic, and on the intimate connection between the people and the country that they inhabit, involved a substantial act of renuncia-

tion. Not only were the Turks renouncing their imperial past and bidding farewell to the lost provinces
of the Ottoman Empire; they were also renouncing the
pan-Turkish and pan-Islamic ideologies that for a
while had stirred many of their intellectuals and had
encouraged some Turkish leaders to seek a new role
for their country as the spearhead of a greater movement aiming at the union of all Turks or, beyond that,
of all Islam. Instead, the Turkish people were defined
as a nationality rather than as a religious or an ethnic
community, and their identity was delimited by their
national frontiers. Although this choice has been challenged in recent years by leaders seeking to revive
those religious and ethnic loyalties, the challenge has
made little headway, and the basic character of the
Kemalist revolution has been reaffirmed.[101]

Yet there have recently been all kinds of Turkish flirtations
with the Islamic world. The extent to which this is a pragmatic
(and perhaps even temporary) response to the lure of petro-Islam
can be judged from a candid statement by a recently retired Turkish
diplomat, Ambassador Nuri Eren, who has declared that it was disenchantment with the West over Cyprus that led Turkey to look to
the Third World, and the Islamic countries in particular.[102] Relations with these countries, however, were "cool if not unfriendly":[103]

Turkey could not espouse their militant anti-Westernism,
and in the international forums they resented Turkey's
pro-Western stance. . . . Since the 1970s, every government that came to power placed closer relations with
the Islamic countries as one of the principal objectives
in its foreign relations. In all the international forums,
Turks began to trail the Muslim group and vote with the
Arabs.
      In wooing the Arabs and the other Muslim coun-
tries, Turkey's principal objective was to recruit their
support on Cyprus.[104]

This is as clear an example of raison d'état (albeit tempered
by emotion) as any. So, too, is the conclusion:

Now that the dust is settling on the emotional aspects
of Turkey's foreign relations, Turkey's opinion gradually appears to understand how it deceived itself in its
search for reliance on the Muslim group. . . . In the

General Assembly vote of 1979 on Cyprus, not one single
Muslim vote was recorded in favor of the Turkish stance.
In all these years, the Muslim countries have remained
adamant about an independent Cyprus under a unitary
government, denying obstinately to the Turkish community its request for a federal status for preserving its
Turkish-Muslim identity. [105]

Nor has Turkey yet received any financial aid from the Arab oil
states, in spite of pleas for help to revive Turkey's failing economy
and in spite of the fact that Turkey supported the Arab position
against Israel.

All this leads Ambassador Eren to argue for a thorough reassessment of Turkish policy:

> Israel is the only country in the area on which Turkey
> can rely in countering a Soviet thrust into the Middle
> East. Again Israel and now Egypt are the two coun-
> tries with which Turkey can cooperate and help the
> politically primitive polities of the Arab world in ef-
> fecting the transition to modern statehood. Yet,
> Turkey, in order to gain Arab support, has jeopar-
> dized her relations with Israel and Egypt. She did it
> at the expense of alienating opinion in the West, and
> particularly American opinion. In the institution of
> the embargo this alienation was of considerable im-
> pact.
> My conclusion . . . was that the Muslim world
> cannot constitute an alternative to Turkey's affiliation
> with the West. First, it has not reciprocated Turkey's
> advances. Secondly, the Muslim world is more divided
> within itself than any other group. They have evinced
> their inexperience in statehood by failing to develop a
> joint world outlook. They have become prisoners to
> the Arab-Israeli issue and have failed to evolve a
> realistic attitude and a constructive policy. . . .
> Turkey must develop a policy of conciliation and co-
> operation in the Middle East region as a whole. [106]

It is difficult to say how widely this view is shared in relevant
political circles in Turkey today. This is less important, however,
than the tone, style, and substance of the pros and cons of the argument, the terms of reference of the debate: what is expressed is
the interests of the Turkish state not as an integral part of an Islamic superentity but as a separate unit, seeking to use the relation-

ship with other Islamic states for purposes defined by its own traditional conceptions of interest and orientation. In this sense, Turkey has not been captivated by the "return of Islam"; its flirtation with the Islamic world is a controlled, deliberate policy, a pragmatic attempt to break out of a concrete political-economic crisis.

In the Arab countries, several attempts have been made to preempt an Islamic revolt by simply coopting Islam into the state. The traditional conservative version can be seen in Saudi Arabia, the radical version in Libya.

In the wake of the revolution in Iran, and the November 1979 events in Mecca, there was a widespread assumption that Islam might strike soon in Saudi Arabia.[107] This assumption was caused partly by the commonly shared perception that Saudi Arabia is a weak state by any criterion of modern stateness. It is probably quite true that the Saudi notion of stateness is quite low. This, however, may be precisely one key reason that the Saudis have so far managed to coopt their Islamic establishment into the ruling elite. When the level of stateness is low, the differentiation of the state from other structures is obscured, and then the focus for what Nettl calls "disestablishment" or "disidentification" is blurred; in other words, when there is not much of a state, there is not much to rebel against. Also, of course, revolutionary incentive is lacking when there are ample resources to be distributed and the proprieties of Islam are already being observed. And as the Saudis never subscribed very enthusiastically to radical Arab nationalism, the latter's failure did not create an ideological vacuum for them.

Ironically, barring the reaction to Arab nationalism, the similarity with radical Libya is striking. Again, ample resources, the cooption of the Islamic establishment, the widespread use of Islamic symbols, and a low level of stateness provide all kinds of protection against a possible Islamic "danger." Indeed, Qadhafi and his colleagues have made a most ambitious effort to bring about a renewed and reinvigorated fusion of Arabism and Islam and to tie this to a populist notion of socialism, all of which they offer as a "Third Theory"; that is, an ideology appropriate to the entire Third World, one that would be preferable to both capitalism and Marxism. The form of the Libyan state has been named __jamahariya,__ an awkward Arabic term roughly translatable as "mass republic."

The Libyans first addressed the Islamic message to the Arabs:

> As a prominent member of the regime, Bashir Hawadi,
> put it, "Arabism is a body and Islam is the living soul
> which moves this body."

This statement was made in the course of a popular meeting which took place in Tripoli in October 1972. The meeting was organized in order to expound what Qadhafi has called his Third Theory. The theory claims to provide an alternative to Marxism and liberalism or capitalism, which are declared to be equally bankrupt. On examination, the Third Theory turns out to be based on Islam and Arabism and, in spite of a lame attempt to assert its universal value, to be really addressed to the Arabs, whose allegiance to Islam is taken to be part of the natural order of things. Thus, in a speech of October 1971, Qadhafi declared:

"The revolution of the Arab Libyan people represents something deep and well-rooted in the region. It is a new chapter in the evolution of the struggle of our Arab nation and of the Arab revolution. It affirms the established and individual character of the heritage of our nation, holds fast to Arabism and Islam, resurrects those values and principles which are most alive in them, and proclaims that the Arab nation is one nation having its place in the world and its role in the civilization of humanity."

At the meeting of October 1972, Hawadi affirmed: "In our belief, the Arab personality must be founded on a total commitment to belief in God and in Islamic values." And, at the same meeting Jallud, the prime minister, ended his speech by saying that, "Arab unity, in so far as it constitutes a strength for the Arabs, is also a strength for Islam: this is something fundamental."[108]

When it became obvious that the Arab countries had passed the peak of Arab nationalism, the doctrine was offered by Qadhafi to the entire Third World:

There is no East and West; there is rather North and South: the North extends from Washington to Peking, the South from Tangier to Djakarta; so that East and West can be considered as the two great camps allied against a third camp which is underdeveloped, or subjected by force. The Moslem world constitutes the centre of gravity of this camp. . . . the important thing is the existence of this doctrinal division in the world, this ideological map of the world.[109]

The very foreword of Qadhafi's theory asserts, "Our religion is the religion of democracy and social justice, for which the noble Koran has called since the appearance of Islam."[110] All this leads to an activism that is almost anachronistic by the standards of Arab nationalism:

> Thus, at the same meeting of October 1972, where Qadhafi explained the fundamental division of the world between North and South, another speaker affirmed that "jihad by the sword by all means for the sake of God: this is what ought to govern our relations with the other [i.e., outside] world in order to spread the message." The speaker went on to say that a limited truce might interrupt the jihad for a time, but it must be resumed whenever the Muslims become strong. The same speaker broached another activist, revolutionary theme when he said that he who raises the banner of Arab unity, and struggles for its sake, is the only legitimate imam or ruler "and all the imams are illegitimate."[111]

The Libyan regime's activism is made possible by the immense petro-resources at the disposal of the Libyan state and the glaring weakness of some neighboring African states (which in turn resent Libya's intervention on their "turf"). In the Middle East itself, the Arab countries consider Qadhafi a latter-day pseudo-Nasser who is a generation behind the times. His ideological message is vague and confused, and seems to have had very little impact. (Significantly, this is true even of Iran or Pakistan.)

The "return" of Islam, then, has struck more forcefully in the Northern Tier than in the Arab countries, for the paradoxical reason that whereas in the former, dilemmas of identity and stateness were resolved earlier, in the latter, Arab nationalism slowed down this process considerably. As has been seen, however, the state is now more than a match for Islam. Will the next wave hit the Arab countries, starting with Egypt, the most statelike among them? This is not impossible, but empirically, of course, much depends on the eventual outcome of the Islamic revolution in Iran as well as future socioeconomic developments in Egypt itself. In any case, there is no logic that dictates the necessity of the Islamic wave spreading throughout the region.

Lewis is probably right in concluding that

> Islam is still the most effective form of consensus in
> Muslim countries, the basic group identity among the

masses. This will be increasingly effective as the
regimes become more genuinely popular. One can
already see the contrast between the present regimes
and those of the small, alienated, Western-educated
elite which governed until a few decades ago. As regimes come closer to the populace, even if their
verbiage is left wing and ideological, they become
more Islamic. [112]

"More Islamic" may, however, mean many things to many
people; it does not have to mean "less statelike." Khomeini's version of "more Islamic" is at odds with Ibn Khaldun's analysis. The
former wishes to realize a form of caliphate in what is really but a
mulk. The latter knew that the mulk, the state, had a logic of its
own—tempered, to be sure, by Islam, but still the logic is that of
the state, not of Islam. This is something that Khomeini refuses
to accept. There is ample reason to believe that Ibn Khaldun's
analysis of politics is better than Khomeini's.

NOTES

1. Cf. Edward W. Said, Covering Islam: How the Media and
the Experts Determine How We See the Rest of the World (New York:
Pantheon, 1981).
2. For example, "Islam: The Militant Revival," Time,
April 16, 1979. There are, of course, partial exceptions: "Upsurge in Islam," New York Times, series beginning on December
28, 1979, or "Militant Islam," The Economist, January 27, 1979.
3. Bernard Lewis, "The Return of Islam," Commentary 61
(January 1976): 39-49.
4. Weekly Media Abstracts (Media Analysis Center, Jerusalem), March 11, 1981, p. 5.
5. There is an enormous literature on this, and the interested reader has a great many good sources. The author concurs
with the following recommendations from James A. Bill and Carl
Leiden, The Middle East: Politics and Power (Boston: Allyn and
Bacon, 1974), p. 25: "There is a wealth of material on the changing religious patterns of the Middle East in general, and on Islam
in particular. Prime among them is A. J. Arberry, ed., Religion
in the Middle East, 2 vols. (Cambridge: Cambridge University
Press, 1969); H. A. R. Gibb, Mohammedanism (London: Oxford
University Press, 1949) is still an excellent introduction to Islam;
Cambridge University Press has published its Cambridge History
of Islam in two volumes (1970), edited by P. M. Holt, Ann K. S.

Lambton, and Bernard Lewis; Edinburgh University Press has now published eight volumes in its Islamic Surveys series. The sixth and eighth volumes can be particularly mentioned here: W. Montgomery Watt, Islamic Political Thought (Edinburgh: Edinburgh University Press, 1968); and W. Montgomery Watt, Bell's Introduction to the Qur'an (Edinburgh: Edinburgh University Press, 1970). See also Bernard Lewis's recent collection, Islam in History: Ideas, Men and Events in the Middle East (New York: Library Press, 1973). A fuller background of Muslim political thought can be found in Erwin I. J. Rosenthal, Political Thought in Medieval Islam: An Introductory Outline (Cambridge: Cambridge University Press, 1958). Reuben Levy, The Social Structure of Islam (Cambridge: Cambridge University Press, 1957); and Maurice and Gaudefroy-Demombynes, Muslim Institutions (London: George Allen and Unwin, 1950) are also useful. For Islamic reform, see Charles C. Adams, Islam and Modernism in Egypt (London: Oxford University Press, 1933); and Malcolm H. Kerr, Islamic Reform: The Political and Legal Theories of Muhammad 'Abduh and Rashid Rida (Berkeley: University of California Press, 1961). For the intricacies of Islam, the Encyclopedia of Islam, New Edition (London: Luzac and Company, 1960-), two volumes published to date, is indispensable."

The following works should be added to the above list: Gustave E. von Grunebaum, Medieval Islam (Chicago: University of Chicago Press, 1952), especially ch. 5, and Modern Islam (New York: Doubleday, 1964; H. A. R. Gibb, Modern Trends in Islam (Chicago: University of Chicago Press, 1946); W. C. Smith, Islam in Modern History (Princeton, N.J.: Princeton University Press, 1957); Joseph Schacht, An Introduction to Islamic Law (Oxford: Oxford University Press, 1964); E. I. J. Rosenthal, Islam in the Modern National State (Cambridge: Cambridge University Press, 1965); Muhsin Mahdi, Ibn Khaldun's Philosophy of History (London: Allen and Unwin, 1957); Elie Kedourie, Islam in the Modern World (Washington, D.C.: New Republic, 1980).

On related historical and behavioral aspects, see Clifford Geertz, Islam Observed (New Haven, Conn.: Yale University Press, 1968); Leonard Binder, The Ideological Revolution in the Middle East (New York: Wiley, 1964); Richard P. Mitchell, The Society of the Muslim Brothers (London: Oxford University Press, 1969); Bernard Lewis, The Middle East and the West (New York: Harper, 1964), and The Arabs in History (New York: Harper, 1964). An extremely interesting but little-known concise study is Arthur Jeffery, "The Political Importance of Islam," Journal of Near Eastern Studies 1 (October 1942): 383-95. For further bibliographical information on this vast subject, see also Gabriel Ben-Dor, "Political Culture Approach to Middle East Politics," International Journal of Middle East Studies 8 (1) (January 1977): 43-63.

6. von Grunebaum, Medieval Islam, p. 142.

7. Lewis, "The Return of Islam," p. 40. Numerous other authorities argue along essentially the same lines.

8. Gabriel Ben-Dor, "State, Society and Military Elites in the Middle East," in the forthcoming volume Hierarchy and Stratification in the Middle East (New York: Social Science Research Council), based on papers presented at the May 1979 conference on that subject.

9. "Convergence," an alternative term to "integration," is put forth by C. A. O. van Nieuwenhuijze in his Social Stratification in the Middle East (Leiden: Brill, 1965), who argues in terms of a "cultural majority principle" rather than conventional theories of integration. Ibid., p. 10.

10. G. Ben-Dor, "State, Society, and Military Elites," pp. 11-12.

11. von Grunebaum, Medieval Islam, p. 169.

12. Quoted in Halil Inalcik, "The Nature of Traditional Society: Turkey," in Political Modernization in Japan and Turkey, ed. Robert E. Ward and Dankwart A. Ruston (Princeton, N.J.: Princeton University Press, 1964), p. 43.

13. Ibid., p. 48.

14. See also H. A. R. Gibb and Harold Bowen, Islamic Society and the West, Vol. 1: Islamic Society in the XVIIIth Century, Parts I and II (London: Oxford University Press); and Norman Itzkowitz, "Eighteenth Century Ottoman Realities," Studia Islamica 16 (1962): 73-94.

15. See, for example, John B. Glubb, "The Role of the Army in the Traditional Arab State," in Modernization of the Arab World, ed. J. H. Thompson and R. D. Reischauer (Princeton, N.J.: Van Nostrand, 1966).

16. Michael C. Hudson, Arab Politics: The Search for Legitimacy (New Haven, Conn. and London: Yale University Press, 1977), pp. 94-95.

17. See Serif Mardin, The Genesis of Young Ottoman Thought (Princeton, N.J.: Princeton University Press, 1961); Uriel Heyd, Foundations of Turkish Nationalism: The Life and Teaching of Ziya Gokalp (London: Lucas, 1950); George Antonius, The Arab Awakening (Beirut: Khayat's, 1961); Sylvia G. Haim, Arab Nationalism: An Anthology (Berkeley: University of California Press, 1962); Zeine N. Zeine, Arab-Turkish Relations and the Emergence of Arab Nationalism (Beirut: Khayat's, 1958); Richard Cottam, Nationalism in Iran (Pittsburgh, Pa.: University of Pittsburgh Press, 1954) and numerous similar works. The earliest stages are particularly well discussed in Gibb and Bowen, Islamic Society and the West, referred to earlier; Bernard Lewis, The Emergence of Modern

Turkey (London: Oxford University Press, 1961); and Niyazi Berkes, The Development of Secularism in Turkey (Montreal: McGill University Press, 1964.

18. Hudson, Arab Politics, p. 99. The reference is to Watt, Islam and the Integration of Society (London: Oxford University Press, 1961), p. 175.

19. Hudson, Arab Politics, pp. 92-93. The reference is to Rosenthal, Islam in the Modern National State, pp. 17-22.

20. Vol. II, C-G (Leiden: Brill, 1965), pp. 177-78.

21. von Grunebaum, Medieval Islam, p. 165.

22. Ibid., pp. 165-66. See also M. A. Shaban, The Abbasid Revolution (Cambridge: Cambridge University Press, 1970).

23. von Grunebaum, Medieval Islam, p. 166.

24. James A. Bill and Carl Leiden, The Middle East: Politics and Power (Boston: Allyn and Bacon, 1974), p. 32.

25. Rosenthal, Political Thought in Medieval Islam, ch. 3.

26. Ibid., p. 62.

27. See, for example, the eleventh-century Siyasat-nama of Nizam al-Mulk; in English, The Book of Government or Rules for Kings, trans. H. Drake (London: Routledge and Kegan Paul, 1960); or Kai Kaus Ibn Iskandar, Qabus Nama—in English, A Mirror for Princes, trans. R. Levy (London: Cresset Press, 1951).

28. Rosenthal, Political Thought in Medieval Islam, p. 67.

29. Hudson, Arab Politics, pp. 42-43.

30. Ibid., p. 43. The Muqaddimah has been translated into English (3 volumes), with a lucid introduction by Franz Rosenthal (New York: Pantheon, 1958). A one-volume abridgment of this (edited by N. J. Dawood) has also been published (Princeton, N.J.: Princeton University Press, 1967). A superb analysis is to be found in Muhsin Mahdi, Ibn Khaldun's Philosophy of History and in Rosenthal, Political Thought in Medieval Islam, ch. 4 ("The Theory of the Power-State: Ibn Khaldun's Study of Civilization"); the subsequent discussion draws heavily upon the latter.

31. Rosenthal, Political Thought in Medieval Islam, p. 109.

32. Ibid., p. 108.

33. Ibid., pp. 108-9. Asabiya is a key term in Ibn Khaldun's sociology, roughly translatable as "group solidarity."

34. Ibid., p. 107.

35. For the definition of the "depraved condition" see Ernst Cassirer, The Myth of the State (Garden City, N.Y.: Doubleday, 1955), p. 140.

36. Rosenthal, Political Thought in Medieval Islam, p. 85.

37. Ibid., p. 86.

38. Ibid., p. 87.

39. Ibid., p. 88.

40. Ibid., p. 92.

41. Ibid., p. 96.

42. Ibid., pp. 97-98. Khilafa is the correct Arabic term for what is generally known in the West as caliphate.

43. Ibid., pp. 103-4.

44. Bill and Leiden, The Middle East Political Power, p. 36.

45. See Jeffery, "The Political Importance of Islam."

46. Fouad Ajami, "The End of Pan-Arabism," Foreign Affairs (Winter, 1978-79): 364. Emphasis added. Incidentally, this author does not believe in the "resurrection" of Islam any more than in its "return": it neither died nor went away.

47. Ibid.

48. There is a copious literature on these (and similar) terms and their political implications. See, for instance, Haim, Arab Nationalism, "Introduction"; and Hisham Sharabi, Nationalism and Revolution in the Arab World (Princeton, N.J.: Van Nostrand, 1964).

49. On this, in addition to previously quoted sources, see Charles D. Cremeans, The Arabs and the World (New York: Praeger, 1962); Majid Khadduri, Political Trends in the Arab World: The Role of Ideas and Ideals in Politics (Baltimore, Md.: Johns Hopkins University Press, 1970); Hazem Z. Nuseibeh, The Ideas of Arab Nationalism (Ithaca, N.Y.: Cornell University Press, 1956); Fayez Sayegh, Arab Unity: Hope and Fulfillment (Old Greenwich, Conn.: Devin-Adair, 1958); Malcolm Kerr, The Arab Cold War, 3d ed. (London: Oxford University Press, 1971).

50. Lewis, The Middle East and the West, p. 94.

51. Elie Kedourie, "Religion and Secular Nationalism in the Arab World," in The Middle East: Oil, Conflict and Hope, ed. A. L. Udovitch (Lexington, Mass.: Heath, 1976).

52. Ibid., p. 182.

53. Ibid., pp. 182-83.

54. P. J. Vatikiotis, "Inter-Arab Relations," in The Middle East: Oil, Conflict and Hope, ed. A. L. Udovitch (Lexington, Mass.: Heath, 1976), p. 145. It might be added that, in the present author's opinion, the success in mastering the first of the three factors eventually enabled the rulers to manipulate the other two more or less successfully—a key point in his argument.

55. Arab socialism is an intriguing and complex phenomenon, which, however, is beyond the scope of this book. A few basic works that include guidance for further reading are Kamel S. Abu Jaber, The Arab Ba'th Socialist Party (Syracuse, N.Y.: Syracuse University Press, 1966); John Devlin, The Ba'th Party (Stanford, Cal.: Hoover Institution, 1966); Sylvia Haim, "The Ba'ath in Syria," in People and Politics in the Middle East, ed. Michael Curtis (New

Brunswick, N.J.: Transaction, 1971); Hamid Enayat, "Islam and Socialism in Egypt," Middle Eastern Studies 4 (January 1968): 141–72; Malcolm H. Kerr, "The Emergence of Socialist Ideology in Egypt," Middle East Journal 16 (Spring 1962): 127–44; Arab Socialism: A Documentary Survey, ed. Sami A. Hanna and George H. Gardner (Leiden: Brill, 1969).

    56. Kedourie, "Religion and Secular Nationalism in the Arab World," p. 192.

    57. Ibid.

    58. Lewis, "The Return of Islam," p. 44.

    59. Ibid.

    60. Ibid.

    61. The Philosophy of the Revolution (Cairo: no publishers, no date), p. 68.

    62. Lewis, "The Return of Islam," p. 46.

    63. Ibid.

    64. This term is borrowed from Clement Henry Moore, "On Theory and Practice Among Arabs," World Politics 24 (October 1971): 106–26.

    65. Ajami, "The End of Pan-Arabism," p. 364.

    66. Ibid.

    67. Ibid. On this, see also Fouad Ajami, "Stress in the Arab Triangle," Foreign Policy 29 (Winter 1977–78): 90–108, where he speaks of "Petro-Islam"!

    68. Ajami, "The End of Pan-Arabism," p. 364. The data in question are those in Tawfic Farah, "Group Affiliations of University Students in the Arab Middle East (Kuwait)," Reports and Research Studies, Department of Political Science, Kuwait University, 1977. Compare with the data in the C.R.A.U. study, Al-Mustaqbal al-Arabi, Beirut, March–May 1980.

    69. See the autobiography of Anwar al-Sadat, In Search of Identity (New York: Harper, 1977).

    70. See Nadav Safran, Egypt in Search of Political Community (Cambridge, Mass.: Harvard University Press, 1961).

    71. Ajami, "The End of Pan-Arabism," p. 370.

    72. Bernard Lewis, "Loyalty to Community, Nation and State," in Middle East Perspectives: The Next Twenty Years, ed. George S. Wise and Charles Issawi (Princeton, N.J.: Darwin Press, 1981).

    73. Gabriel Ben-Dor, "Military Regimes in the Arab World: Prospects and Patterns of Civilization," Armed Forces and Society I/3 (May 1975): 317–27.

    74. See the article by the Iraqi scholar Ayad al-Qazzaz, "Political Order, Stability and Officers: A Comparative Study of Iraq, Syria and Egypt from Independence till June 1967," Middle East Forum 45 (2) (1969): 31–51.

75. Cf. Shimon Shamir, "The Arab World between Pragmatism and Radicalism," in Middle East Perspectives: The Next Twenty Years, ed. George S. Wise and Charles Issawi (Princeton, N.J.: Darwin Press, 1981).

76. Tahseen Basheer, "Intellectual and Cultural Trends," and Gabriel Warburg, "The Challenge of Populist Islam in Egypt and the Sudan in the 1970s," both in Middle East Perspectives: The Next Twenty Years, ed. George S. Wise and Charles Issawi (Princeton, N.J.: Darwin Press, 1981); Israel Altman, "Islamic Movements in Egypt," Jerusalem Quarterly 10 (Winter 1979): 87-94; and E. Sivan, "How Fares Islam?" Jerusalem Quarterly 13 (Fall 1979): 4-5.

77. This from Warburg, "The Challenge of Populist Islam in Egypt and the Sudan in the 1970s," p. 106.

78. Basheer, "Intellectual and Cultural Trends," p. 83.

79. Ibid., pp. 83-84.

80. Lewis, "Loyalties," pp. 27-28.

81. This may be particularly true in the key state of Syria. See Tabitha Petran, Syria (London: Oxford University Press, 1972); Moshe Ma'oz, Syria under Hafiz al-Asad; New Domestic and Foreign Policies (Jerusalem Papers on Peace Problems, No. 15, 1975); Malcolm Kerr, "Hafiz Assad and the Changing Patterns of Syrian Politics," International Journal 28 (4) (August 1973): 689-706; N. van Dam, The Struggle for Power in Syria (London: Croom Helm, 1979); I. Rabinovich, "Continuity and Change in the Ba'th Regime in Syria," in From June to October, ed. I. Rabinovich and H. Shaked (New Brunswick, N.J.: Transaction, 1977), pp. 219-28.

82. James A. Bill, "Iran and the Crisis of '78," Foreign Affairs 57 (2) (Winter 1978-79): 323-42.

83. Cf. Eric A. Nordlinger, "Political Development: Time Sequences and Rates of Change," World Politics 20 (3) (April 1968): 494-520.

84. The stages of this revolution are easily reminiscent of the violent phases of other revolutions surveyed in the literature. See, for instance, Chapter 3, "Revolution," in Henry Bienen, Violence and Social Change (Chicago: University of Chicago Press, 1968), pp. 66-91; and S. N. Eisenstadt, "Sociological Theory and an Analysis of the Dynamics of Civilizations and of Revolutions," Daedalus 106 (Fall 1977): 59-78.

85. Lewis, "Loyalties," pp. 29-30.

86. Ibid., p. 30.

87. See, for example: Richard Cottam, "Revolutionary Iran," Current History (January 1980): 12-16; R. K. Ramazani, "The Iranian Revolution," International Affairs 56 (3) (Summer 1980): 443-57; A. Saikal, The Rise and Fall of the Shah (Princeton, N.J.:

Princeton University Press, 1980); Fereydoun Hoveyda, The Fall of the Shah of Iran (New York: Simon and Schuster, 1980).

88. D. Pipes, "This World Is Political—The Islamic Revival of the Seventies," Orbis 24 (1) (Spring 1980): 9–41.

89. On related issues, see Chapter 12, "Ideology and Religion," in Gabriel Ben-Dor, The Druzes in Israel: A Political Study (Jerusalem: Mognew Press, 1979) and the sources cited there.

90. This is articulated in Ayatollah Ruhollah Khomeini, Islamic Government (no publisher, no date).

91. Karl Mannheim, Ideology and Utopia (New York: Harcourt, Brace, 1954), p. 49.

92. Manfred Halpern, quoted in Ben-Dor, The Druzes in Israel, p. 158.

93. Clifford Geertz, "Ideology as a Cultural System," in Ideology and Discontent, ed. David E. Apter (New York: Free Press, 1964), p. 64.

94. Ibid.

95. Khomeini, Islamic Government, p. 41.

96. Ibid., p. 55.

97. Weekly Media Abstracts, March 11, 1981, p. 6.

98. P. J. Vatikiotis, "Regional Politics," in Middle East Perspectives: The Next Twenty Years, ed. George S. Wise and Charles Issawi (Princeton, N.J.: Darwin Press, 1981), p. 50.

99. Shamir, "The Arab World Between Pragmatism and Radicalism," pp. 68–69.

100. See Serif Mardin, "Center-Periphery Relations: A Key to Turkish Politics?" in Post Traditional Societies, ed. S. N. Eisenstadt (New York: Norton, 1972), pp. 169–90; Political Participation in Turkey, ed. Engin Akarli with Gabriel Ben-Dor (Istanbul: Bosphorus University Press, 1974); Dankwart A. Rustow, "Turkey's Travails," Foreign Affairs 58 (Fall 1979): 82–102; Frederich W. Frey, "Patterns of Elite Politics in Turkey," in Political Elites in the Middle East, ed. George Lenczowski (Washington, D.C.: American Enterprise Institute, 1975), pp. 41–82; and the further, extensive literature cited in these sources.

101. Lewis, "Loyalties," p. 27.

102. Ambassador Nuri Eren, "Comments on Turkey," in Middle East Perspectives: The Next Twenty Years, ed. George S. Wise and Charles Issawi (Princeton, N.J.: Darwin Press, 1981), p. 199.

103. Ibid.

104. Ibid., pp. 199–200.

105. Ibid., p. 200.

106. Ibid., p. 202. Note the reference to the Muslim "inexperience in statehood" from the Turkish perspective!

107. Cf. Haim Shaked, "The Islamic Revolution—Is Saudi Arabia Next?" in Middle East Perspectives: The Next Twenty Years, ed. George S. Wise and Charles Issawi (Princeton, N.J.: Darwin Press, 1981.

108. Elie Kedourie, "Religion and Secular Nationalism in the Arab World," p. 189.

109. Quoted in ibid., p. 190.

110. Ibid.

111. Ibid., p. 191.

112. Lewis, "The Return of Islam," p. 148.

3
Stateness,
Zionism, and
Israel

In discussing Israel, it is almost a matter of protocol
to begin with the following observation; Israel is so
exceptional among other countries of its kind that it
provides a check against hasty generalization arising
from a comparative study.[1]

It is indeed a good idea to observe this protocol, especially in
political matters, but the point ought not to be overstated: Israel
has now lived as a state in the Middle East for well over a generation, and the majority of its population, however defined, is of
Middle East origins.[2] Moreover, the dialectic of stateness and
Judaism offers a useful comparison to the relationship between
stateness and Islam.

Much like Islam, Judaism is also significantly more than a
religion in the Western sense of the term. Like Islam, it seeks to
shape comprehensively the lives of its adherents to resemble the
ideal expressed in the commandments of God. And, again like
Islam, Judaism also stresses the survival of the integrity of the
community, where its ideals may be realized. In that sense, the
idea of separating church and state ("Render unto Caesar . . . .") is
as intrinsically alien to Judaism as to Islam;[3] while no Islamic
state in the Middle East has such a constitutional separation, Israel,
as is well known, has neither constitution nor separation.[4] On the
other hand, the enormous differences between Islamic and Jewish
history have had a thorough impact: "The . . . major Middle Eastern religions are significantly different in their relations with the
state and their attitudes to political power. Judaism was associated
with the state and then was disentangled from it; its new encounter
with the state at the present time raised problems which are still
unresolved,"[5] whereas "Islam from the lifetime of its founder was
the state, and the identity of religion and government is indelibly

stamped on the memories and awareness of the faithful from their own sacred writings, history and experience. "[6]

The disentanglement of Judaism from the state has been felt even on the etymological level: Israel today defines itself as the "State of Israel," using the term _medina_. But this is a complex term, and certainly does not represent an authentic heritage. This complexity is reflected in Nettl's somewhat misleadingly sharp formulation:

> An example of a very precise cultural internalization
> of the notion of state is found in Israel. Because of the
> intervening and unique concept of country (_eretz_) in com-
> mon usage, the state (_medinat_) becomes merely the ac-
> tive institutionalized principle of autonomous authority,
> while government (_memshalah_) is the temporary, party-
> based incumbent. [7]

If there is really a "very precise cultural internalization of the no tion of state" in Israel, this is a recent phenomenon. Daniel J. Elazar, an orthodox Jewish scholar and one of the best-known political scientists in Israel, observes:

> There have been periods in which the Middle East has
> broken up into relatively small national units. There
> have also been eras in which the Middle East has been
> under imperial rule. . . . Sometimes imperial peace
> involved autonomous (and here I use the Hebrew word)
> _medinat_. The word _medina_, implying a modern "abso-
> lutely sovereign" polity, is now translated as "state,"
> but in its original Biblical usage it referred to entities
> that had political authority, but were not independent.
> Etymologically, the closest English equivalent would
> be "jurisdictions." The term _medina_ only acquired
> the connotations of sovereignty in the 18th or 19th cen-
> tury, as a result of the encounter of the Jews in Europe
> with modern nationalism. [8]

Note the instructive contrast in the etymology of "the state" in Arabic (dawla) and Hebrew (medina): in the Islamic context, as has been seen, the origin of dawla is the rule of an individual or a dynasty in all or part of the Islamic empire (ruled, obviously, by Muslims), whereas in the Jewish context, medina derives from autonomous Jewish jurisdiction of a fragment of a non-Jewish em- pire. This must have thoroughgoing consequences for political cul- ture. [9] It has also contributed significantly to the very slow evolution of stateness in the Zionist movement.[10] As Segre puts it, "The secular Zionists, despite their love for Zion and their strong sense of Jewish dignity, did not want to be judged on any metaphysical parameter. Their pride was to be 'realists' even if their aim sounded dreamlike."[11] This is reflected in the annals of Zionism. From the very start ideologues were deliberately noncommittal on the issue of the state. "When the Zionist movement was founded in the late 19th century, there was no clear cut decision that a sovereign state was to be its goal in the ancient homeland."[12] There were several reasons for this: some were purely philosophical, but some were significantly, blatantly political.

On the philosophical side,

> The Jewish political tradition has never focused on the sovereignty issue because, as a matter of religious doctrine, sovereignty could only belong to God. Humans on this earth could only exercise the powers granted or allowed them as a consequence of their covenants with the Almighty. Therefore, rather than discuss questions of sovereignty, an issue not in human hands, Jewish political discussions have focused on the exercise of powers.[13]

This religious/metaphysical tradition is periodically revived in present-day Israel, giving rise to somewhat brutal criticisms of the "idolatry" involved in sanctifying the value of a secular Jewish state at the expense of observing the commandments—the proper "Jewish way of life." This is articulated most vocally by the prominent maverick Orthodox intellectual, Professor Yeshayahu Leibowitz:

> There are certain Jews in the State of Israel for whom the people is God, the state a religion, nationalism the law and a supreme value. They are Fascists, some of them conscious ones, many unconscious, and they are attached with passion to the idea that the Jewish people are defined according to their State. . . . There are many Jews among us who raise [the concept of the land] to a level of holiness. This is idolatry, pure and simple. . . . The land is neutral, like anything else in this world. Only One is holy . . . and apart from Him nothing is holy, neither in history nor in nature nor in man; but it is possible to sanctify all things through the service of the Lord.[14]

Thus the metaphysics. In practical terms, also, the Zionist efforts were conducted along lines that explicitly excluded (or at least omitted) the concept of statehood for a long time, although in practice, as Dan Horowitz and Moshe Lissak argue in their authoritative study: "Against this background, the concept of the 'Jewish community in Palestine' (the Yishuv) emerged. Perceived as an autonomous political system in embryo, the Yishuv was often defined as a 'state in the making' or 'a state within a state.' "[15]

For many this is hard to believe even today; but on the political-diplomatic level, the Jewish "state" was almost taboo for several decades. Michael R. Marrus, who conducted a thorough examination of this question, argues this point:

> Zionism poses an odd paradox: rich in ideology, ambitious in its intentions for Jewish national life, it has still to realize its most fervently declared goals; yet its most important achievement—a Jewish state—occurred in the area where it was ideologically weak. It is curious that Jewish nationalism, which paralleled other nationalisms in so many respects, diverged from them so sharply on the state idea. While other national movements seem frequently obsessed by this notion—speaking variously about the creation, the liberation or the purification of the state—Zionism only slowly drew the state idea to the core of its doctrine. Historically, it was not until the second half of the 1930s that a state emerged as a respectable priority for the World Zionist Organizations. For various reasons, partly tactical, but partly also ideological, it took time for the state to crystallize as an officially declared goal of the movement. It was only when events both within and without the Zionist arena drastically narrowed choices that the focus upon a state seemed both reasonable and desirable. [16]

The founder of political Zionism, Herzl, is often quoted for his famous prophecy following the First Zionist Congress, held in Basel, 1897: "If I were to sum up the Congress in a word—which I shall take care not to publish—it would be this: At Basel I founded the Jewish state."[17] (Emphasis added.) Those who like to quote this phrase normally discuss the prophetic truth contained in the statement. Yet from the point of view of this study, it is perhaps equally important to inquire why Herzl took care not to publish the idea of the Jewish state.

This care was neither accidental nor idiosyncratic, nor did it have much to do with the metaphysics of the Jewish religious tradition. Rather, it was dictated by pragmatic diplomatic/political considerations. One is tempted to point to the operation of the logic of raison d'état in a movement that dared not identify stateness as its ultimate goal (Endziel). Marrus concluded:

> But Herzl's discretion on this matter—the care not to publish—clearly made sense: the idea of a state was thoroughly discussed at Basel, and in the end opinion turned decisively against it. Nothing was said about a state when the Zionists formally declared their aims, and the 1897 Basel Programme, which was to embody the movement's goals for twenty years, contained no reference to it whatever. Rather, the Zionist platform groaned under the weight of the following: "Zionism aims at the creation of a home [Heimsatte] for the Jewish people in Palestine to be secured by public law [offentlich-rechtlich gesichert]."
>
> Far from being a linguistic accident, this ponderous definition was born in committee, in a laboured effort at compromise. Essentially, some delegates wanted to see a state enshrined as a goal of Zionism, while most did not—mainly fearing the reactions of the Ottoman authorities to such an egregious display of imperial separatism. Palestine was, after all, part of the Turkish empire, and so it made sense to speak cautiously about Jewish goals. [18]

Indeed, the energies of practical Zionism were increasingly channeled into building a viable Jewish infrastructure in Palestine. [19] Stateness, nevertheless, always lurked in the background, on the level of the relationship with the Arabs in Palestine. [20] And, of course, there was the seminal Balfour Declaration of 1917, which seemed to satisfy the original Zionist goal of "a home for the Jewish people in Palestine, to be secured by public law." The declaration itself speaks of "a national home for the Jewish people." Naturally, this deliberately vague formulation was open to a variety of interpretations.

In the famous and curious Faisal-Weizmann agreement (January 3, 1919) the talk is of the relationship of an "Arab state" with a future Jewish entity—which is merely referred to as "Palestine."[21] Even in the Zionist view, stateness was still absent, although great expectations were raised:

> From a minority of no special standing in a few provinces of the Turkish Empire, the Jews of Palestine became the nucleus of a projected Jewish National Home,

united by common political aspirations, with the ambition, at first greatly inflated, of sharing in the gover-
nance of the country, or at least maintaining wide
autonomous rights within it. [22]

Elaborate attempts to refrain from using the term "state" did
not do much to allay the fears and suspicions of the Arabs, which
came to take such a violent form that David Ben-Gurion was pushed
to an abyss of pessimism:

Everybody sees a difficulty in the question of relations
between Arabs and Jews. But not everybody sees that
there is no solution to this question. No solution!
There is a gulf and nothing can fill this gulf. It is possible to resolve the conflict between Jewish and Arab
interests (only) by sophistry. I do not know what Arab
will agree that Palestine should belong to the Jews—
even if the Jews learn Arabic. And we must recognize
this situation. If we do not acknowledge this and try to
come up with "remedies," then we risk demoraliza-
tion. . . . We, as a nation, want this country to be
ours; the Arabs, as a nation, want this country to be
theirs. [23]

Still a clash of nations; nothing about states. And what was
the view of the promulgators of the Balfour Declaration, the British,
on its relationship to statehood? Balfour himself supposedly told a
friend in 1918 that he hoped "the Jews would make good in Palestine
and eventually found a Jewish state." [24] Lloyd George said the Imperial War Cabinet contemplated an eventual "Jewish Commonwealth." [25] Not surprisingly, all this may have led Weizmann in
1919 to his famous definition:

I defined the Jewish National Home to mean the creation
of an administration which would arise out of the natural
conditions of the country—always safeguarding the interest of non-Jews—with the hope that by Jewish immigration Palestine would ultimately become as Jewish as
England is English. [26]

Even this, however, may have been more a cultural than a
political conception. Nahum Sokolov, for example, observed that

the achievement of a political success with this or that
Power must never be mistaken for the real aim of Zion-

ism. Its real aim is the regeneration—physical, economic, moral—of the Jewish people. That is a constructive task of the highest value from the point of view of humanity, and those who set their hands to such a task need many high qualities. [27]

The most authoritative, however—and still quite ambiguous—explanation of the British understanding of the Balfour Declaration was attempted by Lloyd George:

As to the meaning of the words "national home," to which the Zionists attach so much importance, he understood it to mean some form of British, American, or other protectorate, under which full facilities would be given to the Jews to work out their own salvation and to build up, by means of education, agriculture, and industry, a real centre of national culture and focus of national life. It did not necessarily involve the early establishment of an independent Jewish State, which was a matter of gradual development in accordance with the ordinary laws of political evolution. [28]

Thus, a Jewish state was not seen as necessary in the then foreseeable future, but it was not ruled out, either.

But this semantic hairsplitting along intellectual lines could not continue indefinitely in the face of brutal historical realities. Perhaps its final accord may be seen in Weizmann's somewhat confused reaction to the suggestion of partition made in the Report of the Peel Commission in Palestine (1937): "I was asked how the idea struck me and I naturally answered that I could not tell on the spur of the moment, nor would I give my own impressions except after consultation with my colleagues. Actually, I felt that the suggestion held out great possibilities and hopes."[29] And this was the reaction of the most prominent Zionist leader of the time to the idea of a Jewish state in a partitioned Palestine, 40 years (!) after Herzl's statement that he (Herzl) had founded the Jewish state! What follows in Weizmann's memoirs sounds even more incredible:

Something new had been born into the Zionist movement, something which had to be handled with great care and tenderness, which should not be permitted to become a matter of crude slogans and angry controversy. I remember saying not long afterward to a colleague: "A Jewish State, the idea of Jewish independence in Palestine, is such a lofty thing that it ought to be treated

like the Ineffable Name, which is never pronounced in
vain. By talking about it too much, by dragging it down
to the level of the banal, you desecrate that which
should be approached only with reverence."[30]

Four decades after the First Zionist Congress, Weizmann
still viewed the idea of a Jewish state as something new that "ought
to be treated like the Ineffable Name"! Yet the tide of history had
turned, and there was no way for Weizmann, or anyone else, to
alter its course.

A few weeks later, apparently Weizmann had made up
his mind. After a long discussion with the sympathetic
Reginald Coupland one evening at Nahalal, in Palestine,
Weizmann stepped out into the darkness and called out
to the local farmers using the words of Herzl, written
forty years before: "Comrades, today we laid the basis
for the Jewish state."
　　　Thereafter, there could be no turning back. The
Peel Report turned all but a few Zionist groups from
the habit of long-term aspirations and wishful thinking.
The Twentieth Zionist Congress which met in Basel in
the summer of 1937 authorized the leadership to negotiate partition with the British, and the Jewish state
became a definable goal.[31]

By the late 1930s, the Yishuv was finally united behind the explicitly stated goal of a Jewish state, which itself had been heatedly
disputed as recently as the 1931 Zionist Congress, whereas in the
early 1930s many prominent Labor Zionist leaders considered the
call of Jabotinsky and his Revisionists simply demagogy. Eventually, Jabotinsky's idea that the only meaningful Zionist goal was a
state (independent and with a Jewish majority) came to be accepted:
not because of any ideological evolution, but due to concrete political conditions that rapidly and visibly deteriorated. This is persuasively argued by Marrus:

If crisis brought the Jewish state to the political forefront in 1931, a deepening of this crisis, affecting Jews
almost everywhere, completely reshaped discussion
before the outbreak of the Second World War. By 1939
virtually the entire Yishuv had rallied to the goal of a
Jewish state, and the World Zionist Organization, so
torn over the dispute over the Endziel in 1931, became
firmly committed to it. Far from having defeated a

> move toward a Jewish state, therefore, the 1931 Congress turned out to be one of the very last occasions when Zionists could seriously dispute with each other over the question.
>
> Abroad the most significant development was Hitler. Nazism, of course, would transform utterly the way in which Zionism was received—both in the Jewish and non-Jewish world. From a debatable historical experiment, the <u>Yishuv</u> became for thousands of Jews a practical necessity. Gravely menaced by a lack of Jewish immigrants in 1931, the <u>Yishuv</u> now braced for a flood of Jewish refugees—for whom Palestine was increasingly the sole means of escape. Threatened with being a Jewish backwater in the 1920s, Palestine within a short time became a principal focus of Jewish concern.[32]

This trend was reinforced by the fact that the British (due to their own <u>raison d'état</u>) progressively but visibly reinterpreted their mandatory obligations in a way that threatened to deal Zionism a mortal blow; restricted Jewish immigration to Palestine was the most significant and serious consequence of British policy.[33] Obviously, urgent alternatives were needed to the reliance placed by a semiautonomous Jewish community in Palestine on a reluctant and hostile British mandatory power.

The idea of the Jewish state was revived or rather articulated under these changed circumstances, partly as a response to the ideas emanating from the British themselves (primarily through the partition recommendations of the Peel Commission); it was not so much an intellectual or cultural notion as the product of historical necessity.

> A Jewish state came to be seen as a categorical imperative. Only a state could mobilize resources necessary for the defence of Jews in the increasingly turbulent Palestine of the late 1930s. And only a state could guarantee the control over Jewish immigration which, since the advent of Nazism, had become a paramount concern of Jews, just as it was a primary fear of the Arabs. A Jewish state had always been the intention of some Zionists, but for most it had languished far in the background of national thought. Now, however, when Jewish life was so seriously imperilled, the state appealed to almost all.[34]

There is a voluminous literature on the impact on eventual
Jewish statehood of the Holocaust in the Nazi inferno of Europe, but
Marrus is entirely correct in arguing that its impact on the evolution of the idea of the Jewish state in Zionist thinking is definitely
overstated:

> It is well to stress that this important shift in Zionist
> policy took place before the systematic murder of Euro-
> pean Jews. It was not the Holocaust which tipped the
> scales in the direction of the Jewish state idea, what-
> ever its subsequent effect on the realization of that goal.
> European Jews were in trouble long before the Nazis
> began to kill in large numbers, and Palestinian affairs,
> while linked to events in Europe, did not depend com-
> pletely on them. Still, the official codification of the
> new goal did not occur until May 1942, at the Biltmore
> Conference of Zionists in New York, which issued the
> most important Zionist statement during the war—a
> declaration, in effect, of Jewish war aims. The con-
> ference urged "that Palestine be established as a Jew-
> ish commonwealth integrated in the structure of the
> new democratic world." But this preceded an assess-
> ment of the Holocaust.[35]

This was indeed a curious evolution of stateness. Culturally,
the notion of state had been disentangled from Judaism. Intellec-
tually, statehood lurked tacitly, implicitly—one might say surrepti-
tiously—in the background, for fear of alienating others with explicit
statements of apparently overambitious goals. A lack of clarity in
the minds of the Zionist leadership as to the form and timing of the
creation of optimal conditions for realizing the social, cultural, and
humanitarian goals they considered supreme also contributed to this
lack of explication. It was the outcast Jabotinsky and his faction
who persistently argued that the entire idea of creating new, free,
proud, liberated Jews in their own homeland was not viable without
a state to supply the security and the institutional apparatus necessary for the attainment of this lofty ideal.

The weaknesses of the intellectual and cultural components of
stateness in Zionism paled into insignificance against the pressing
historical imperatives. Of course, the institutional structure of the
Jewish community in Palestine did not necessarily reflect the ideological arguments within the Zionist movement. On the contrary,
while the hesitations about the intellectual notion of stateness were
manifold, the Jewish community in Palestine (the Yishuv) evolved
a complex and effective organizational infrastructure, which formed

the nucleus of the efficient state machinery ultimately rendered necessary by the decision to declare statehood.[36]

To a certain extent, this state in the making or state within a state was even independent of the question of the relationship between state and nation. Thus, Dr. Arthur Rupin, a prominent Zionist leader in Palestine and a member of the binational-state-oriented <u>Brith Shalom</u> group, explicitly stated: "We seek to rid ourselves of the mistaken notion that has ruled Europe for a hundred years and has caused a world war, to wit, that a state can contain only one nation."[37] Nevertheless, it was the one nation represented by the Yishuv that developed the statelike institutional apparatus.

This phenomenon was studied from the point of view of modern social science in a most sophisticated way by Horowitz and Lissak.[38] As mentioned previously, they speak of a state in the making or a state within a state, and demonstrate that it consisted of an institutional framework that "in many spheres of political and social activity operated in a statelike manner."[39] They insist, however, on using the term "quasi-state," because three traits distinguished the Yishuv as a political system from a full-fledged state. (This, by the way, adds an additional theoretical aspect of "statelike authority without statelike sovereignty" to Nettl's conceptual variable.)

> First, the Yishuv was a minority in a dual social-political system. Moreover, not only was Mandatory Palestine a binational political unit, but large sections of the country had a mixed population; there were almost no continuous areas of Jewish settlement without an Arab population.
>
> Second, in terms of the functions it performed, the system was of a partial nature. In particular, it lacked judicial functions, with no legal code or courts of its own. Other areas, such as postal and telegraph services, customs, and the maintenance of the transportation infrastructure, were a monopoly of the Mandatory government. In the sphere of security the Yishuv had several paramilitary organizations, mainly the Hagana, but these organizations did not usually engage in enforcing law and order.
>
> Finally, the Yishuv was dependent on the Diaspora. Without the latter's resources of manpower, funds, and political support the Yishuv would not have been able to amass economic power or to maintain its political institutions.[40]

The decision taken in the 1930s and 1940s by the Zionist movement to opt for statehood eventually had to be implemented through the machinery of the Yishuv which, in terms of institutional behavior, had simply anticipated the eventual macro decisions of the Zionist leadership by a good many years. While the transition from Yishuv to state was by no means always as smooth as is sometimes described in the literature (to the extent that the process of integrating the military undergrounds into a state army even involved incidents bordering on civil war), it is probably correct to say that the institutional basis available was more statelike than in any other newly independent country.

> The transformation of the Yishuv from a quasi-state into a state in 1948 involved demographic changes that made possible the creation of a society with an overwhelming Jewish majority and the acquisition of sovereign status entailing the three functions of a sovereign state: legislative, executive, and judicial. On the other hand, the special relationship between the Yishuv and the Diaspora, persisted—along with the need for the Diaspora's resources. Nevertheless, the political implications of this connection were reduced by the separation of the functions of immigration and settlement—in which the Diaspora continued to take an active part through the institutions of the Zionist movement—from other spheres of policy making that passed into the exclusive jurisdiction of the Israeli government. [41]

There were, then, several functions that the state could not immediately take over. This was due not only to the special relationship with the diaspora, but also to the internal contradictions of the Yishuv system. Thus, while the state benefited from the ready-made institutional core, it had to contend with the countervailing centrifugal forces inherent in the particularistic nature of the elements that combined to form the Yishuv. While the system was characterized by a universalistic, statelike center, it simultaneously allowed—in fact, facilitated—the fragmentation of authority along party lines. This fragmentation involved a wide range of social and cultural services and generated what were virtually party "fiefdoms." A lengthy struggle ensued over the control of these fiefdoms, won eventually (but not unconditionally) by the state over particularistic forces: a process that Amitai Etzioni, in an apt phrase, calls "the decline of neo-feudalism." [42] This neo-feudalism was expressed in more elegant, if less specific terms by Horowitz and Lissak as "extreme flexibility":

The extreme flexibility which characterized the institutional system of the organized Yishuv was inconsistent with the organizational patterns characteristic of the executive branch in sovereign states in Western democracies. The concept of orderly government in a sovereign democratic system, as it developed in Western Europe and North America, implies a system of obligatory universalistic rules as well as the existence of authorities to ensure the observance of these rules.[43]

Eventually, however, the transition from Yishuv to state on the institutional/structural level was made with far less disruption than might reasonably have been expected. The heritage of the political center developed by the Yishuv proved to be both adaptable and resilient:

> The central phenomenon marking the transition from a "state in the making" to a sovereign state was political stability in circumstances of social change. This stability depended on the political center's ability to solve some major problems which it faced when independence was achieved: the imposition of authority on formerly dissident or separatist groups; the appropriation of quasi-governmental functions from particularistic political bodies; the assumption of new governmental functions and the enforcement of binding legal norms; and the absorption of the new immigration of the 1950s. Several factors helped the leadership of the Yishuv to cope successfully with these problems and to avoid crises that could have threatened the integrity of the entire system: the existence of rules of the game which had been acceptable by the vast majority of political groups before the establishment of the state; the center's ability to mobilize resources in the Diaspora; and the circumstance of the state's establishment at the height of a military struggle which compelled all political bodies in the state to accept the decisions of the central government.[44]

In other words, the institutions of the Yishuv included a strong statelike nucleus that preceded the state—a theoretically deviant case not really covered in the literature. The man who presided over this transition was David Ben-Gurion, the dominant political figure of Israel's first 15 years of existence. Although the explicit notion of a Jewish state was first raised in the Zionist

movement by his opponents, Jabotinsky and the Revisionists, it was
Ben-Gurion's fortune to declare the independence of the Jewish state,
to struggle with the difficulties of defending and institutionalizing
that state in its initial formative years, and to develop a school of
Zionist thought, which he called Mamlachtiout, explicitly concerned
with stateness. Ben-Gurion's views, theories, and arguments with
opponents served to put the problem of stateness in Israel in the
sharpest possible focus, and his disciples have kept it that way: in
fact, Ben-Gurion's spirit continues to hover over all Israeli questions of stateness, exerting an enormous influence over friend and
foe alike.[45]

Ben-Gurion's statesmanship and career in politics reveal a
most complex character. He started out as a Marxist socialist and
turned into an étatist social democrat. He was secretary general
of the all-powerful Trade Union Federation (Histadrut), but later
spent much of his time attempting to reduce the Histadrut's power
and influence. Virtually identified with his party, Mapai, he was
almost constantly alienated from his colleagues in the party leader
ship. He was supposed to be the party's greatest electoral asset,
but when he quit the party to run on his own, in 1965, he suffered a
crushing defeat. When, three years later, his disciples, Dayan
and Peres, decided to lead the seceded faction back into the fold of
Labor, Ben-Gurion decided to stay in the wilderness with an even
smaller faction of unknown faithfuls: a faction that went on to join
with his archrival, Begin, to establish the Likud! In addition to this
irony, not only did the Likud win the 1977 election and conclude the
peace treaty with Egypt, but Begin, the man Ben-Gurion had casti-
gated for his extremism, was to be honored with the Nobel Peace
Prize!

Ben-Gurion the political thinker was a man of great contrasts.
To many outside observers he seemed an extremely determined,
hawkish leader, but he was the one to accept total withdrawal from
the Sinai and the Gaza strip in 1957, and after 1967 he advocated a
withdrawal from all the conquered territories (except Jerusalem
and later, the Golan Heights). He was the determined leader who
declared the independence of the state in 1948 against great odds
and despite a great deal of reluctance among his colleagues, yet he
could be very hesitant, even pessimistic. He was the one who coined
the famous phrase "It does not matter what the Gentiles say: what
matters is what the Jews do," yet in practice few Israeli statesmen
were more conscious than he of world public opinion, and it was
Ben-Gurion who enunciated the doctrine that Israel ought not to be
involved in warfare without the assured support of at least one superpower. Aronson (partly on the basis of Teveth's research) gives the
following insight into Ben-Gurion the political thinker:

Even if Teveth does not state them outright, the picture he portrays leads to the following substantive and behavioral conclusions about Ben-Gurion's goals and methods [sic]. First, like other Zionists, Ben-Gurion totally rejected Jewish life in the Diaspora—culturally, socially, and politically. Second, his Zionism was, to a large extent, a personal struggle with hostile (non-Zionist) Jewish, Turkish and Arab environments, with Zionists who paid lip service to his ideas but did not implement them, and with Zionists who tried to achieve too much too soon. Having developed abroad a negative approach to his nation's "normal" way of life and having watched the few Jews who lived under Turkish rule in Palestine, Ben-Gurion was suspicious about the Jews' ability to transform themselves. Nevertheless, he was determined to transform himself and to create a political instrument that would implement his ideas. Third, he wanted a social-democratic, secular Jewish society based on egalitarian, just, and moral principles, and derived from the Bible rather than from Diaspora traditions, especially from the social and political ethos of the prophets. Finally, he envisioned a piecemeal, personal progress toward such a society, rather than a political miracle, diplomatic or military, that would secure Jewish predominance in Palestine.

This "pessimism" in Ben-Gurion's perception of the traditional Jewish way of life constrained him psychologically, in my opinion, when obstacles were expected to be encountered by the Jews in Palestine. But at the same time, it drove Ben-Gurion to create a fighting nation. He adored fighters and settlers, who symbolized for him the growing success of his main aim—to create a socially balanced, physically working land-oriented society capable of defending itself. The "defense" itself, the use of military power, the implementation of doctrines of sovereignty—in practice, all the concrete manifestations of principles were hindered, without Ben-Gurion's publicly admitting it, by his fear of the non-Jewish environment, by his "pessimism" with regard to traditional Jewish habits and by his piecemeal strategy of accumulating power, rather than working back to reality from legal, political and military goals. Ben-Gurion's behavior was determined by cognitive postulates derived from understanding, learning, and analyzing reality while trying to change it. [46]

In what follows, it will be argued that the perceived pessimism was but the awareness of the contrasting traits and conflicting demands of the Jews as a nation scattered in the diaspora, on the one hand, and the demands of realpolitik concerning Jewish statehood in Palestine, on the other. It will also be argued that his reasoning from reality to goals (rather than the other way around) and his cognitive-postulative thinking based on historical reality were classic examples of the logic of stateness in a politician. It will be further argued that his cumbersome, inconsistent, and ambivalent articulation of raison d'état was to a large extent responsible for the subsequent ideological confusion of his disciples and the general public in Israel.

Initially—that is, until the Arab revolt in Palestine in the mid-1930s[47]—Ben-Gurion, like other Labor Zionists, thought of the Arabs in terms of socialist cooperation against the feudalist-capitalist elites ruling the Arabs.[48] Like most other Zionists (and unlike Jabotinsky), he had the idea of Jewish statehood as an immediate goal all but forced upon him by history, particularly by the need to respond to the Peel Commission's partition plan. This need provoked tremendous controversy in the Zionist movement in general, and particularly in Labor Zionism. Ben-Gurion's role and arguments in this controversy clearly demonstrated the extent to which he had been converted to stateness, and showed the beginnings of what was to become his profound belief in partition. He argued the case for partitioned states as a basis for a peaceful accommodation over the question of Palestine, an idea he would cling to for the rest of his life:

> More than in other times, I believe in an Arab-Jewish agreement in the foreseeable future. And if we bring hundreds of thousands of Jews to our State and consolidate ourselves from the economic and military point of view, there will be a basis for a free agreement regarding the abolishment of frontiers between us and the Arab [Partitioned] State. . . . Their true national interests will impel Arabs to compromise with us in exchange for mutual use and enjoyment of the areas of both our States.[49]

Behind this reasoning lay a profound idea that challenged several sacred nationalist and socialist articles of faith: the idea that nationalist movements were less likely to reach a reasonable compromise (even if they shared common social goals) than were states pursuing legitimate interests.

He advocated a new idea that became a cardinal tenet in
his conception of Jewish-Arab relations: Arab-Jewish
rapprochement could be achieved only _after_ a Jewish
state had been established. Once a Jewish state had
consolidated Jewish economic and military power, one
could expect the Arabs to realize that a strong Israel
could benefit them directly. [50]

Therefore, Ben-Gurion proceeded, in the midst of great opposition, to defend and support the idea of a partitioned state as
suggested by the Peel Commission, on the grounds that this would
give the Jews state instruments.

This report . . . gives us a wonderful strategic basis
for our stand, for our right . . . the first document
since the Mandate which strengthens our moral and
political status. . . . It gives us control over the Coast
of Palestine; large immigration; a Jewish Army, systematic colonization under State control. [51]

The need to obtain possession of such instruments as soon as
possible had to override all other concerns, whether or not the possibility of establishing a Jewish state in the foreseeable future was
real: "No one without faith in the great Zionist vision would find
the strength to reject a concrete offer to establish a Jewish State
immediately in part of the country." [52]
    Note that the concreteness of a Jewish state in even part of
the country is more important for Ben-Gurion than the completeness of the historical homeland, the continuation of the special relationship with the British mandatory power, and the continued coexistence of a binational Arab-Jewish society within the same borders. All these arguments were raised by opponents of both Left
and Right in the Zionist movement, and all were rejected by Ben-
Gurion. In particular, most of the influential figures in Zionist
socialism maintained that the resolution of Arab-Jewish national
contradictions ought to precede the establishment of statehood,
whereas Ben-Gurion maintained that partition into states was the
best vehicle for national reconciliation.
    He similarly rejected all arguments along the lines that the
Jews were not yet ready for statehood and that they needed the continued protection of the British and/or the League of Nations. Nor
did he accept the Revisionist arguments that partition had to be rejected in favor of a Jewish commonwealth based on a Jewish majority in _all_ of Palestine (Transjordan included), and that Jewish rejection of partition would ultimately lead the British to realize the

weakness of the Arabs as a mainstay of British imperial policy in the area. The Revisionists were willing to wait for an ultimate Jewish majority in all of Palestine; Ben-Gurion was willing to accept a partition of Palestine in order to have a Jewish majority in a part of it. The socialists wanted national reconciliation as a precondition of statehood; Ben-Gurion wanted statehood as a precondition for national reconciliation. From this point on, stateness, in Ben-Gurion's thinking, would clearly outweigh nationalist or socialist ideological considerations.

But he was not only an original thinker: when it came to affairs of state, he was a great believer in realpolitik, despite its demands of timing and reasonable risks in decision making. As Aronson says,

> Ben-Gurion was a "postulative" statesman; guided by a strong sense of sequencing and timing, he cognitively arrived at a set of principles and priorities. His political method, at the height of his intellectual and political power, was based upon his instincts for power, his understanding of where power lay or what might determine one's sovereignty and defense, and his habit of studying matters in depth, gathering data and analyzing it over a relatively long period until his opinion was set. [53]

In other words, postulating upon the lessons of history was good as a guide for action only when the interests of state made this imperative. At times this led Ben-Gurion to bold and determined measures; at other times he proved to be unexpectedly (and often apparently inconsistently) conciliatory, much to the confusion of the Israeli body politic:

> On May 14, 1948, when he decided, against the advice of many political friends, to proclaim independence and await the invading Arab armies almost empty-handed, Ben-Gurion knew that he took a great risk, but he regarded other possibilities as even more risky in the long run. History, he believed, does not repeat itself, and the rare moment of Soviet-American understanding in favor of Jewish sovereignty in a part of Palestine might disappear forever. It was up to the power of will—his own—and the power of his nation to fight to use favorable political circumstances against heavy military odds. This method created an image of an aggressive, "hawkish" leader. In reality, his postulates usually brought about a pragmatic compromise, mostly a territorial status quo, to the dismay of his most ardent followers. [54]

State-oriented thinking, for Ben-Gurion, meant clear priorities. Above all, it meant the need for a comprehensive, universal institutional framework, which he first sought in the Histadrut but found eventually in the state. To him even the loftiest national or social goals were meaningless if the instrument of their realization was functionally too weak. The strengthening of the instrument had to be given first—and almost absolute—priority. In some ways this led Ben-Gurion to take a rigidly étatist attitude, one curiously devoid of other ideological content (much to the dismay of numerous party ideologues and intellectuals in the country); in other ways it led him to profound distinctions that he never fully articulated.

Unquestionably, Ben-Gurion was a believer in a territorial state in the historical homeland. He never had doubts as to the rights of the Jews in this regard, nor was he greatly concerned one way or the other with arguments that these Jewish rights were not exclusive and absolute, that others (such as the Palestinian Arabs) had such rights, or the like. His first priority was the establishment, security, and prosperity of a Jewish state. According to his vision, the goals of such a state were not territorial; therefore success could not be judged in territorial terms, but only by the criteria of the "practical politics of the Zionist-Israeli ethos." This vision, in turn, as Aronson observes, "had two facets of major importance: the wish to consolidate Israel as the working success story of Zionist ideology and the desire to create a Jewish man, qualitatively new in political, social, and cultural terms."[55]

In this sense, the state had to command absolute loyalty; a nation, of course, could easily become both corrupt and misunderstood (as eventually was the case, according to Aronson, with the Israel of Ben-Gurion's successors in the 1970s), a potentiality greatly increased by brutal realities such as the persistent Arab-Israeli conflict:

> Ben-Gurion's Jewish state was an instrument to achieve
> social, cultural, and moral values. For the Zionist
> right and members of the younger generation, it was a
> purpose for itself, the embodiment, in sovereign and
> religious symbols, of Jewish traditions, experiences,
> and rights. Since this mixture of right-wing, religious,
> and state-oriented emotional, responsive, manly and
> legalistically bound leaders now took over, a vast major-
> ity of Jews—those who might not be satisfied with reli-
> gion, the state, the conflict, and settlements in the West
> Bank as the sole manifestation of their complex heri-
> tage—a trend reverting to social, humane values might
> be expected if the conflict permitted it. Yet the historical

structure and the psychological asymmetry of the conflict are not promising in this respect. A high degree
of penetrating other peoples' psyches is needed to syn-
chronize pragmatic retreats from ideological and substantive demands on both sides, and an almost inhumane
restraint of built-in constraints in negotiations is needed
to control the temptation to view gains by the other side
as in a zero sum game. [56]

As far as Ben-Gurion himself was concerned, however, stateness as an instrument was a clear conception. The State of Israel
was in the Land of Israel (the only commonly accepted Jewish term
for what the rest of the world tends to call "Palestine"), but was
not identical to it. The goals the state had to realize had to do with
the elevation of the Jewish people to freedom, dignity, security,
sovereignty, and creativity. While these could be attained only in
a state of their own, the size, territory, and boundaries of that
state could not be expected to play a decisive role, for such spatial
and geographic considerations had little to do with the essentially
educational task of a state in transforming the collective experience
and psyche of a people. If Ben-Gurion had a myth, it had to do with
the people of Israel, not the Land of Israel. [57] One critical consequence of this was that the romantic lure of the completeness of the
Land of Israel (which he consistently resisted) was subordinate to
the raison d'état of the State of Israel. If Ben-Gurion was ever
caught in the mystique of the land, it was in the dream of settling
the Negev desert (which comprised almost two-thirds of pre-1967
Israel, and where he made his home in the latter years of his life).
The Negev was the desert he really wanted to conquer, not the Sinai:
the latter was important only in strategic terms, as were all other
territories. Says Aronson:

> In 1956, Israel launched a preventive war against Egypt,
> hoping to bring about a change in Egyptian behavior and
> to control, if possible, certain spaces that were empty
> but strategically important in the context of the constant
> Israeli-Egyptian friction since 1954. It is no accident
> that I have mentioned empty territories of only strategic
> importance, not of historical and ideological importance.
> This latter aspect would become crucial for the govern-
> ments after Ben-Gurion. He himself, however, had
> reached a compromise between the demands of Zionist
> ideology, which regarded all of Palestine as the historic
> homeland of the Jews and as the modern solution to their
> problems, and the movement's tactics and other goals

in the mid–1930s, when he had accepted the Peel Commission partition plan.[58]

Analysis of Ben–Gurion's strategy in the 1948–49 war reveals
a similar restraint, this time bringing up yet another crucial postu-
late of Ben–Gurion's as a component of the raison d'état of the Jewish state:

> During the War of Independence, Ben–Gurion again
> proved willing to compromise on the territorial issue.
> His reasoning seems to have been along these lines:
> the main objective of Zionism was to establish Jewish
> sovereignty over territory in Palestine and bring it
> under Jewish military control, with the support and, if
> possible, aid of the extraregional powers. This terri-
> tory would be settled by a growing Jewish majority com-
> posed mainly of the existing Jewish community and refu-
> gees and displaced persons in urgent need of the Zionist
> homeland. Later, other Jews would immigrate. At the
> same time, according to his experience and evaluation
> of emerging forces in the modern world, it was essen-
> tial that there be as few Arabs as possible in the terri-
> tory under Jewish control.[59]

Ben–Gurion's cold-blooded state logic astonished many
Israelis. An articulation of national interests, pure and simple,
would have dictated taking, and maximizing, control of the vast
spaces of the Jewish homeland in Arab hands (particularly the Old
City of Jerusalem, of enormous symbolic significance to the Jewish
people from time immemorial). If Ben–Gurion was right, however,
that in the long run Jewish national interest could be articulated,
realized, and protected only under the aegis of the state, then the
interests of the latter had to be the overriding consideration, even
where territorial issues were concerned. Since the state of Israel
had been born in war, Ben–Gurion knew enough about statecraft to
understand that the eventual borders in a peace settlement would be
dictated more by the outcomes of battles than by neatly drawn lines
inspired by nationalistic reasoning or historical imperatives. All
this seemed clear enough in his own mind, but due to manifold political pressures, the articulation of these precepts to the Israeli public
was somewhat confused (with predictable ultimate consequences).
These contradictions are clearly brought out in Aronson's detailed
analysis:

> The prime minister did not tell the Israeli public all
> this in its exact meaning. The postulate of not ruling

Arabs was not emphasized. Instead, he stressed that
the borders were dictated by the military outcome of
the War of Independence. When it accepted partition,
Israel gave up its historic rights to areas dear to the
Judaeo-Zionist tradition. However, when the Arabs
rejected partition and relieved the Jews of their commitment to the plan, Israel was kept from exercising
its rights to improve the strategic situation caused by
Arab aggression. Israel's right to expand its "historical" territory was restricted by pressures exerted by
the extraregional powers, by Arab military strength,
and by perceptions of Arab willingness to come to some
agreement. Anglo-American pressure at the end of the
war was enough to keep Ben-Gurion from expanding into
the Sinai. Instead, he annexed the Eilat region, which
Israel had not captured during the fighting but which was
allotted to the Jewish state under the Partition Plan.

Brigadier General Yigal Allon, commander of the
southern front in the War of Independence, leader of the
kibbutz underground during the Mandate period, and
member of the leftist nationalist Achdut Ha'Avoda party,
disagreed. He claimed that by deciding not to encircle
or destroy the Egyptian army and to accept no more than
an armistice, Ben-Gurion missed a historic opportunity
to impose a peace settlement on Cairo. The pragmatic
decision not to attempt to impose peace on hostile nations, but instead gradually to create a framework of
cooperation through a general armistice, while allowing
Israel to recover from a bloody war and to concentrate
upon domestic rehabilitation and absorption of immigrants, was described by the nationalist left and right
as a national catastrophe.

The decision not to extend Israeli territory in the
east was also attacked as leading to "generations of woe."
This historic error was attributed to Israeli military
weakness and naiveté in believing that peace could be
achieved under the circumstances. Achdut Ha'Avoda
and the nationalist right led by Menachem Begin, which
had never accepted partition, accused Ben-Gurion of a
"historic failure" for not capturing the West Bank and
East Jerusalem. Ben-Gurion, who privately did not
think Arab control of the West Bank an unmitigated disaster, publicly blamed both Israel's objective weakness, which had influenced the cabinet majority against
his own wishes, and the extraregional pressures. In

time, his version of events was accepted, and the debate over the lost opportunities of the War of Independence was closed. However, by casting the argument
in these terms he legitimized the aspiration to revised
borders for as long as the conflict continued and if and
when Israel was forced to fight the Arabs again.[60]

Aronson cites the testimony of a former Israeli ambassador
to Washington, Ephraim Evron, who at that time was Ben-Gurion's
personal aide. According to him, in 1949 Ben-Gurion observed:
"Luckily, we were not able to capture the whole of Jerusalem during the War of Independence. This would have been too much for
us, and the world wouldn't allow us to keep it anyhow."[61]

There is a most intriguing account of the times and their
dilemmas in the memoirs of Ben-Gurion's prized disciple, Moshe
Dayan, who gives, among other insights, a most instructive description of two key decisions taken by Ben-Gurion. The reasoning
inherent in the arguments of both Ben-Gurion and Dayan are almost
textbook exercises in the application of the logic of raison d'état to
a war situation.

The first decision was to enter a series of talks with the Jordanians under most unsatisfactory conditions. Dayan recounts:

> At a meeting with the prime minister on December 18,
> 1948, Ben-Gurion stressed [to Dayan] that "our primary
> aim now is peace," and he warned against our being
> "flushed with victory." He added: "Immigration de-
> mands that there be an end to war. Our future need is
> peace and friendship with the Arabs. Therefore I am
> in favor of talks with King Abdulla, although I doubt
> whether the British will let him make peace with us."[62]

Even more instructive was the dilemma raised by the refusal
of the Jordanians to live up to their part of the armistice agreement,
and their persistence in keeping the all-significant Old City of
Jerusalem closed to Jews. Says Dayan:

> On Jerusalem, however, we remained divided in our
> views. I proposed that we take action to enforce the
> Armistice Agreement, using the army to open the roads
> to Mount Scopus, the Western Wall, and through Latrun.
> Unless this was done, the joint decision reached at
> Rhodes would be worthless, an empty promise. After
> all, it was not up to the Arabs but to us to give tangible
> expression to our rights, and our failure to do so was
> tantamount to surrendering those rights.

Ben-Gurion asked me if such military action would not bring about a renewal of the war. I told him I did not think so. I judged that even if it came to an open military clash and the use of force to break open a corridor to the Western Wall and Mount Scopus, it would remain an isolated episode and not touch off general hostilities. Moreover, it was possible that when the Jordanians saw that we were ready to take determined measures, they would themselves fulfill the terms of the agreement, as they had done with the division of no-man's land in southern Jerusalem.

Ben-Gurion did not accept my proposal. His main reason was that we now had to concentrate on the targets of peace—the care and rehabilitation of our immigrants, the settlement of the land, above all the injection of life into the desert regions—and the overall development of the country. . . . In Ben-Gurion's mind, the book of war was closed—for the time being at least. His eyes were now turned to the realization of the Zionist dream, the essence of which was immigration—the return of the Jewish exiles—and the revival of the land. [63]

A similarly complex picture emerges from analyzing Ben-Gurion's policy of retaliation and deterrence in the early 1950s. [64] The strategic requirements and educational imperatives of the state are again curiously juxtaposed, as is demonstrated in Ben-Gurion's credo of retaliation:

One of the reasons I believe in the policy of retaliation is that it will deter the enemy. But there is another reason, educational and moral. Look at these Jews. They come from Iraq, from Kurdistan, from North Africa. They come from countries where shedding Jewish blood was cheap, where others had the legitimate right to torture and beat them. . . . They are used to being the helpless victims of the Gentiles. Here [in Israel] we must show them that their blood is not cheap; that there is a Jewish State and Army that will not permit [their oppressors] to do with them as they please; that their lives and properties have value; that they walk erect and with pride. We must demonstrate to them that whoever assaults them will be punished, that they are now citizens of a sovereign state that is responsible for their lives and their security. [65]

This juxtaposition characterized Ben-Gurion's entire career: to the end of his days he continued to believe that the establishment of the State of Israel and the long history of the Jewish people somehow had not yet been fused into nationhood. In other words, Ben-Gurion also believed, much as theoreticians like Friedrich did, that the state had to create its own nation (and not the other way around). In a characteristic outburst in a 1969 interview with Perlmutter he declared:

> This is not a nation, not yet. It is an exiled people still in the desert longing for the flesh of Egypt. It cannot be considered a nation until the Negev and Galilee are settled; until millions of Jews immigrate to Israel; and until moral standards necessary to the ethical practice of politics and the high values of Zionism are sustained. This is neither a mob [Erev Rav] nor a nation. It is a people still chained to their exilic past. Redeemed but not fulfilled. [66]

But on this score, also, much confusion ensued. The activist policy of retaliation ("the mailed fist," in Ben-Gurion's terms), the need for self-reliance, serious consideration for the extraregional great powers, and the eventual hope of peace with the Arabs (though without a very profound analysis of concurrent developments in the Arab world), made for a volatile mixture. Here it seems that Aronson overstates the case:

> In general, Ben-Gurion succeeded in developing a political consensus about the pragmatic policy he was able to present in fundamental ideological terms. He maneuvered between the demands for unattainable peace and war, between territorial compromise and protracted conflict, between the exigencies of day-to-day security and the challenge of basic, long-range security. [67]

In the relevant years, the "political consensus" was based less on pragmatic policy and more on Ben-Gurion's leadership. In security matters, however, he did not always project a clear interpretation of raison d'état. Much of the ensuing confusion is captured in Aronson's account:

> Ben-Gurion's policy provided only indirect affirmation of the territorial status quo. The prime minister attributed much importance to developing and populating Israel's empty south, the Negev. He argued repeatedly

that the 1949 boundaries gave Israel enough space to realize Zionism's main goal: providing a refuge for persecuted Jews and concentrating as many Jews as possible in a sovereign Israel. He hoped this would create the socially, psychologically, and culturally new Jewish type. However, there was a glaring contradiction in the argument. The national ideology stressed full Jewish sovereignty over the state's territory, that is, its exclusive Jewish character. It also stressed securing the borders of the state and protecting Jews from persecution. Logically, then, it follows that the physical security of the inhabitants of the sovereign Jewish state must be ensured in the fullest sense of the word. Given the Arabs' constant provocations, their open hostility, and their relations among themselves, it could be argued that the 1949 borders secured neither Jewish sovereignty nor the physical survival of individual Jews, let alone Israel's legitimacy.

Ben-Gurion's arguments and aims imposed serious constraints on his policy. [68]

No wonder that so many Israelis were taken aback in 1956 by his blatant willingness for withdrawal and in 1967 by his dovish pronouncements. The 1967 war, in particular, seemed to destroy many of his postulates. It appears that Ben-Gurion's strange, idiosyncratic—almost mystic—methodology in developing his notions of state interest, and his reluctance to articulate clearly its parts while in power, prevented him from developing a doctrine, or even an intellectual framework, of stateness as a legacy for his successors.

Historically, cognitive experience, as manifested in Ben-Gurion's case, based upon ceaseless reading and soul searching and presented in disguised, difficult to read terms and actions, is difficult to transfer to the next generation, which absorbs and distorts the experience according to its own experience and background. Ben-Gurion's constant search for a compact, viable power base to serve his postulates—a sovereign, socially reformed, humanitarian Jewish existence—created a growing rejection of his personal regimen in the same power base and outside it, as the secondary leadership adapted itself to new social realities in a post-pioneering Israel. The image of a socially, culturally, and psychologically reformed sovereign

Jewish state, created by Ben-Gurion in order to change
the nature of his nation, became divorced from Jewish
realities in Israel. A mixture of the fighting Jew, who
indeed was raised by the pioneers and who adopted Ben-
Gurion's political and military slogans rather than his
complicated set of postulates, who rejected ruling Arabs
and territorial exaggeration and preferring pragmatic
defense postures, was later blurred with traditional
Jewish fears, emotionalism, and bargaining habits.
Ben-Gurion's latent dependence on foreign powers and
"the world," his historically postulated understanding
of a compromise between Jewish rights and Arab presence in and around Palestine (which he reluctantly admitted publicly but which set limits on his "proud,"
"sovereign," and autonomous behavior) created a gap
between the substance of his policy and its appearance,
and was not acceptable to the more optimistic, more
autonomous younger generation or to the ideological,
self-righteous Jewish right inspired by the unique experience of post-World War I anti-Semitism. [69]

The confusion of Ben-Gurion's legacy was compounded by the
equally complex nature of the domestic aspects of his state doctrine.
Here, the complexity stemmed from the ambiguous realities and
perceptions of the party-state-society triangle. On this level, too,
Ben-Gurion early broke away from his socialist colleagues, who
were by and large irrevocably committed to the maintenance of a
"state within a state." The Labor-dominated Histadrut continued to
expand its activity in education, health care, all aspects of the
economy, and for some time, even defense and security. A tremendous struggle ensued, in which Ben-Gurion took a strong stand.
His position, however, was far from free of contradiction and paradox. Initially, as Perlmutter has said:

The Labor movement maintained its hold over the
newly-established state machinery by using its autonomous structures to control functions formally assigned
to the state bureaucracies, including labor relations,
health, education, and even the integration of some
600,000 newly-arrived immigrants.
David Ben-Gurion opposed these tendencies almost single-handedly. To him the establishment of the
State of Israel required an end to the Yishuv's particularistic, personality-dominated, elitist practices. Ben-
Gurion's conceptions were paradoxical. He was himself

an elitist, a statist, and an anti-populist nationalist. Yet, in his mind, the Leninist conception of a Parteistaat [sic] was diametrically opposed to that of the labor collective (especially its left-wing Ahdut Haavoda parties). Ben-Gurion was set to destroy the party-state linkage. With the formation of the state, Ben-Gurion set himself the task of diminishing the role of the Histadrut-Hityashvut collectivistic, non-statist practices. He became a statist par excellence because he was a nationalist before he was a socialist. A formalist, he believed in a government of laws and procedures, not a government of personalities and col- lective action. In fact he intended to use Mapai to mod- ify its own hegemonic aspirations and to strengthen the newly-created formal and bureaucratic structures of the State of Israel. [70]

As an elitist, he stood alone; as a statist, he was alienated from his socialist colleagues; as an antipopulist, he was opposed to Jabotinsky's successors, [71] the Beginistas of Herut, who forged an almost mystical link with the masses of Asian and African immi- grants. As a statist for whom the state had priority over the nation (he was a nationalist only in this qualified sense), he was often alien- ated even from the worldwide Zionist leadership. And there was an overwhelming paradox in a man trying to use his party as a base of power from which to destroy the party-state linkage. No wonder, given so many contradictions and so much alienation, that the sec- ondary leadership of his party not only failed to follow his example, but eventually teamed up to destroy him. "Ben-Gurionism," such as it was, became the heritage only of the "Young Turks," led by Dayan, who understandably often failed to make much of his heritage on account of the exceedingly weak theoretical foundations.

The Zionist movement's belated adoption of the goal of state- hood had thoroughgoing (and negative) implications for Zionist theory. Perlmutter correctly argues that

the formation of the state preceded any clear definition of the relationship between state and society. Even after the state was a reality, the pragmatists of the labor movement failed to create any political theory, occupied as they were with the practical aspects of nation building and security. [72]

To this dismal "state of the theory,"

David Ben Gurion was no exception. Although he had
some pretensions as a political philosopher, he never
worked out a clearly stated theory of Mamlachtiout.
Nonetheless, he perceived that, despite their protesta-
tions to the contrary, the leaders of the labor movement
and Mapai were mainly preoccupied with dominating
both state and society. It was his aim to prevent the
state from becoming the pawn of a parochial labor Zionism. While Ben-Gurion believed that the political order
(the state, the military) should subordinate and even replace partisan political organizations, he was also aware
that political power for individuals stems from such organizational bases. He understood that the best way to
achieve his goals, therefore, was to use the system he
deplored to accumulate power. [73]

To this very day, most Israelis remember Ben-Gurion's
legacy of stateness as Mamlachtiout. This generic term, however,
means different things to different people. Perlmutter gives one
broadly accepted interpretation:

This cardinal concept of state and societal relations in
Israel was Mamlachtiout, a term whose literal transla-
tion is as complex as its connotations. In Hebrew,
Mamlacha literally means kingdom; Mamlachtiout means
kingship. The concept derives from the Jewish kingdoms
of the Old Testament in which the political meaning of
kingdom has a universalistic, non-particularist overlay.
It is possible to translate Mamlachtiout as statism, but
the term is better understood as an operative political
concept that connotes a set of intellectual and political
aspirations. Mamlachtiout cannot be construed in the
sense of the Weberian traditional (kingship) authority
structure, but in its pure form, it is what Weber would
have called the legal-rational form of authority. As
such, it supersedes the patrimonial, pre-bureaucratic,
"voluntaristic" Yishuv-Zionist concept of the relationship between state and society. To Ben-Gurion Mamlachtiout meant the creation of a political order. And
since the most exalted Jewish historical political entities were the kingdoms of David and Solomon, Mamlachtiout meant the creation of a political order in the
third Jewish Commonwealth in Eretz Israel. [74]

It can be argued that <u>Mamlachtiout</u> meant not just the creation of a political order, but a specific kind of political order, one that emphasized the state at the expense of everything else. Ben-Gurion expressed this in complex and often very misunderstood phrases and slogans, such as "From class to Nation" and "Not a Class Party, but a Service Party." He partly won the battle in universalizing most state services and in increasing the saliency of the state in Israeli politics; but he lost in eventually having to transfer power to an elite that did not subscribe to his views. The task of carrying on Ben-Gurion's work was supposedly left to his loyal "Young Turks" and Moshe Dayan. But his prized pupil was a man of no lesser complexity, and his career, too, was one of paradox: the perennial hawk of Labor governments became the perennial dove of the Likud government (1977–79) under Ben-Gurion's archrival, Begin, and returned, in the 1981 elections, to his most characteristic role—the maverick, individualistic lone wolf. [75] His importance became manifest at the time of the 1967 war. By then, Ben-Gurion seemed to have developed numerous doubts about him, but the war changed everything. Ben-Gurion was isolated in a political wilderness.

> After the Six Day War, the "old man," as he was called years before, became old indeed, politically. He was caught in the contradictions that made up his foreign and defense policy between 1949 and 1963: his concepts of sovereignty and self-reliance could be interpreted as if they led toward an Israeli rule in Palestine <u>as a whole</u>, including Arabs. His pessimism, as far as the abilities of the IDF and pressures by foreign powers to return territories were concerned, proved false for the time being. When he <u>spoke up and said that Israel should return all of the territories captured in 1967 in exchange for peace, thus revealing his basic priority of not ruling Arabs</u>, he was regarded as the fallen old leader who envied Eshkol's achievements.

Thus, Ben-Gurion himself started to correct his own traditional course. He added East Jerusalem and the Golan Heights to the territory that should remain in Israeli hands, yet, until his death in 1973, he kept arguing that Israel should return its conquests in exchange for peace. He found himself opposing a new national consensus created after June, 1967, and he lost his influence altogether. As a matter of fact, Dayan never consulted him before the war or after. Nevertheless, Ben-Gurion was fascinated by Dayan and

his apparent success and was hopelessly at odds with
the much more cautious Eshkol. He thus preferred to
criticize Dayan indirectly, then left current politics
behind altogether. Times had changed, but his in-
stincts still told him that Israel's bid for autonomy,
coupled with occupation of vast Arab lands populated
by many Arabs, was an extremely risky exercise. Perhaps it was one that could be carried out by a real power,
but not a tiny Jewish state.

Ben-Gurion had helped make many Israelis think
of themselves as a proud, if possibly autonomous, old/
new brand of Jewishness. Dayan seemed a successful
incorporation of that dream. Could Ben-Gurion tell
them openly that he doubted it? He preferred silence. [76]

Dayan's thinking on state affairs was quickly shown to be entirely different from Ben-Gurion's. If Ben-Gurion was a "cognitive-
postulative"[77] leader, Aronson says, Dayan "used to be . . . the
manly-responsive" type, one who "is inclined to react to the other
side's challenges almost automatically, as a matter of principle,
fearing that the other party will interpret a lack of response as a
sign of weakness and will be tempted to escalate its challenges."[78]
The argument is reiterated that what Aronson calls Ben-Gurion's
"cognitive-postulative"[79] approach is characteristic of statelike
thinking. The "manly-responsive" approach (to which Mrs. Meir
was at times also prone!),[80] on the other hand, is much lower on
the scale of stateness, and tends to mix the logics of state and nation, as can be clearly seen in Dayan's assessment of the 1967 war:

In six days we have achieved war aims, which were the
outcome of the causes of the war that was enforced upon
us by the Arabs. Today, we are facing no war aims,
but the goals of peace. We want a state of Israel that
will retain its uncompromising Jewish character, demo-
graphically and structurally. We want borders that will
ensure Israel's security. We want to have equal international rights, including the freedom of shipping. We
want borders that will reflect the connection between the
Jewish people and their historical land. We want a
state that will be recognized by its neighbors. We want
peace treaties that will also solve the Palestine refugee
problem. [81]

Not only are the declared goals obviously contradictory, they
reintroduce "the connection between the Jewish people and their

historical land" as a criterion for the borders of Israel, whereas for Ben-Gurion the newly "acquired" territories were to be used to change the legitimacy and security of the borders of the state as he knew them: the state again coming before the nation. Moreover, the goals were enunciated with a remarkable lack of attention to the goals of the adversary.

To be fair, Dayan could at times show remarkably detached insight into the motives and fears of the Arabs, and even came to acquire a reputation as the government's expert on Arab affairs, one who understood Arabs and knew how to negotiate with them. On the other hand, in moments of enthusiasm (as in the post-1967 euphoria), Dayan seemed to disregard Arab state interests altogether and instead looked for "psychological" explanations:

> There is something deplorable and there is something positive in this so-called Arab mentality. The negative aspect is the inclination of the Arabs to cheat and to deceive themselves, and others consciously. This starts with a false or incorroct report given by a field commander either to explain a failure or to make a hero of himself, by exaggerating his situation and the number of Jews killed. It ends with the president of Egypt or the king of Jordan, who know that the information was falsified, but still accept it. Again [they do this] either to explain their failure or make heroes of themselves. . . .
> Arab mentality does not interest me as a psychological issue. It explains to me why the Arabs do not want peace . . . not because reality makes it difficult for them, but because their mentality shields reality from them. [82]

This is a singular departure from the logic of stateness. Given a low degree of state logic in one's own reasoning, there is a tendency also to regard the adversary in nonstatelike terms. It may not be a farfetched speculation that in this particular instance Dayan suffered from the consequence of a long historical process of omission: because Zionism was late to develop a theory of the Jewish state, it was also late to develop a theory of the Arab states; this was not really rectified, even by Ben-Gurion. In fact, Ben-Gurion's continued emphasis on the state as a generic concept after 1949 temporarily postponed any pointed ideological questions that the Zionist movement had previously asked. Such questions were raised with great intensity all over Israel after 1967. What would be the relationship of Judaism as a culture and a way of life of the Jews to the family of states upon their return to Zion?

> What would then replace the known patterns of Jewish
> life? . . . Was the Jewish State intended to be an end
> in itself, a Utopia . . . through which life was to be
> transformed? Or was it to be primarily and more mun-
> danely the means by which national political power, of
> the advantages of which the Jews had been deprived for
> twenty centuries, was to be restored?[83]

Though Ben-Gurion repeatedly spoke of educating the "new
Jewish man," one who would be liberated, proud, independent,
courageous, and productive, he never managed to fuse his lofty
ideals with the traditional Judaism understood by Jewish masses
everywhere. Though pragmatic Zionism produced brilliant social
innovations such as the kibbutz and the moshav, it was not clear
whether this was due to Zionist ingenuity or to Jewish genius. The
entire question of the "Jewish state" as against "the state of the
Jews" was never seriously tackled, much less resolved.[84]

> It was to be expected that the question, the Jewish ques-
> tion of Israel, would explode in all its intensity with the
> establishment of the State. Against all logic, however,
> it did not: for three main reasons. The first was the
> Arab hostility, which created in the new and fragmented
> Israeli society a strong reflex of unity for survival. The
> second was the astonishment of the Israelis, old settlers
> and newcomers alike, at the reappearance of Jewish po-
> litical sovereignty, a dream searched for for so long
> that when it materialized, all "men were like dreamers,"
> in the words of the Psalmist. The third reason was
> Ben-Gurion, who not only acted as midwife to the State
> but imposed on all parties, much against their will, the
> historic decision of not deciding on any essential prob-
> lems of the State: not on a constitution, not on the
> national borders, not on the ideological character of
> the State. This policy of non-decision-making was dic-
> tated as much by national wisdom as by party interest:
> only by not deciding could Mapai, a social-democratic
> party with 34 per cent of the seats in parliament, act
> as a national party. But it was an attitude which saved
> Israel from grave internal dissension in the first very
> difficult years of her existence.[85]

Ben-Gurion's notion of stateness, in this sense, may have de-
generated into an ideologically obscure interpretation of étatisme
which left all too many basic problems in abeyance. Etatisme preempted ideology:

In the 1930s the political formation of parties, structure and movement were closely linked to ideological
aspirations. . . . The concern now was with running
a state, winning elections, the welfare of the society,
dealing with friends and foes, dedication to the excellence of Zahal (the Israel Defence Force) and above
all political domination. These were no longer ideological events. [86]

Even so, Ben-Gurion's practical emphasis on partition as
shaping an acceptable state and his pragmatic approach to its territorial connection with the Land of Israel, at least created a virtual
acceptance of the fait accompli resulting from the 1948-59 war, re-
leasing energies for pragmatic tasks. The 1967 victory shattered
the status quo, and revived serious debate on the most fundamental
existential questions concerning the Jewish state:

It relieved the State from the Arab menace of physical
destruction; the conquest of populous Arab areas
obliged Israel to define itself in relation to its enemies:
what it meant to be "Jewish" or Israeli in the occupied
areas, how the "redemption of the land" could serve to
be justified by the redemption of the people. The victory of 1967 should have been used to solve past problems, such as the danger of Arab guerrillas, the question of the demilitarized zones with Egypt and Syria,
the implementation of the Jews' right to visit their own
holy places in Arab Jerusalem (as envisaged in the
Jordan-Israel Armistice Agreement). Instead, it was
used to create new ones: occupation of Syrian and
Egyptian national territories, occupation of the whole
of Jerusalem with the holy places of both Christianity
and Islam, destabilizing of not yet recognized borders,
a deepening of the Middle East conflict.
Thus, to the old, insoluble problems new ones
were added, but in a situation which no longer permitted postponing the fundamental debate on the nature and
task of the Zionist state. The absence at the helm of
government leaders with an historical vision and personal authority—like Ben-Gurion—made the situation
all the more difficult. Just as most of the initiative
for the Zionist movement had in the past come from
the outside—that is, reaction to anti-Semitism, to
social and economic pressures, to Arab hostility—so
it was hoped that this time the initiative for a settlement

> would come from the Arabs, and that the new strength
> of Israel would attract the necessary support from the
> Diaspora and the friendly Western countries to solve
> its other problems, or at least create new conditions
> in which to face them. [87]

The contributions from all sides to the resulting debate retained many elements of statelike considerations. Increasing doses of nationalist-historical arguments, however, on the one hand, and utopian-social-humanitarian arguments on the other, were also introduced. This created conspicuous cleavages inside the major parties on most key questions, generating interminable factional disputes, [88] and also produced two new explicitly ideological movements: the maximalist "Land of Israel Movement" (LIM)—part of which eventually joined the Likud, only to split again in the wake of the Camp David agreements—and the minimalist, rather amorphous, "Peace Now" Movement (PN). Also, an orthodox religious variation of LIM produced Gush Emunim (GE), [89] giving rise to what Perlmutter calls "neo-Zionism."[90] The principal challenge was to Ben-Gurion's legacy that the reality of partition was a sufficient parameter for defining the boundaries of the state. It also wiped out many of the historical differences between Ben-Gurion's disciples and their traditional revisionist opponents. The results could hardly have been more paradoxical: Begin signed a peace treaty with Egypt, but he probably could not have had it ratified in the Knesset if he had relied on his own party; whereas Yigal Allon, long considered a "dove" as the author of the infamous (to the Likud) "Allon plan," could not bring himself to support the Camp David accords.

In wiping out the reality of the partition, the traumatic events of 1967 struck at the very roots of the Ben-Gurion heritage. His socialist opponents in general, and the United Kibbutz Movement—Ahdut Haavoda faction in particular—were never very comfortable with Ben-Gurion's emphasis on the reality of the partitioned state. A dose of realism was retained, to be sure, but the renewed mystique of the land—socialist settlement, nationalism, and "dynamic Zionism"—was strongly felt, as can be seen in the words of one of the chief policy formulators of the Zionist Left, Israel Galilee: His "venture of settlement and its development, the settling on land, creates a sense of rootedness, a sense of belongingness that in turn makes the nation in Eretz Israel into a responsible organism defending his homeland (moledet)."[91]

This is again a journey back: from the state, to the homeland, to settlement, to the "religion of labor." There is also a strong sense of historical mysticism, as enunciated by Galilee, himself a secular, perhaps even radical, socialist:

> In all we did and said [Ahdut Haavoda and United Kibbutz
> Movement before the establishment of Israel] the ele-
> ment of uncertainty had had its most positive impact.
> Uncertainty as an element of power. When I delve into
> the history of Zionism I reach the conclusion that not a
> small element of Zionism was conceived from dreams,
> feelings and sentiments. And [what] I don't hesitate to
> say in this connection is that Zionism was inspired by
> historical consciousness . . . and [a] mysticism that
> are derivative from the historical sources of Jewish
> people: the Bible, modern Hebrew literature and the
> lessons of our own history. All that we have to do now
> is to learn from the powerful sources of our aspirations
> and wishes which are not in contradiction to political
> reality and limitations which we are not allowed to
> ignore. [92]

Admittedly, political reality and its limitations are still
acknowledged. There are even some elements of cognitive-postulative thinking. What is missing is the state. When the state is
mentioned by one of Galilee's former colleagues, a founder of LIM,
it is only in the context of creating strength to overcome the inescapable realities that make changes in boundaries so difficult. This
is no longer Ben-Gurion's partitioned state.

> The choice is not really in our hands; there is no alter-
> native of going back to the old boundaries. We are con-
> demned to be strong. . . . One thing all members of
> the Movement have in common is a sense of strength,
> and this is not chauvinism or overbearing pride, but
> comes from a feeling that either the State of Israel
> will be strong or it will not exist. [93]

The strength of the state here is tantamount to an independent
variable that is capable of changing political reality; that the strength
of the state stems partly from legitimized boundaries is not even
mentioned. In fact, for LIM the state as such is no longer the central concern; it is the Land of Israel, with its historical and national
connotations, that occupies their minds. The state should serve the
nation by repossessing the land in its entirety. As the LIM mani-
festo states,

> The whole of Eretz-Israel is now in the hands of the
> Jewish people, and just as we are not allowed to give
> up the State of Israel, so we are ordered to keep what

> we received there from Eretz-Israel. We are bound to
> be loyal to the entirety of our country—for the sake of
> the people's past as well as its future, and no govern-
> ment in Israel is entitled to give up this country. [94]

In this conception, the state loses its rights (and its privilege
to develop its own interests and the policies derived from them). It
has a duty to serve the interests of the nation. Raison d'état is replaced by raison de nation. Explains Isaac:

> Implicit here is the notion that a power higher than
> state sovereignty limits the power of the state, and
> that the land belongs not to the citizens of Israel, but
> to the entire Jewish people, which are not represented
> in its government, and which can therefore not act in
> its name. [95]

This is Ben-Gurion's logic turned completely upside down, putting
back "the clock of history" (as he perceived it) by decades.

In particular, LIM and its numerous ideological satellites
vociferously attacked the "truncated state" Ben-Gurion had created
and which he attempted to legitimize via partition. In fact, "partition" became a dirty word. Rather than a historical compromise
arrived at on the basis of the political reality in a particular region
of states, it was viewed as an alien, almost colonial, imposition:

> Partition, LIM argued, is a foreign concept, imposed
> on Israel by the British and the UN. The movement in-
> sisted on the "legitimacy" of Israel's claims over the
> territories taken in the 1967 war. "Territories for
> peace," the government's slogan, was seen as a be-
> trayal of Zionism for it apparently accepted the idea
> that the territories were "Arab." Territories cannot
> be bargained as they were in 1937, 1947, and 1956,
> LIM members said: partition is no longer the line of
> contention, separation and conflict. Once the terri-
> tories are integrated the argument over boundaries
> will become moot. [96]

This is again a retrogression of several decades in the evolution of the idea of the Jewish state. In fact, LIM went so far as to
challenge the basic assumption that in a partitioned Israel the goal
of Jewish statehood had been accomplished and that now, via the
utilization of this instrument (the Jewish state), the cultural/educa-
tional goals of creating a "new Jewish man" were attainable. Instead,

grandiose new goals were set, sometimes in phrases that sounded perilously close to Arab propaganda claims. This is summarized by Isaac thus:

> [From] the Movement's perspective Zionism's goal was indeed statehood and normalization of the Jewish condition, but these goals had not yet been achieved. Zionism had as its goal the ingathering of all the Jews of the world, with the exception of a small number who would be assimilated and lose their identity in their countries of origin, and this goal had clearly not been realized, Israel having little more than a fifth of the world's Jews living within her borders. Zionist faith was thus the answer to the "demographer-Zionists" as they were scornfully called by Movement members, for the Movement, in its official position, advocated granting full rights to the Arabs of the new territories once they were absorbed into Israel. But all the world's Jews could only be ingathered within an "undivided Land of Israel." The twin goals of Zionism were thus inextricably connected: the settlement of the "entire land" required the "aliya" of the world's Jews and the world's Jews needed the entire land to provide them with the conditions making settlement of millions of additional immigrants possible. [97]

But LIM ideology and personnel were not drawn exclusively from either revisionist circles or romantic socialists. A fair number of Ben-Gurion's former disciples and colleagues from his Rafi faction were also among the founders, injecting a somewhat mythical geopolitical perspective into the debate. Says one of these, Zvi Shiloah:

> I have not based my views on a historical conception of borders, because there have been many boundaries and all of them are historical. We need a geopolitical conception. We need a conception of a "great Israel" extending from the Mediterranean to the Persian Gulf. . . . The concept of space has not been grasped yet in Israel. . . . We must develop the geopolitical vision to recognize that it is essential to control large spaces, so that people cannot talk of Israel as a small obstacle in the Near East. The unity of Arab states is in any case a fiction, but once Israel becomes a big wedge between them, even the fiction disappears. [98]

Only Ben-Gurion's worst temporary hallucinations (after the euphoria of the 1956 war) come close to this disciple's vision. Finally, one more dimension of Ben-Gurion's partitioned state was vehemently attacked by LIM: that the stateness of Israel be tempered by Jewish ethics, and that it be "a light unto the nations." Isaac quotes a former underground commander, Eldad, who preached his particular message in a regular weekend column in one of the country's popular newspapers (and who, according to Perlmutter, "proudly proclaimed himself as a Jewish Fascist"):[99]

> The existence of the partition of the country is a function of the division of the existential soul of Zionism in its different layers. In these layers, from the beginning, there was a deep fragmentation, with guilt feelings towards the cosmopolitan ideals of socialism and liberalism, which were to liberate the world from nationalism—maybe even from the plague of the nation-states—and which would liberate the Jews entirely from their separate unique existence. . . . This is a typical schizophrenia. We have guilt feelings that we presumably have betrayed these universal ideals by turning to Zionism, which is of necessity "reactionary" for it is a return to sometimes irrational roots. . . . Had it only at least been possible to implement "utopian Zionism" in "ways of peace" through convincing the Arabs that we bring blessings to them too, and socialist liberation and progress! But in vain! To go with psychological language, what is left is frustration—the feeling that perhaps Zionism is after all a reactionary movement.[100]

All this had a profound impact on most Zionist parties, whereas

> the influence of the Peace Movement [was] restricted to the left-wing kibbutz movement and Mapam, not because a majority within the parties or in the general public were maximalists, but because the [movement's] championing of the formation of a Palestinian state restricted and curtailed its momentum and political appeal. It will flourish after 1973.[101]

Perhaps it could not flourish by then, but only after Sadat's visit in 1977, in the new form of the "Peace Now" movement (if it can be called that):

> The inception of PN was also linked both to a social crisis and organizational phenomenon. The "crisis" was

Sadat's visit to Jerusalem which aroused the hopes of
many Israelis for peace. When three months had lapsed
and negotiations seemed to have reached a stalemate, a
few small groups of Israelis, the chief of which consisted of reserve officers, students of the Hebrew University in Jerusalem decided "to do something" about
peace. They came out with a public letter which was
designated to the Prime Minister, demanding that territorial concessions should be made for the purpose of
obtaining peace. The young officers were not the only
group proclaiming to accelerate the peace process and
retreat from occupied lands. They were preceded by
(a) senior high-school students about to be recruited
into the army protesting against their presumed participation in an "unnecessary war" (b) activists of various parties (especially within the left-wing Shelli and
the DMC) who were dismayed with professional politics
and decided to launch "civil" campaigns in order to influence foreign policy outside their parties' setups.
These attempts, however, have not materialized into
a viable political movement.

    The PN leaders came, in the main, from three
sources: the army, the political parties and a previous
Peace Movement. They too were in the same age group
(mostly young) and had similar socialization patterns.
. . . The ideology of PN was linked with that of the
Peace Movement which was founded in the aftermath of
the Six Day War as a countermovement to the Land of
Israel. Its major advocacy was to regard the occupied
territories as a vehicle for peace and not as a means
for implementing the Zionist cause. On the contrary,
Israel's keeping the territories had been regarded as
an affront to all basic moral values, whether Jewish,
Zionist or humanitarian. . . . In its own estimation
it had the support of perhaps five percent of the Israeli
public. [102]

In all this argument, "reason of state" increasingly dimin-
ished, to be replaced by reasons of God, nation, and humanity.
Some of Ben-Gurion's "reasons of state" persisted in the mind of
a man who played a key role in the 1967-73 period, as well as in
the Israeli team negotiating the peace treaty with Egypt. The man
was Moshe Dayan, whose thinking appears to have been extremely
complex throughout this time, especially on questions of land and
territory. Some of the components of his thought maintained ele-

ments of the Ben-Gurion heritage, while others were thoroughly penetrated by the logic of LIM. Perlmutter assesses some of Dayan's enormous impact in the following complex way:

> Between 1967–1973, Moshe Dayan wielded influence far beyond his role as defense minister. To Israel, but especially the international community, Dayan embodied the Israeli victory of 1967, as well as Israel's willpower, determination and stubbornness. His charisma and reputation surpassed any single member of the Labor government and its coalition partners. To the Israelis, Dayan symbolized their second liberation since 1948. Dayan could and did make a considerable contribution to the formation of the second partition state. Although he never subscribed to LIM maximalism, his political senses told him that the Arabs will not accept the dictates of 1967.
>
> Dayan's authority was welded into several areas. He was the spokesman for Israeli political aspirations. His statements represented greater authority than Mrs. Meir in international quarters. Dayan was not a simple defense minister. In Ben-Gurion's tradition he was no longer a disciple. Dayan, not unlike Ben-Gurion, but not with the determination and talents of the latter, set Israel's future goals. He was Israel's leader, the mentor of its newly established relations with Arabs (the Open Bridges Policy), the most authoritative voice on the nature and structure of Israel's new frontiers.[103]

The message emanating from Dayan was, however—to use an understatement—less than clear:

> Dayan has frequently been accused in Israel of wavering and inconsistence, of changing his position from month to month, and there is no doubt that it is possible to find contradictory quotations in his speeches. For example, in December 1970, asked if he preferred a larger binational Israel to a smaller one with a Jewish majority, he said he preferred a larger country for defense reasons, "but if it threatens the essence of our Jewish state, then I prefer a smaller one with a Jewish majority." This not only contradicted Dayan's more frequently expressed attitude toward the future of Judea, Samaria and Gaza (where the "demographic threat" was concentrated) but also contradicted the

basis upon which Dayan customarily argued, namely
the fulfillment of the historic task of Zionism. [104]

Perlmutter attempts to develop a comparison between Dayan's
thought and that of his old mentor:

In the Golan and Sinai, settlement means both dynamic
Zionism (in Sinai, Dayan planned a city port he named
Yamit that would become a city of some 250,000 population) and military security. This is the Ben Gurion
legacy; Jews to settle in _empty_ spaces, in deserts.
For Ben Gurion, the Negev was Israel's southern frontier; for Dayan it was Sharm el-Sheikh at the tip of the
Sinai desert. As he has said sometimes in 1973, "If
we have peace without Sharm el-Sheikh, I prefer Sharm
el-Sheikh, without peace." He pursued the old Zionist
policy and doctrine of settlement and security. In the
West Bank, Dayan was concerned with the "nature of
peace," not with security, but with the facts on the
map, with _faits accomplis_. Dayan's concept of Open
Bridges meant once more the eradication of frontiers,
"no passports, no visas" between the West and the
East of the Jordan River. In contradiction to Allon,
settlement in the West Bank was not to be strategic.
Dayan was a skeptic when it came to strategic settlement, arguing that the next strategic problem stems
from the first strategic solution, i.e., you build a
new "strategic settlement" to defend your former
frontier, it now becomes a new frontier to defend.
For Dayan the breaking and dissolution of frontiers was essential. Here he goes beyond his mentor,
Ben Gurion. Ben Gurion was frontier minded. Ben
Gurion was a formalist. He also was more cautious
in dealing with the international community. For
Ben-Gurion, the Jewish State would create the instruments for peace.
Dayan's concept of peace was more sophisticated,
more subtle. Jews and Arabs must live together without barriers between them if peace is to prevail. Ben
Gurion still lived under the shadow of the mighty British Empire, Naziism and the holocaust, all without a
power center, a state. Dayan, released from these
bonds, and head of a victorious liberating army, was
not liberating the partitioned state of 1947 but extend-
ing the frontier of its successor state. Dayan, in

command of a state with a mighty military, exuded
greater confidence, less humility and caution than
Ben Gurion.[105]

Throughout his public career Dayan left numerous doubts as
to where he really stood on issues such as those related to settlements, land, peace, and compromise. Ben-Gurion's legacy of
stateness and the lure of LIM's raison de nation coexisted uneasily
in his mind, and consequently he never ceased to puzzle his listen-
ers in Israel, the Arab world, and across the globe. In a speech
to LIM, for example, he states:

> We have not abandoned your dream and we have not for-
> gotten your lesson. We have returned to the Mountain,
> to the cradle of our people, to the inheritance of the
> Patriarchs, the land of the Judges and the fortress of
> the Kingdom of the House of David. We have returned
> to Hebron and Shechem, to Bethlehem and Anatot, to
> Jericho and the fords of the Jordan at Adam Ha'ir.[106]

At other times, however, Dayan objects to LIM's rhetoric:

> It is my opinion that in every area we must examine
> what can be done and must be done now in order not
> to waste time and the governmental authority we now
> possess with the Arabs but even any discussion with
> them. In my view, the solution lies in action, not
> declarations of annexation.[107]

On occasion, he entertained realistic ideas concerning peace,
but he was also a pessimist. "We should regard our role in the administered territories as that of the established government—to plan
and implement whatever can be done, without leaving options open
for the day of peace—which may be distant."[108]
And Isaac assessed Dayan's views of 1972 as follows:

> Co-existence of Jews and Arabs is only possible under
> the protection of the Israeli government and army. . . .
> The departure of the government of Israel and its army
> from the Strip and the West Bank means in fact also de-
> barring Israel from these places. (The official Israeli
> position was that Jewish settlements were possible in
> areas that might ultimately be returned since in a con-
> dition of peace there was no reason why Jews could not
> live under Arab sovereignty.) Dayan urged: "We must

persist in implementation of our vision and not be afraid of realizing Zionism, for it is in our hands to build our future." As for the demographic problem, Dayan suggested that the Arabs retain Jordanian citizenship while the territories remained under Israeli sovereignty.[109]

Up to 1977 Dayan increasingly cooperated in the attempts to subvert the fait accompli of partition, which had been engineered by Ben-Gurion. Caught up in LIM's mystique of Israel's need for an almost unlimited freedom to maneuver and to impose its own territorial wishes on the regional political reality, he argued:

The question before us is not a question and solution of foreign policy but first and foremost a question of inner will and inner faith and the answers can only be given by ourselves. First and foremost is the question, "What are we and what do we believe in?"[110]

Thus, the opportunity

also imposed a test—concerning our belief in ourselves and our knowledge of what we want. If we believe and want it, the map of the Land of Israel can be determined by ourselves. If we are prepared for political and military struggle and if we are ready to carry the full burden of the struggle, I believe we can carry it through. It is in our power to withstand military tests and a political struggle, providing we can unite in seeing it the same way, the leadership and the public and the Jewish people.[111]

One might say that Dayan partially returned to his original legacy only as foreign minister in Begin's government (1977-79), when he had the opportunity for the first time to negotiate for peace with a major Arab leader, Sadat, who thought in the cognitive-postulative/statelike manner of Dayan's old mentor.[112] To obtain this opportunity, Dayan was finally forced to make a decisive break with his Labor background, and joined a government led by the arch-rival of the movement in which he had spent his entire political career.

The Dayan-Begin relationship is of great importance in view of the fact that Dayan would eventually become Begin's key, and probably only, foreign policy advisor.

Although a Ben-Gurion disciple, a product of Labor
Zionism, Palmach, and the agricultural cooperative
settlement, Dayan's hawkish pragmatism appeals to
Begin, the ideological and historical militant. During the era of the National Unity Government (1967-
1970), Dayan and Begin forged a special and enduring
relationship, and even before the elections, Begin offered Dayan a key Cabinet position if he joined Likud.
For Begin, Dayan's integration is a historic achievement. He now possessed Ben-Gurion's disciple,
Labor's most brilliant and controversial figure, the
Israeli with the greatest international reputation and,
above all, his opposite—a tactician whose concept of
security would not be challenged by Begin, the Likud
government or the nation. Dayan also commanded
considerable support among the NRP (National Religious Party) young militants. [113]

This was the culmination of extreme étatisme. The Ben-Gurionist
party/state symbiosis was completely abandoned.

Begin, surprisingly enough, subscribes to several of Ben-
Gurion's postulates—at least those related to the primacy of the
state over particularistic interests and organizations. This is due
partly to Jabotinsky's heritage, partly to the immense stress Begin
puts on patriotism, and partly to the weakness of the organizational
structures affiliated with Begin's movement, as opposed to the persistent strength of the rival Labor movement (broadly defined).
More than any other Israeli prime minister, Begin emphasizes the
external appearance of the majesty of the state—the flag, the anthem,
and the like.

His methodology of statesmanship, consequently, is markedly
different from Ben-Gurion's cognitive-postulative orientation, which
starts with the reality of the state. Rather, as Aronson argues:

The legal-ideological approach embodied by Mr. Begin
works from preconceived "rights" and goals back to
reality, trying to transform it accordingly. This approach is based on historical experience and a cultural
vision derived from the hazards and the emptiness of
Jewish life in the Diaspora and in Israel itself. The
"logical" or "legal" method here dictates a fight over
principles, which are indivisible. "Rights" are usually not a subject for negotiations and could be pursued
by convincing oneself, and third parties about them.
Being also self-centered, but not progressive and

cognitive, the postulates of this approach ignore the
"rights" of the other party to the conflict or offer that
party "rights" in the overall framework of its own
"rights." The legal–ideological approach in this case
is conservative (i.e., pessimistic) about the "real in-
tentions" of the other side and about human nature in
general, as is the manly-responsive approach. Bargaining is sometimes thought useless, sometimes self-
deceptive and thus self-defeating. Inwardly oriented,
its main concern is to educate, convince, and lead the
nation to fight for goals for the future as developed
from experiences of the past.[114]

As Perlmutter has it, Begin, being of the same generation as
Ben-Gurion, is "the last old Mohican of the grand old Zionist generation born in the diaspora."[115] He is also an authoritative,
charismatic leader in the Ben-Gurion mold: externally, if anything,
Begin enjoys the paraphernalia of statesmanship even more than did
his life-long rival:

> Begin, again like Ben-Gurion, is a Herzlian Zionist.
> Theodor Herzl, the founder of Zionism, was a
> nineteenth-century Viennese writer, dreamer and
> Don Quixote, but with a realist's view of politics.
> . . . This political Zionism—diplomacy with the
> great powers over the establishment of a Jewish
> state—was the Herzlian legacy that held overwhelm-
> ing appeal for both Ben Gurion and Begin.
> Here the similarity between Ben Gurion and
> Begin ends. The real chasm between the two is wide.
> They were deeply divided on the strategy to achieve
> Jewish political and territorial independence. Ben
> Gurion represented the mainstream of political Zion-
> ist thought. Both he and former President Chaim
> Weizmann aspired to establish a state populated, if
> possible, only by Jews.[116]

Perlmutter correctly identifies the key difference between the
two, arguing, on the one hand, that for Ben-Gurion

> population and sovereignty were seen as related vari-
> ables. . . . a Jewish autonomous state would be
> carved out of historical and mandated Palestine that
> was now settled by Jews. Therefore, Ben Gurion ad-
> hered to the concept of the partition of Palestine (he

supported three British partition proposals) into distinct and separate Jewish and Arab states. [117]

For Begin, on the other hand, who follows the well-articulated
LIM logic, partition is an anathema, a curse to be avoided at almost
any cost:

> For Begin, following the dogma of Revisionist Zionism,
> the territorial and political integrity of Palestine is in-
> divisible. . . . For Begin, the problem of the composi-
> tion of the population in the Jewish state is secondary to
> a concern with its territory. For his part, Begin would
> prefer a Jewish majority over all of formerly western
> Palestine. In its absence, however, he claims the po-
> litical indivisibility of the territory between the Medi-
> terranean and the Jordan River; its settlement by Jews;
> and the eventual establishment of Jewish hegemony and
> political domination over those parts of western Pales-
> tine truncated by the 1947 U.N. Partition into separate
> Jewish and Arab states. [118]

Two facts made the initial Dayan-Begin alliance possible: the
fact that first priority was given to peace with Egypt; and that Dayan
also supported (at least partially) the idea of not returning to a partitioned Palestine. On the second point, Dayan secured a promise
that (for reasons of state) the government would not annex the territories, at least as long as there was a chance of negotiations with
the Arabs. On the first point, once the "Sadat initiative" was
launched, Begin found it easier than many Labor Zionists to let
reasons of state lead to the necessary concessions, whereas the
latter were thoroughly mesmerized by the mystique of settlement—
even in the Sinai, which could not by any reasonable definition be
considered part of the Land of Israel. Also, as Theodore Draper
puts it,

> Mr. Begin was truly willing to arrive at peace with
> Egypt. The occupation of the Sinai was the primary
> issue between Israel and Egypt, but the Sinai had
> never been regarded as part of the historic land of
> Israel. Mr. Begin, therefore, could let it go in good
> conscience. . . . The deal that Mr. Begin had in mind
> was return of the Sinai to Egypt in exchange for (or
> tacit consent to) Israel's right to Judea and Samaria. [119]

So Dayan could act as an efficient key negotiator (with Weizmann) in the Egyptian-Israeli deal. He could also in good conscience

participate in formulating the "autonomy" plan for Judea and Samaria. (Note that this plan totally avoids all political questions related to stateness!) It soon became clear, however, that further progress in peace making necessitated taking serious steps to break the Palestinian deadlock,[120] even if only through a forceful, unilateral implementation of the autonomy plan. Both Dayan and Weizmann were ultimately unable to avoid confronting the fact that when it comes to determining what constitutes the Land of Israel, Begin is propelled entirely by "reasons of nation," and those who have to negotiate by reasons of state are simply overwhelmed and are unable to continue. Hence, both resigned.

Zionism here diverges into irreconcilable paths: the one of the caliphate, and the other of the mulk (to use Ibn Khaldun's terms). Ben-Gurion championed partition as a basis for peace, for he argued the logic of state and hence the reality of political constraints upon territorial aspirations. Begin rejects partition as a basis for peace, for he argues the logic of nation and hence stresses history and rights to all the homeland. Perhaps "never the twain shall meet"— not even in a Dayan, who at times held to both logics.

NOTES

1. Ben Halpern, "The Role of the Military in Israel," in The Role of the Military in Underdeveloped Countries, ed. John J. Johnson (Princeton, N.J.: Princeton University Press, 1962), p. 317.

2. See Raphael Patai, Israel Between East and West (Philadelphia: Jewish Publication Society, 1953), and the elaborate sociological study by Sammy Smooha, Israel: Pluralism and Conflict (Berkeley: University of California Press, 1977).

3. See S. Zalman Abramov, Perpetual Dilemma: Jewish Religion in the Jewish State (Rutherford, N.J.: Fairleigh Dickinson University Press, 1976); Ervin Birnbaum, The Politics of Compromise: State and Religion in Israel (Rutherford, N.J.: Fairleigh Dickinson University Press, 1970).

4. Cf. Don Peretz, The Government and Politics of Israel (Boulder, Col.: Westview Press, 1979).

5. Bernard Lewis, "The Return of Islam," Commentary 61 (January 1976): 40.

6. Ibid.

7. J. P. Nettl, "The State as a Conceptual Variable," World Politics 20 (July 1968): 578.

8. Daniel J. Elazar, "Options, Problems and Possibilities in the Light of the Current Situation," in Self Rule/Shared Rule: Federal Solutions to the Middle East Conflict, ed. Daniel J. Elazar

(Ramat Gan: Turtledove, 1979), p. 5. See also, Elazar's article "Government, Biblical and Second Temple Periods," in Encyclopedia Judaica Year Book, 1973, pp. 210-15, and idem, The Jewish Political Tradition and Its Contemporary Uses (Columbus: Ohio State University Press, forthcoming). Many stimulating ideas on this are to be found in Ch. 4, "Traditional Jewish Thought," in Dan V. Segre, A Crisis of Identity: Israel and Zionism (New York: Oxford University Press, 1980), pp. 51-73.

9. A few of these are explored in G. Ben-Dor, "Political Culture Approach to Middle East Politics," International Journal of Middle East Studies 8 (January 1976): 43-63, and the sources there cited.

10. See the authoritative David Vital, The Origins of Zionism (London: Oxford University Press, 1975); Walter Laqueur, A History of Zionism (New York: Weidenfeld and Nicolson, 1972); Ben Halpern, The Idea of the Jewish State (Cambridge, Mass.: Harvard University Press, 1961); The Zionist Idea, ed. Arthur Hertzberg (New York: Atheneum, 1959); also Theodor Herzl, Der Judenstaat: The Jewish State, trans. Harry Zohn (New York: Herzl Press, 1970), and Chaim Weizmann, Trial and Error: The Autobiography of Chaim Weizmann (New York: Harper, 1949).

11. Segre, A Crisis of Identity, p. 53.

12. Elazar, "Options," p. 6.

13. Ibid., p. 7.

14. Y. Leibowitz, "The World and the Jews," Forum 4 (Spring 1959): 83-90.

15. Dan Horowitz and Moshe Lissak, Origins of the Israeli Polity (Chicago: University of Chicago Press, 1978), p. 2.

16. Michael R. Marrus, "Zionism and the Idea of a Jewish State," Social Praxis 4 (Winter 1976-77): 197-214.

17. The Diaries of Theodor Herzl, ed. and trans. Marvin Lowenthal (New York: Grosset and Dunlap, 1962), p. 224, quoted in Marrus, "Zionism and the Idea of a Jewish State," p. 199. See also Vital, The Origins of Zionism, Ch. 13.

18. Marrus, "Zionism and the Idea of a Jewish State," p. 199. Marrus adds in this connection (p. 42): "In the great debate over the Endziel in 1931, Weizmann was able to quote Nordau in 1916 saying that the aim of Zionism was not to found an independent Jewish state."

19. Horowitz and Lissak, Origins of the Israeli Polity.

20. See Neil Caplan, Palestine Jewry and the Arab Question, 1917-1925 (London: Frank Cass, 1978).

21. For the full text see Middle East Focus 4 (May 1981): 26-27.

22. Moshe Burstein, Self-Government of the Jews in Palestine Since 1900 (Tel Aviv, 1934), p. 79; quoted in Caplan, Palestine Jewry, p. 15.

23. Quoted in Caplan, Palestine Jewry, p. 42. See also David Ben-Gurion, My Talks with Arab Leaders (New York: Third Press, 1973.

24. Marrus, "Zionism and the Idea of a Jewish State," p. 210.

25. Howard M. Sachar, A History of Israel from the Rise of Zionism to Our Time (New York: Knopf, 1976), p. 110.

26. Weizmann, Trial and Error, p. 244.

27. Quoted in Marrus, "Zionism and the Idea of a Jewish State," p. 213.

28. Halpern, The Idea of the Jewish State, pp. 168-69.

29. Weizmann, Trial and Error, p. 385; quoted in Marrus, "Zionism and the Idea of a Jewish State," p. 210.

30. Ibid.

31. Marrus, "Zionism and the Idea of a Jewish State," p. 211.

32. Ibid., pp. 208-9.

33. Ibid., p. 210. This analysis is repeated in numerous other studies of British policy in mandatory Palestine, and all the available documentary evidence bears it out. See, for example, Nicholas Bethell, The Palestine Triangle (New York: Putnam, 1979) and Michael J. Cohen, Palestine: Retreat from the Mandate (New York: Holmes and Meier, 1978).

34. Marrus, "Zionism and the Idea of a Jewish State," p. 210.

35. Ibid., pp. 211-12. For the text of the Biltmore Program, see Middle East Focus 2 (January 1980): 22, and Walter Z. Laqueur, The Israel Arab Reader, ed. Walter Z. Laqueur (New York: Bantam Books, 1969), p. 79. On conditions in Palestine at the time, see J. C. Hurewitz, The Struggle for Palestine (New York: Norton, 1950).

36. Horowitz and Lissak, Origins of the Israeli Polity, p. 2.

37. This was said in 1929, quoted in ibid., p. 139. See also Amos Elon, The Israelis: Founders and Sons (London: Weidenfeld and Nicolson, 1971), Part I.

38. Horowitz and Lissak, Origins of the Israeli Polity. See the rich bibliographical material contained therein for further sources. On the transition from Yishuv to statehood, see S. N. Eisenstadt, Israeli Society (London: Weidenfeld, 1967). For the transition from military underground movements to a state-controlled army, see Amos Perlmutter, Military and Politics in Israel: Nation-Building and Role Expansion (New York: Praeger, 1969). On the origins of the Labor Movement which was to dominate Israeli politics for 30 years, see Yonathan Shapiro, The Formative Years of the Israeli Labour Party: The Organization of Power, 1919-1930 (Beverly Hills, Cal.: Sage, 1976); Yosef Gorni, Ahdut Haavoda 1901-1930: The Ideological Principles and the Political System (in Hebrew) (Tel-Aviv: Hakibbutz Hameuhad, 1973); Myron J. Aronoff, Power and Ritual: The Israel Labour Party (Amsterdam: Van Gorum, 1977);

and Peter Y. Medding, Mapai in Israel: Political Organization and Government in a New Society (Cambridge: Cambridge University Press, 1972). A good narrative and most detailed bibliography are to be found in Nadav Safran, Israel, The Embattled Ally (Cambridge, Mass.: Bellknap Press, 1978).

39. Horowitz and Lissak, Origins of the Israeli Polity, p. 2.

40. Ibid.

41. Ibid.

42. Amitai Etzioni, "The Decline of Feudalism: The Case of Israel," paper presented at the Annual Meeting of the American Political Science Association, St. Louis, Missouri, September 1961. See also, A. Perlmutter, "Anatomy of Political Institutionalization: The Case of Israel and Some Comparative Analyses," Harvard University, Center for International Affairs, Occasional Papers in International Affairs, No. 25 (Cambridge, Mass., August 1970).

43. Horowitz and Lissak, Origins of the Israeli Polity, p. 196.

44. Ibid., p. 211.

45. There is an enormous secondary literature on Ben-Gurion. The present author's ideas on his notions of stateness were greatly influenced by Shlomo Aronson's "David Ben-Gurion: Israel's Democratic Bismarck and His Heirs, 1949-1967," in his Conflict and Bargaining in the Middle East (Baltimore, Md.: Johns Hopkins University Press, 1978), which contains a most useful series of annotated footnotes and bibliographic material, and thus listing these items here is superfluous); and by a series of papers given by Amos Perlmutter, Israel: The Partitioned State and Its Challenges, 1917-1980, at the Lehrman Institute in New York, 1979-1980. These are "Redemption, Colonization and Partition: The Political Strategy and Struggle of Yishuv in Palestine, 1917-1947"; "Israel: The First Partitioned State, 1949-1967: Statism vs. Partyism"; "The Second Partitioned State, 1967-1973"; and "The Collapse of the Conception and the Unwon War: 1973-1980."

Some key primary sources are David Ben-Gurion, "Israel Among the Nations," State of Israel Government Yearbook, 1952-53 (Jerusalem: Government Printing Office, 1954); Ben-Gurion Looks at the Bible, trans. J. Kolatch (Middle Village, N.Y.: Jonathan David Publishers, 1972); Ben-Gurion Looks Back: In Talks with Moshe Perlman (New York: Simon and Schuster, 1970); David Ben-Gurion: In His Own Words, ed. A. Ducovny (New York: Fleet Press, 1968); Israel: Years of Challenge (New York: Holt, Rinehart and Winston, 1963); The Jews in Their Land, trans. M. Nurock and M. Louvish (London: Aldus Books, 1966); Letters to Paula, trans. A. Hodes (London: Valentine Mitchell, 1971); My Talks with Arab Leaders, ed. M. Louvish, trans. A. Rubinstein and M. Louvish (New York: Third Press, 1973); Rebirth and Destiny of Israel (New

York: Philosophical Library, 1954); and Recollections, ed. T. Barsten (London: Macdonald, 1970); Israel: A Personal History, trans. N. Myers and U. Nystar (New York: Funk Wagnalls, 1971).

A detailed biography based on Ben-Gurion's papers is Michael Bar-Zohar, Ben-Gurion (in Hebrew) (Tel Aviv: A. Oved, 1977). An analytical look at his early life is to be found in Shabtai Teveth, David's Desire: The Young Ben-Gurion (in Hebrew) (Jerusalem: Schocken, 1977). This author was also greatly intrigued by the passages on Ben-Gurion in the autobiography of his most famous and complex disciple, Moshe Dayan, Moshe Dayan: Story of My Life (New York: William Morrow, 1976).

46. Aronson, Conflict and Bargaining, p. 378. Incredibly, this detailed and enormously important evaluation is buried in a footnote!

47. See the authoritative study by Yehoshua Porath, The Palestinian Arab Nationalist Movement, 1929-1939, Vol. 2 (London: Cass, 1977), and the sources there cited.

48. David Ben-Gurion, We and Our Neighbors (in Hebrew) (Tel Aviv: Davar, 1934).

49. This was said in 1937. Quoted in Perlmutter, "Redemption, Colonization and Partition," p. 25.

50. Ibid.

51. Quoted in ibid.

52. Quoted in ibid., p. 26.

53. Aronson, Conflict and Bargaining, p. 10.

54. Ibid., pp. 10-11.

55. Ibid., p. 6.

56. Ibid., p. 356.

57. How different the conceptions of his successors were can be learned from the superb analysis in Rael Jean Isaac, Israel Divided: Ideological Politics in the Jewish State (Baltimore, Md.: Johns Hopkins University Press, 1976).

58. Aronson, Conflict and Bargaining, p. 7.

59. Ibid., p. 8.

60. Ibid., pp. 8-9. Many of the issues relating to the General Armistice Agreements putting an end to the war of 1949 are analyzed in a theoretical framework in Michael Brecher, The Foreign Policy System of Israel (London: Oxford University Press, 1972); and idem, Decisions in Israel's Foreign Policy (London: Oxford University Press, 1974).

61. Ibid., p. 379.

62. Dayan, Story of My Life, p. 33.

63. Ibid., pp. 147-48.

64. On the Israeli policy of retaliation, in addition to the aforementioned sources, see Michael I. Handel, Israel's Political

Military Doctrine (Cambridge, Mass.: Harvard University, Center for International Affairs, Occasional Papers, 1973); and Dan Horowitz, "Flexible Responsiveness and Military Strategy: The Case of the Israeli Army," Policy Sciences 1 (2) (Summer 1970): 191-205. See also the multivolume Moshe Sharett, Personal Diaries (Tel Aviv: Maariv, 1978) (in Hebrew) for a fascinating account of the incessant arguments on this point between Ben-Gurion and his foremost critic in his party.

65. From Bar-Zohar, Ben-Gurion, Vol. 3, quoted in Perlmutter, "Israel: The First Partitioned State," pp. 26-27.

66. Ibid., p. 40.

67. Aronson, Conflict and Bargaining, p. 10.

68. Ibid., p. 9.

69. Ibid., pp. 355-56.

70. Perlmutter, "Israel: The First Partitioned State," p. 3. For the classic study of Israel as a Parteienstaat, see Benjamin Akzin, "The Role of Parties in Israeli Democracy," Journal of Politics 17 (November 1955): 507-46.

71. See Marrus, "Zionism and the Idea of a Jewish State," for a discussion of this controversy.

72. Perlmutter, "Israel: The First Partitioned State," pp. 4-5.

73. Ibid., p. 5.

74. Ibid., p. 4.

75. An enormous amount has been written about this enigmatic figure. For primary sources see his Story of My Life (also in the Hebrew original) (Tel Aviv: Dvir, 1976); "Israel's Border and Security Problem," Foreign Affairs 33 (January 1955): 110-18; A New Map: Different Relations (in Hebrew) (Haifa: Shikmona, 1969); A Diary of the Sinai Campaign (New York: Harper, 1966). See also Shabtai Teveth's biography, Moshe Dayan (Jerusalem: Schocken, 1971), English ed. (Boston: Houghton Mifflin, 1973). Dayan has, throughout his career, also given innumerable interviews to the Hebrew and English press.

76. Aronson, Conflict and Bargaining, pp. 80-81. Emphasis added. On the italicized point, Aronson, p. 392, writes as follows:

In an interview with the American correspondent, John McCowen Roths, of the Saturday Review, Ben Gurion said: "Peace, genuine peace, is our most vital need, and to achieve it every sacrifice would be worthwhile, including withdrawal to the pre-1967 borders. If I were now prime minister, I would initiate this principle." Referring to specific conquered territories, Ben-Gurion told the American correspondent: "Sinai? Sharm-el-Sheikh? Gaza? The West Bank? Let them all go. Peace is more important than real estate. We

do not need territories. With adequate irrigation, the
Negev can support all the Jews in the world who desire
to come."

Quoted by D. Bar-Nir, "Ben-Gurion: Peace, Not Real Estate,"
New Outlook 14 (June-July 1971): 63; cf. Bar-Zohar, Ben-Gurion,
pp. 1579-80 n.

77. Aronson, Conflict and Bargaining, p. 349.

78. Ibid., p. 350.

79. Ibid.

80. Ibid., p. 349.

81. Dayan, New Map, p. 18 (quoted in Aronson, Conflict
and Bargaining, p. 389).

82. Dayan, New Map, p. 48 (quoted in Aronson, Conflict
and Bargaining, p. 391).

83. Vital, The Origins of Zionism, pp. 373-74.

84. An excellent explanation of this is Segre's A Crisis of
Identity: Israel and Zionism, which lists the relevant other works
extensively. For a modest effort of the present author, see Ch. 16,
"Israel and the Druzes: The Politics of Ambiguity," in Ben-Dor,
The Druzes in Israel, pp. 230-44; also the sources there cited.
The post-1967 ideological debate is superbly studied in Isaac, Israel
Divided: Ideological Politics in the Jewish State (Baltimore, Md.:
Johns Hopkins University Press, 1976).

85. Segre, A Crisis of Identity, p. 30.

86. Perlmutter, "The Second Partitioned State," p. 31.

87. Segre, A Crisis of Identity, pp. 30-31. Many Israelis
would argue that the latter half of this assessment is somewhat
overstated. On the general sense of confusion, see Gabriel Ben-Dor,
"Crisis in Israeli Society," Middle East Focus 41 (May 1981): 19-23.

88. Isaac, Israel Divided; Perlmutter, "The Second Partitioned State."

89. See Isaac, Israel Divided, on this. Also Yael Yishai,
"Party Factionalism and Foreign Policy: Demands and Responses,"
Jerusalem Journal of International Relations 3 (Fall 1977): 53-70;
idem, "Interest Groups and Foreign Policy in Israeli Politics: The
Problem of Land and Peace," paper delivered at the International
Political Science Association Congress, Moscow, August 1979);
Ehud Sprinzak, "Extreme Politics in Israel," Jerusalem Quarterly
5 (Fall 1977): 33-47; Janet Oden, "Gush Emunim; Roots and Am-
biguities," Forum 24 (Spring 1976): 39-50. And a series of papers
published by the Jerusalem Institute for Federal Studies, Center for
Jewish Community Studies (Jerusalem): Janet Aviad, "Peace Now"
(January 1980); Mordechai Nisan, "Gush Emunim and Israel's Na-
tional Interest" (January 1980); and Mervin F. Verbit, "Gush
Emunim, Peace Now and Israel's Future" (April 1980).

90. Perlmutter, "The Second Partitioned State," p. 6. See also Yehoshofat Harkabi, Arab Strategies and Israel's Response (New York: Free Press, 1977), pp. 79-168. On the factional struggles inside the Likud government, see Ezer Weizman, The Battle for Peace (New York: Bantam Books, 1981).

91. Interview, Davar Hashavua, May 10, 1977, p. 13 (quoted in Perlmutter, "The Second Partitioned State," p. 23).

92. Ibid., p. 24.

93. Quoted in Isaac, Israel Divided, p. 110.

94. Quoted in ibid., p. 101. "Eretz-Israel" or the "Land of Israel" is the Jewish term for "Palestine," most recently in its mandatory boundaries.

95. Ibid.

96. Perlmutter, "The Second Partitioned State," p. 8.

97. Isaac, Israel Divided, p. 110.

98. Quoted in ibid., p. 104.

99. Perlmutter, "The Second Partitioned State," p. 12.

100. Isaac, Israel Divided, p. 19.

101. Perlmutter, "The Second Partitioned State," p. 5.

102. Yael Yishai, "Interest Groups and Foreign Policy in Israeli Politics: The Problem of Land and Peace," pp. 4-5. See also Isaac, Israel Divided, pp. 73-102. The letter in question was published in the Jerusalem Post, March 8, 1978. The DMC (Democratic Movement for Change), led by Professor Y. Yadin, was the large protest movement of the Center, winning 15 seats to the Knesset in 1977, only to split shortly thereafter with one faction joining the government and the other remaining in opposition. By 1981 the "party" disappeared, leaving behind only a tiny two-man faction.

103. Perlmutter, "The Second Partitioned State," pp. 45-46.

104. Ibid., p. 45.

105. Ibid., pp. 47-49. Dayan's views on strategy and settlement are from an interview in July 1973 (ibid., p. 68). For the present author, the key point is "for Ben-Gurion, the Jewish State would create the instruments of peace."

106. Quoted in ibid., p. 44.

107. Isaac, Israel Divided, p. 219; quoted in Perlmutter, "The Second Partitioned State," p. 50.

108. Quoted in Isaac, Israel Divided, p. 220.

109. Ibid.

110. Quoted in ibid., p. 240.

111. Quoted in ibid.

112. Aronson, Conflict and Bargaining, p. 1352.

113. Perlmutter, "The Collapse of the Conception and the Unwon War 1973-1980," pp. 56-57. See also Perlmutter, "Begin's

Strategy and Dayan's Tactics: The Conduct of Israeli Foreign Policy," Foreign Affairs 56 (2) (January 1978): 357-72.

114. Aronson, Conflict and Bargaining, pp. 350-51.

115. Perlmutter, "The Collapse of the Conception and the Unwon War 1973-1980," p. 53.

116. Ibid., p. 54.

117. Ibid., p. 55.

118. Ibid., pp. 55-56.

119. "A Revealing Memoir of Camp David," New York Times Book Review, May 12, 1981, p. 35.

120. See Gabriel Ben-Dor, "Stabilizing Peace in the Middle East: Israel, the Palestinians and the Arab States," International Spectator 33 (December 1979): 778-83.

4
Stateness and
Inter-Arab Relations

Since most of the Middle East is populated by Arabs, the large majority of the states in that region are Arab states. Therefore, by definition, much of the regional politics of the area have been and will continue to be dominated by the complex, ambiguous, and turbulent relations among the Arab countries—a key political factor that shapes regional political life.[1] Indeed, no political force in the area can ever hope to escape its impact. It may also be noted that perhaps in no other element of the Middle East political arena has the lack of stateness had such destabilizing consequences.[2]

The turbulence and tensions involved in inter-Arab relations are well known, and are due only partially to the impact of the conflict with Israel. Decades of high ideological tensions,[3] heated rhetoric, and serious quarrels have created an extremely skeptical political climate in the Arab world. This is demonstrated to some extent by the data recently gathered by the Center for Research on Arab Unity (CRAU) located in Amman and Beirut, published in the March-May 1981 edition of CRAU's Beirut monthly, Al Mustaqbal al-Arabi ("The Arab Future").[4]

According to the findings, it is concluded that 78 percent of the respondents—6,000 persons in ten Arab countries—contend that there exists a cultural entity defined as "the Arab Homeland," whereas 22 percent doubt that.[5] Even so, the analysis of the findings indicates that among the respondents there are profound differences in the most basic definitions of the Arab homeland and Arab unity.[6]

As many as 38 percent of the respondents consider inter-Arab conflicts to be the most pressing problem facing Arabs today, compared with 31 percent who consider the Arab-Israeli conflict the most urgent problem, while 22 percent are most concerned with the tackling of domestic socioeconomic problems and the "lack of democracy" in their countries.[7]

Significantly, only 4 percent believe that Israel constitutes the major foreign obstacle to unity, compared with 34 percent who blame the Soviet Union and 60 percent who blame the United States.[8] Furthermore, as many as 87 percent of the respondents contend that "Arab rulers" are to be blamed for the lack of Arab unity—fully, or at least partially. On this issue, no more than 42 percent of the respondents feel that unification attempts have yielded positive results; 33 percent are undecided, while as many as 25 percent go so far as to state that the attempts at unification have been "disadvantageous to the Arab cause,"[9] an astonishingly high number, unimaginable only a few years ago.

Seventy-seven percent of the respondents state that their countries are unable to cope with present challenges without assistance from other countries. At the same time, as many as 82.5 percent label current inter-Arab cooperation unsatisfactory and, in fact, an almost incredible 51 percent prefer non-Arab countries to Arab countries as sources of such assistance![10]

> The co-ordinator of the research concludes that the romantic support to Arab unity is gone; that supporters of Arab unity prefer—in the short run—a partial unity; that there is a surprising lack of enthusiasm for unity among the high level professionals, media people and university teachers and that there is the danger that the clash between religious and secular unity will further undermine any Arab unification attempts.[11]

Lest there be a credibility gap here, it might be well to cite a Jordanian newspaper, which suggests that "one of the functions of the C.R.A.U. is to restore credibility and status to the empty notion of Arab unity."[12] If the figures are any indication, then the mainstay of the drive for Arab unity, the intelligentsia in the Arab countries, is deserting the cause in significant proportions, thus strengthening Ajami's argument that Arabism is losing ground to the state on the one hand, and to Islam on the other.[13]

The emerging picture of disillusionment with the political aspects of the drive to Arab unity is reinforced by the inter-Arab economic gap and its political implications. Tuma's analysis[14] of the gap and its implications helps explain the increasing disenchantment with the results of Arab unity. (It may be added parenthetically that the very consideration of economic differences as a significant factor in assessing the benefits of inter-Arab relations is indicative of the new, increasingly statelike thinking about these matters in the Arab world today.) The inequality between the oil-rich (and mostly population-poor) Arab countries, on the one hand, and the more

densely populated Arab countries, on the other, is well known. [15]
Inter-Arab relations have so far had little impact on the basic structural features of the various economies of the Arab countries. [16]
According to the annual report of the Arab Monetary Fund for 1980,
the external debt of the non-oil-producing Arab countries amounted
to $36 billion in 1979, compared with $8 billion in 1974 and $28 bil-
lion in 1978. [17] The report adds that debt servicing alone for these
countries reached as high as $5.9 billion in 1979, compared with
only $1.2 billion in 1974. The report concludes that this burden is
becoming unbearable, to the point of possibly even reducing the
availability of future external loans. [18]

Tuma proposes that such inequality is, in fact, the order of
the day, and is consistent with inter-Arab economic patterns observed over time. [19] Indeed, a significant increase in equality—
should that occur—would be a development requiring an elaborate
explanation. This inequality is due in part to more or less objective historical and environmental conditions, and in part to ideological and institutional factors that make a trend to greater equality improbable, rhetorical expectations notwithstanding. For instance, differential endowments in the region (especially in the Arab
countries) have been protected and even increased in the relevant
countries by legislation that restricts mobility. Thus, all prevailing social, economic, and political institutions and conditions considered, Tuma expects inequality to increase even further, rather
than diminish—again, despite all official pronouncements to the contrary. "Policy matters in the Mideast weren't intended to promote
equality and that attitude reflects religion, political ideology, cultural values and traditionalism, all of which generate tolerance toward inequality and militancy against equality."[20]

The fact is that in recent years the incomes earned by the oil-
producing countries in the Arab world (and hence also their per
capita income and their marginal propensity to invest) have increased
more rapidly than in their poorer Arab counterparts—even oil-
producing Egypt—which tend to have a significantly higher rate of
growth in population. Also, inter-Arab economic aid constitutes
only a small fraction of the available surplus capital, and is too
small to affect the pattern of capital distribution. [21] Tuma claims
that the

> major shortcomings of the intra Arab aid program are
> that they usually distribute the benefits in favor of the
> donor rather than of the recipient country; they are
> politically determined and are—in the context of Mid-
> east fragmentation—uncertain as to their continuity
> and magnitude. [22]

Tuma concludes[23] by pointing to the "potential for further instability and conflicts," which is rooted in this pattern of economic distribution and behavior. And yet, this pattern ought not to surprise the observer of Arab politics. The poor countries pursue their raison d'état in seeking to maximize economic benefits from inter-Arab cooperation. Thus, they attempt to mobilize as many resources as possible, from as many contributors as possible, with as few political strings as possible. The donor countries, however, naturally wish to maintain their freedom of action and to maximize their political gains. Therefore economic resources are transferred selectively, slowly, and under the greatest possible control, and automatic future commitments are minimized in order to avoid yielding further resources without commensurate additional political gains. This is rational behavior according to textbooks on political economy,[24] and it is exactly the type of policy that a raison-d'état-oriented calculation yields. The lack of "fit" is only with the kind of policy one would expect (or rather, would have expected years ago) from textbooks on Arab nationalism.[25] There is no economic salvation in Arab nationalism. In the case of its former leader, perhaps it would not be an exaggeration to suggest bluntly that "by opting out of the Arab-Israeli conflict, Egypt has fulfilled a necessary condition for her economic recovery."[26]

This is a far cry from the ambitions inherent in modern Arab nationalism. A full circle has been all but completed; the ideological tensions in inter-Arab relations have generated a situation in which the costs of participating in the struggle for the causes of Arab nationalism outweigh the benefits. The ideological tensions have also become an intolerable burden for the Arab states.

> The dominant feature in the modern history of inter-Arab relations is the struggle for leadership in the name of Arab unity. Ideologically, that is, regional Arab politics have been concerned with the problem of Arab unity, the supreme, or ultimate, objective of Arab nationalism. Closely linked to this, since 1948, has been a collective position toward Israel. Theoretically, the two issues are interrelated, but practically, quite separate. They, moreover, often obfuscate and gloss over the more practical problem of the relations between Arab states, governments or regimes and leaders.[27]

The modern history of inter-Arab relations begins in 1949, with the end of the first Arab-Israeli war. There is also, however, a premodern history, in which the genesis of the inter-Arab system can be identified:

Before 1920, inter-Arab relations were confined to the Fertile Crescent area, where the victorious Entente Powers had defeated the Ottoman state and put an end to its domination over these parts. Separatist Arab movements converged within the orbit of the Hashemite-led Arab Revolt out of the Hejaz to provide the first governing cadres in the new British and French mandated territories of Iraq, Syria and Transjordan.[28]

The inter-Arab system, however, in its formative years was limited by necessity. Prior to the mid-1930s, most key Arab states (Egypt, Syria, Iraq) were only semiindependent, under various forms of European tutelage,[29] while the only two fully independent Arab states, Yemen and Saudi Arabia, were basically concerned with domestic (mainly tribal) issues, and played but a minor role in inter-Arab affairs. The more central Arab countries were still involved in the struggle for independence.

Even though the quest for independence consumed most nationalist energies, it did not completely preclude the possibility of inter-Arab rivalries. Vatikiotis enumerates the most important instances:

The independent Arab Kingdom of the Hejaz under the Sherif Hussein, for example, was literally undone and integrated by the Saudis in 1924. Soon after that, in 1926, a political row, involving some use of force, over pilgrimage arrangements to the Holy Shrines in Mecca and Medina, broke out between Egypt and Saudi Arabia. The dispute, however, was linked to the issue of the Caliphate to which the Egyptian monarch aspired. The blatant aggrandizement of Saudi Arabia at the expense of the Hashemites was being countered by the other major contender for regional, or Arab power, Egypt. The chosen arena for this struggle was the issue of Islamic solidarity, the Caliphate, and related matters.

There were, moreover, disputes between the Saudis and Iraqis over tribal activity which were not settled until 1936. The Iraqis for their part, after formal independence in 1932, sought a wider Arab role by improving their relations with Arabia, the Yemen, and Egypt. This was in part the inevitable response of a Hashemite ruler in Baghdad and his governing class of Sunnis who were and still are the politically dominant minority in Iraq over a politically underprivileged and suspect heterodox, Shia, majority.[30]

Iraq became nominally fully independent in 1932. Britain and France then proceeded to renegotiate their treaties with Egypt, Lebanon, and Syria,[31] resulting in arrangements that allowed the latter a significantly greater degree of independence in regional affairs (1936). This development coincided with the pan-Arabization of the Palestinian question following the 1936-39 Arab Revolt in Palestine. Not only did solidarity with the cause of the Palestinian Arabs play a powerful role in raising the level of Arab national consciousness, but the willingness of the British government to negotiate with the rulers of the Arab countries in order to search for a settlement inside Palestine (beginning in the October 1936 request for Iraqi mediation) also regionalized the Palestine conflict on the official diplomatic level. The conference held in Bludan, Syria, in 1937 was the first inter-Arab forum signaling the pan-Arabization of the confrontation with Zionism:

> Egyptians, Saudis, and Yemenis may not have been
> equally deeply concerned over the fate or problems of
> the Palestinian Arabs. They were more interested in
> checking the influence of Iraqi, Transjordanian, and
> Syrian politicians in the affair. But the involvement of
> all these countries in the Palestine problem was given
> official recognition at the end of 1938 when the British
> government announced the convening of a conference to
> which were invited not only representatives of the two
> rival communities in Palestine but also those of the
> Arab states. This unilateral act by HMG so to speak
> "regionalised" the issue, and rendered it prey to inter-
> Arab political rivalries. The latter were to surface
> more thunderously in the 1948 Palestine War. Further-
> more, it limited the freedom of British action over
> Palestine, and granted the right of intervention by Arab
> states in the conflict. From a local conflict, Palestine
> became a regional one, and Egyptian, Hashemite, and
> Saudi rivalries were injected into it.[32]

One reason for this—the British attempt to encourage greater Arab cooperation in order to mobilize the Arab countries to Britain's side in the looming confrontation with Germany—had an even greater impact during the Second World War. Although in this period the central Arab countries were interested chiefly in taking advantage of the shifting balance of power so as to maximize their freedom from the European powers (on the whole, successfully), some of the inter-Arab activity related to Palestine continued to involve Transjordan, Iraq, and Syria. The Hashemite Transjordanian monarch, in particular, made great efforts to dominate the inter-Arab scene where Palestine was concerned. At the same time, the Hashemite rulers of Iraq and Transjordan aired two plans (King Abdullah's Greater Syria plan, involving Syria, Transjordan, and Palestine, and the Iraqi Fertile Crescent Union, involving Iraq, Syria, and Transjordan), but both were doomed by Egyptian and Saudi opposition, inspired by fear of Hashemite domination of the heartland of the Arab world.[33] From these struggles, Egypt, Iraq, and Saudi Arabia emerged as the chief competitors for the leading position in the Arab world, with Transjordan also competing on the Palestinian issue. Eventually—with British support—these leading Arab powers formalized the sovereignty and independence of the Arab countries in the (antifederal) League of Arab States, founded in 1945.[34]

In the wake of the Second World War, there were several dramatic transformations: the number of independent Arab states began to increase rapidly (Libya, Sudan, Kuwait, Tunisia, Morocco, Algeria, South Yemen, Bahrain, Qatar, and the Gulf States); the European presence in the Arab world quickly declined;[35] a general trend to radicalization emerged;[36] and defeat by Israel led to frantic inter-Arab activity. Thus, properly speaking, modern inter-Arab history begins in 1949.

Throughout the stages of the development of the inter-Arab system, a fairly consistent agenda of main issues can be identified. These are the axes around which the system has come to revolve. Although it is evidently impossible to measure this quantitatively with any degree of accuracy, it appears that the political issues, in rough order of importance, are as follows:[37]

1. Arab unity. Sometimes this has been taken almost literally, and at others has been postponed to the indefinite and unforeseeable future. From the mid-1950s on, however—the era of qawmiyya (pan-Arab nationalism)—it played an ever-present and predominant role as the initial point of reference.[38]

2. The struggle for leadership and hegemony.[39] The traditional protagonists were Egypt, Saudi Arabia, and the Hashemites in Iraq and Jordan. Later, the post-Hashemite regime in Iraq continued to play an important role,[40] while Jordan's importance has declined and Syria's has increased.[41]

3. Attitudes toward outside powers—in general, and toward the competing superpowers in particular.[42] This may be tied in with other issues, but often simply takes the form of a struggle over orientation and alignment with (or between) the major blocs or superpowers.

   4. Attitudes toward Israel and the Palestinians. This is but one of several issues and does not seem to rate higher than fourth in importance, although it is, admittedly, not measurable and besides, fluctuates from time to time. It is noteworthy that, conventional wisdom to the contrary, other than at the purely rhetorical level this issue is far from being a unifying force in the Arab world; in fact, it tends to be divisive, creating controversies, tensions, and cleavages. [43]

   5. A series of bilateral conflicts. Although basically limited to a variety of territorial and other practical issues between certain Arab countries, at times these conflicts have engulfed other parts of the Arab world (for instance, Iraq versus Syria over the Euphrates river dam; Morocco versus Algeria over the Sahara; Iraq versus Kuwait over territory; border clashes between Egypt and Libya; clashes between North and South Yemen).

   6. Specific internal issues in single countries. Due to the interdependence and penetrability of the Arab countries, these have often become focuses of tension for the entire Arab world, attracting sometimes massive outside intervention (thus, Lebanon in 1958 and 1975-76, the Yemen in 1961 and the following half-decade, Jordan in 1970-71, and Oman in the 1970s). [44]

   7. Attitudes toward the Northern Tier countries. The disruptive effects of this issue were manifest in the Syrian-Turkish tensions of 1957, the Iranian-Iraqi confrontation up to 1975 between the Shah and the Ba'ath regime, and the Iranian-Iraqi war initiated by the Iraqi invasion of 1980, all of which have contributed to the disturbing fragmentation of the Arab world into competing blocs.

   In addition to these primary political issues, there is always petropolitics: that is, the economic issue of the struggle over resources and its political implications. [45] Around these eight axes there has revolved lively and fluid inter-Arab political activity, which has gone through significant stages of transition.

   Until the late 1960s the first issue—the attainment of Arab unity—was the transcendental goal that totally disrupted any possibility of "normal" Arab politics. Thus pan-Arabism captivated and mesmerized an entire generation at the expense of the state. The commitment to Arab unity and "revolution" (defined at times in terms of modernization) preempted any other goal.

   At the height of its power, pan-Arabism could make
   regimes look small and petty; disembodied structures
   headed by selfish rulers who resisted the sweeping invasion of Arabism and were sustained by outside powers
   that supposedly feared the one idea that could resurrect
   the classical golden age of the Arabs. [46]

A complex problem resulted, plaguing Arab nationalism, inherent in its very duality as expressed in the uneasy coexistence of qawmiyya and wataniyya (loyalty to the state). This duality has had, strangely enough, both a destabilizing and a paralyzing effect on modern Arab policies. Other than the immense hold of Islam, Arab nationalism completely dominated the institutional and ideological center for decades, and left practically no room for anything else. The supreme irony in it was, however, as in many other dialectical processes or movements, that while the appeal of qawmiyya was strong enough to destabilize all competing or alternative political structures, it was not strong enough as a "practical ideology."[47] Ajami cites Heikal as having once

> made the distinction between Egypt as a state and Egypt as a revolution, and . . . defended the right of the "Arab revolution" to interfere in the internal affairs of Arab countries. . . . He has recounted a conversation he had with Secretary of State Kissinger during the latter's shuttle diplomacy in the Middle East in which he told Mr. Kissinger that Egypt was not merely a state on the banks of the Nile, but the embodiment of "an idea, a tide, a historical movement." To this Mr. Kissinger is reported to have said that he himself could not deal with latent tangible forces, or negotiate with an idea.[48]

Kissinger's reply contained a profound truth. The political impossibility of the idea was not merely its unsuitability as a negotiating partner, but also its unsuitability as a practical ideology. It could destroy but could not build; it could create internal conflict but could not resolve it; it could prevent peace with Israel but could not create an Arab policy vis-à-vis the Israeli problem;[49] it could captivate the Palestinians in "the dialectics of dependence," but could not settle the Palestinian issue.[50]

In short, either the idea had to triumph so thoroughly as to make it an overwhelming political reality (which did not and could not happen) or it had to be de facto abandoned. The transitory situation between these two poles debilitated and denormalized Arab politics for over a generation, and so the unstable nature of the Arab political system destabilized the entire region. A corollary of this situation (although not necessarily exclusively depending on it) was the long series of domestic upheavals that made the politics of the Arab countries almost synonymous with instability, violence, and the ubiquitous coup d'etat. According to Amos Perlmutter's count, in seven key Arab countries between 1939 and 1969, 41 military coups were attempted—23 of which were successful.[51] Many of these were recurrent second or third coups. There were also innumerable cases of unrecorded conspiracies, underground activities, violent acts of repression, assassination, and other such blatantly obvious characteristic manifestations of unstable politics in illegitimate polities.

The military regimes did attempt to stem the tide: Nasser's regime tried on three occasions to create a political backbone in the form of mass parties—with resounding failure. Similar attempts, with basically identical results, were made by other military regimes. Elsewhere, alliances were forged with previously existing political parties. None of these courses of action could create stability within the constraints of abnormal politics. The serious quest for the new, established state (nation-state being one option) was really the only viable alternative,[52] but it could not be undertaken until the high tide of radical nationalism (which put the conservative monarchies so badly on the defensive) receded. This was not to be for some time, until the late 1960s saw the trend change. In the meantime, the spell of qawmiyya and its corollaries was influential in at least three core areas of Arab politics: destabilizing the inter-Arab system and hindering the building of states and the conducting of normal relations between them; destabilizing political life within the various Arab countries; and precluding progress toward resolving, settling, or stabilizing Arab-Israeli relations.

The significant stages of transition in Arab politics, referred to above, can usefully be outlined as follows:

Stage I: 1949-55

The first stage was characterized by the wave of radicalism striking at the anciens régimes in the Arab countries in the wake of the 1948-49 war against Israel. A radical, revolutionary tide produced a change of regimes in the key countries of Egypt and Syria.[53] Inter-Arab conflict reflected numerous traditional rivalries, mostly along bilateral lines.

Stage II: 1955-61

The most important development in the second stage was the assumption of active leadership of the Arab world by the most popular Arab country, Egypt.[54] This ambitious effort raised unprecedented expectations that the "unity of ranks"[55] (a military analogy intended to describe eventual merging sovereignties) was a goal attainable in the foreseeable future. This period marked the high tide of messianic pan-Arab nationalism. Radical nationalist revolutions swept away the old regimes in Iraq and Sudan in 1958. Jordan and Lebanon seemed to be in danger of falling to Nasserist forces that same year. Above all, the "finest hour" of Arab nationalism arrived, with Egypt and Syria establishing the United Arab Republic (which, however, fell apart in 1961).[56] Nevertheless, the old regimes in Lebanon and Jordan survived with outside (Western) aid, while the new revolutionary regime in Iraq soon began to quarrel with Egypt along the traditional lines of rivalry for leadership and hegemony.

Stage III: 1961-67

His disappointment with the failure of the United Arab Republic made Nasser cautious about future unification attempts. He thus coined the phrase "unity of purpose,"[57] another military analogy, intended to demonstrate that soldiers do not all have to march in one formation in order to reach the same objective. The idea was to create, by evolution and revolution, more compatible Arab regimes pursuing more or less identical goals, and to contemplate unity by way of merging sovereignties only after these appropriate conditions had been created. Nasser shunned the renewed unification attempts of the Ba'athist regimes that came to power in Syria and Iraq in 1963.[58]

During this time, the Arab world was sharply splintered. Intense ideological tensions existed between the socialist-progressive-military regimes on the one hand and the conservative monarchies, on the other. They culminated in war in the Yemen, where, eventually, as many as 70-80 thousand Egyptian troops were committed to "the republicans," while the other side was massively supported by Saudi Arabia and Jordan.[59] The so-called socialist bloc was also sharply split. Ideological tensions, numerous coups d'etat and mutual subversion were the order of the day, and stability was at its lowest point. All this combined to produce a veritable "Arab Cold War."[60]

With the advent of the hyperradical neo-Ba'ath regime in Syria in 1966,[61] Nasser was haunted more and more by the possibility of being provoked, against his better judgment, into a premature war with Israel.[62] From 1965 on, he increasingly relied on the analogy of "unity of action," which in practice meant (limited) inter-Arab cooperation through Arab summit meetings, coordination of military plans, and the like. (His judgment was to be vindicated in 1973.) Even so, Egypt was dragged into the 1967 war, due to inter-Arab considerations, and at a terrible cost.[63] The inter-Arab system had created a situation in which Nasser's "political stance . . . was offensive and the military posture was defensive. When the fighting came, it became clear that the Egyptians could not militarily cover their political bets."[64]

Stage IV: 1967-70

The debacle of 1967 led to much soul searching in the Arab world in general, and in Egypt in particular. As Ajami has pointed out, "the defeat had underlined the vulnerability of the Arab system of state, the bankruptcy of the Arab order and its guardians, whether radical or conservative."65 It is striking, however, that the Egyptian and Jordanian regimes survived the defeat, and Syria experienced a relatively smooth transition to a new regime in 1970. The bankruptcy was not so much of the states, nor even of the regimes, but rather of the order of priorities derived from the previously prevailing messianic orientations. This was, then, a transitional period, culminating in a new order after a time lag between 1967 and 1970. The delayed effects, as it were, were felt only some three years after the war, in the wake of a final wave of "consolidating turbulence." The transition was marked by a last (at least until now) wave of coups d'etat: in 1968 in Iraq (where the incoming Ba'ath regime has held power ever since, notwithstanding much opposition); in 1969 in Libya and the Sudan (both regimes are still in power, the latter surviving several major coup attempts, notably the bloody 1971 affair); in 1970, bloodlessly in Syria (and as much attributable to the fiasco in Jordan as to the one on the Golan Heights). Assad's regime has now held power—although, as has recently become evident, far from unchallenged—for longer than any other in modern Syrian history. Another feature of this transitional phase was the increasing saliency of the Palestinians in inter-Arab affairs— an aspect that will be elaborated upon in the next chapter.

The 1967 war demonstrated that there was no Arab unity capable of producing either a viable military front or a practical political stand vis-à-vis Israel. The shock of 1967 eroded and eventually shattered the Arab blocs that had emerged in the previous decade. By 1970, it was apparent that very slowly but significantly a note of pragmatism was creeping into inter-Arab politics. Key Arab countries—chiefly Egypt—pursued their conflict with Israel increasingly in terms of their own specific problems, relating it to their own territories, defense burdens, domestic stability, and costs. When Egypt embarked on the "War of Attrition,"66 it did so alone, with no substantial support from the other Arab countries. The cautious diplomatic moves surrounding the War of Attrition also revealed a new spirit emanating from Cairo.

Egypt and Saudi Arabia found a way to reconcile their differences and finally terminated their confrontation in Yemen. The change in this period was most significant in Egypt. The year 1970 marked the acceptance of the third Roger's initiative (by Nasser— not yet Sadat), the end of the Egyptian-Israeli War of Attrition, which paved the way for a determined Egyptian search for a negotiated settlement with Israel, under American auspices, as a result of the military stalemate. (The war can be seen not only as a general rehearsal for the 1973 conflict; the real genesis of the October War is to be found in the War of Attrition, its failure, and the resulting deadlock.)[67] In an era of inter-Arab detente, the initial stages of the 1973 war brought together a diverse Arab coalition; in the late stages, however, the Egyptian-Syrian axis quickly fell apart, with Egypt pulling the rug out from under the feet of its ally as soon as Egyptian raison d'état seemed to justify this.

Stage V: 1970-75/76

The fifth stage witnessed the withering of the Arab Cold War, and new patterns of politics appeared to such an extent that using the term "watershed" seems amply justified. There was a striking increase in the stability of the Arab regimes in terms of their ability to survive, and to reduce and to resist successfully coup d'etat attempts. Sadat succeeded the high priest of the old politics, Nasser, consolidating power in 1971. Except in the Yemen, not a single Arab regime was forcibly overthrown in this period. Some (Algeria in 1979, where Boumedienne had ruled from 1965; Saudi Arabia, where shrewd and adroit King Faysal was assassinated in 1975) even survived relatively easily the supreme test of political stability, a crisis of succession. Furthermore, several military governments have gone a long way toward partial and gradual civilianization (either by adopting the Egyptian-style technocratization-bureaucratization model[68] or, as Itamar Rabinovich puts it,[69] the Syrian-Iraqi-style "Army-Party Symbiosis"), thus giving rise to postmilitary regimes,[70] most of which have struck roots in a more "institutionalized" style of politics.[71] The rulers have learned to master much better the art of government technology. These years saw a certain decline in ideological tensions and a rise in pragmatism; the idea of unity was clearly postponed to the indefinite future.[72] Egypt's place in the center of the inter-Arab system shifted, and a more polycentric system emerged in which many of Egypt's traditional assets (tradition of leadership, geostrategic importance, a charismatic leader, the strongest Arab army, the largest pool of manpower, a position of importance on the international scene) were either challenged, became irrelevant, or were overshadowed by Egypt's pressing and large-scale internal problems.[73] Saudi Arabia, Syria, even Algeria and Libya, contributed to the system's polycentricity, along with the increasing importance of oil (which, however, has a potentially destabilizing role in the system, chiefly because of its asymmetrical distribution).[74]

This stage was also characterized by further cooperation on the tactical, pragmatic level (the Cairo-Riadh-Tehran axis, the Syrian-Jordanian alliance, and even the Egyptian-Syrian partnership in the 1973 war). The Israeli issue after 1973 became more salient, and attitudes to it increasingly matched those toward the United States on the one hand and the Soviet Union on the other. Three blocs could be identified along such lines: a bloc seeking a political settlement in cooperation with the United States (Egypt, Saudi Arabia); the "rejection front," desiring to subvert political settlements, to a certain extent in cooperation with the Soviet Union (Iraq, Libya); and a middle group, hesitant and vacillating, though in temperament closer to the rejection front (Syria, Algeria). [75]

These blocs were far more fragile and heterogeneous than the ones of the previous decade. The middle group contained Algeria, which is geographically remote and is concerned with Africa and the Third World rather than with inter-Arab politics. [76] The Syrian regime was by conviction a rejectionist power, which had to restrain its natural inclinations due to its military isolation from Egypt, the fratricidal feud with the Ba'ath regime in Baghdad, its recurring domestic problems, [77] its military weakness vis-à-vis Israel, and the fact that, unlike the unequivocally rejectionist states, it had a common border with Israel. As for the political-settlement-oriented bloc, which sought an alternative to a military solution (that is, an alternative to war) on the basis of the Security Council Resolution 242 of November 1967, it more or less agreed to the need to negotiate under American auspices and mediation. By the end of the period, however, the arguments surrounding the 1975 interim settlement between Egypt and Israel (Sinai II) began to reveal the enormous cracks in this bloc (the true significance of which became evident only in the next stage). The seriousness of the differences between Egypt and the Gulf states becomes increasingly evident:

> Of all the Arab states, Egypt is the largest, the most politically stable, the most legitimate within her boundaries. This enabled Egypt to give pan-Arabism concrete power, and then, when she tired of it, to turn inward. The oil states had wanted from Egypt an abandonment of the pan-Arabist ideology and acceptance of the logic of the state system, and they got that. What Sadat's diplomacy was to show was that states—or, more precisely and aptly, the leaders of states—could read their interests differently and independently. [78]

As mentioned above, however, at least Nasser's conception of unity of action was vindicated during the initial stages of the 1973 war. The coordinated Egyptian-Syrian military initiative, combined with Arab petropolitics, [79] gave excellent results (as far as Sadat was concerned, at any rate) and opened up favorable diplomatic opportunities.

Stage VI: 1975/76–

In the mid–1970s new inter–Arab tensions arose. The Lebanese civil war of 1975–76 (in a country where stateness has remained more remote than ever), the Egyptian–Israeli interim settlement in 1975, the rising bilateral tensions between Egypt and Libya, Morocco and Algeria, Syria and Iraq, and other focuses of conflict caused renewed turbulence in inter–Arab relations. Tranquillity was gone for the time being. On the other hand, all the regimes survived the inter–Arab upheavals, which no longer sufficed to undermine legitimacy. Moreover, even in the midst of heated inter–Arab debates and conflict, Arab rulers continued to think in terms of raison d'état. Indeed, many of the tensions of the second half of the 1970s seem to have been caused by, or were centered around, raison d'état, pure and simple. Although this was on occasion disguised in the terminology of the Arab Cold War, it is notable that in many cases even this was dispensed with. It is also noteworthy—and nothing could demonstrate more clearly the changing patterns of the times—that while in the 1960s the proverbially cautious conservative monarchies were at odds with Egypt on account of its strong dedication to qawmiyya and its active, leading role in promoting the political manifestations, in the late 1970s they accused Egypt of abandoning the ship and betraying the ideals of Arab nationalism altogether. Egypt, ex–leader of pan–Arabism, almost one third of the entire Arab world, has become a pariah. [80]

After an initial period of "fence–sitting" by the Saudis and their Gulf allies, the interim settlement in the Sinai and the Sadat initiative fractured the political–settlement bloc. Egyptian–Libyan tensions were unprecedented and included a round of border skirmishes (1977). [81] The rejectionist bloc has also been badly fragmented, due to the Iraqi–Syrian rivalry and also to the confusing effects of the Iranian–Iraqi war, which has two of the rejectionist leaders (Iraq and Libya) on opposite sides. The Soviet invasion of Afghanistan has further obfuscated the question of great–power orientation in the Arab world, though Syria—propelled by its isolation and accumulating domestic difficulties—has signed a treaty of friendship and cooperation with the Soviet Union.

All the while, extensive behind–the–scenes relations between Egypt and the rest of the Arab world continue. The Iranian–Iraqi war and the mounting fear of the revolutionary regime in Iran have created the potential for a partial Egyptian–Saudi rapprochement. The continuous rise in the importance of oil and of oil revenues hastened to shift the center of gravity in the region from the Suez Canal zone to the Persian Gulf. [82]

Sadat's visit to Jerusalem was certainly motivated by Egyptian raison d'état. True, Sadat may have counted upon his ability to generate a momentum that would carry to his support his "natural" allies in the Arab world, eventually enabling Egypt (as Sadat himself put it) to lead the Arabs in peace as it had previously led them in war. Until his very last day he seemed to have significantly miscalculated on this point. The fact that he had miscalculated, however, neither prevented him from pursuing the course which he judged favorable from the point of view of Egyptian interests, nor did it enable his opponents in the Arab world to undermine his legitimacy in Egypt itself. Thus, the Sadat initiative and its aftermath are to a significant extent the logical culmination of the process unleashed by the 1970 watershed. This process, of course, is far from being irreversible; it does, however, have an internal logic of its own. All in all, the sharp turn for the worse in inter-Arab relations in the second half of the 1970s does not, then, contradict the thesis concerning the real nature of the much more basic turning point in the first half of the decade.

Unquestionably, further ups and downs in inter-Arab relations may be expected. Widespread conflicts and tensions are frequently prevalent even in relatively normal state systems. The point is that these ups and downs are mostly a matter of quantitative change; the earlier watershed, on the other hand, signified qualitative change.

If this diagnosis is correct, then the 1970 watershed (which is but the culmination of a complex stage in the lengthy process of the rise of stateness in the Arab world) signifies, to the extent that any limited period can do so, the transformation of the Arab state system to a stage of qualitatively greater normalcy.

It is not easy to formulate generalizations based on an analysis of these stages of the development of inter-Arab relations. Nevertheless, along with insights contained in the literature, several tentative conclusions suggest themselves.

1. William Zartman presents a thesis according to which inter-Arab relations oscillate between the phases of "the unity of purpose" and "the unity of ranks."[83] In the unity-of-ranks phase there seems, on the surface, to be harmony among Arab countries, based on the lowest common denominator, which amounts to "doing nothing." In the phases of the unity of purpose, alliances are far more limited in character and comprise fewer states. Among these states, however, the ideological and other ties are more basic and serious. Zartman goes on to argue that there is a strong correlation between the intensity of inter-Arab conflicts—indicated by the oscillation between these two phases—on the one hand, and the intensity of the Arab-Israeli conflict on the other. Thus, in periods of unity of purpose, when inter-Arab conflicts are intensified, a military conflict with Israel is more likely and, even without open warfare, the level of Arab-Israeli tension is likely to be very high. On the other hand,

in periods of unity of ranks, there are generally far fewer tensions. Although Zartman does not exactly explain the dynamics of oscillation from one phase to another, he does argue that the factors that explain this behavior are generally internal and intrinsic to the Arab countries, even though they sometimes touch directly upon the Arab-Israeli conflict. In any case, they are not directly connected to events outside the Middle East. [84]

A detailed examination of the alliances and alignments in the Arab world was conducted by Evron and Bar-Simantov in 1975. [85] A thorough analysis (qualitative and quantitative) led them to two basic propositions:

> (1) The structure of inter-Arab relations is primarily determined by "purely Arab" factors. Two factors are especially noteworthy: the various power relationships in the Arab world and the need to balance changes in them; and the internal instability that characterizes some of the actors in the Arab world. Neither the great powers nor Israel, Turkey or Iran determine the patterns of inter-Arab relations; rather, it is the Arab countries themselves that dictate the character of the inter-Arab system. (2) The establishment or dismantling of coalitions in the Arab world is primarily a function of the structure of inter-Arab relations; Israel and the great powers play only a secondary role in this matter. [86]

In a vein parallel to the present author's analysis of the agenda of inter-Arab relations, Evron and Bar-Simantov find that there are six basic variables that determine the structure of coalitions in the Arab world: the first and most important is the inter-Arab-state factor, which encompasses considerations of strategy, ideology, territory, and economic and military-power relationships in the inter-Arab state system; the second variable comprises domestic considerations of the Arab states; the third is the Palestinian factor; the fourth is great-power rivalry; Israel ranks only fifth; and sixth is the interaction with non-Arab regional states. [87]

Here, too, very low priority is assigned to the Israeli factor (the Palestinian factor, however, which is here considered separately, rather than part of the Israeli problem as in the Ben-Dor formulation, ranks higher), while top priority is given to the state considerations of the individual Arab countries. An interesting conclusion drawn by Evron and Bar-Simantov is that coalitions in the Arab world are extremely fluid: they are assembled quickly and dismantled just as rapidly. The life expectancy of the average coalition

is only about two years. [88] On the basis of the history of the various
Arab coalitions and an analysis of all the possible alliances, Evron
and Bar-Simantov have formed several opinions that are relevant
to the present analysis. They conclude that "changes in the inter-
Arab system often lead to the expansion of areas of conflict . . .
and even to the extension of these conflicts to other regional conflict systems."[89] On the other hand, they claim that Israel has
played only a secondary role in the formation of Arab coalitions,
although since 1967 it has become a more important factor.[90]
Evron and Bar-Simantov also suggest that in the future Israel may
become more sensitive to Arab coalitions, to the extent that they
become increasingly effective. [91]

There seems to be a difference of emphasis between Evron
and Bar-Simantov on the one hand and Kerr and Zartman on the
other. The latter two claim that it is primarily the inter-Arab system that determines the intensity of the Arab-Israeli conflict.
Evron and Bar-Simantov find that there is little correlation between
the way coalitions are put together and act, and the Arab attitude
toward Israel. Rather, they indicate that the opposite state of affairs is true; that is, that what happens in the Arab-Israeli conflict
affects inter-Arab relationships. One might add that to a certain
extent this conclusion is congruent with their finding that destabili-
zation in one structure of relationships in the Middle East subsystem tends to disturb the stability of other structures. [92] Writing in
the mid-1970s, in the wake of the October War, Evron and Bar-
Simantov regarded the Cairo-Riyadh axis as the most important
coalition in the Arab world. Historically, Egypt, Iraq, and Saudi
Arabia had been the centers of coalition building in the Arab world,
and Saudi Arabia's influence was rapidly growing. [93] Evron and
Bar-Simantov finally observed that "further research is required
on the subject of whether the rate of change in explicit or tacit
coalitions raises or lowers the level of stability in inter-Arab relations and in the subsystem as a whole."[94]

Analyzing the 1967-73 period, Dishon found qualified but substantive evidence that "greater acceptance of national sovereignty
and the abandonment of rigid forms of cooperation" yielded "a larger measure of solidarity for the Arabs in 1973 as compared to
1967."[95] This was demonstrated in three areas: the oil embargo,
financial aid, and military aid. Even so, up to 1973 Dishon found
it valid to continue to speak of Egypt as "the key country."[96]

He notes too that during this period there were three unsuc-
cessful attempts by leaders of other Arab states to wrest from
Egypt the role of chief spokesman in inter-Arab affairs: by Algeria's
Boumedienne, by the leadership of Iraq, and by Libya's Qadhafi. [97]
Thus, Egypt continued to exert its qualified leadership; it could

neither be dislodged from its central position nor impose its will on others. "At no time during these years was Egypt strong enough to make the Arab world at large adopt policies for which a fairly wide consensus did not exist in any case. At all times, Egypt remained strong enough to prevent any prospective rival from replacing it at the centre of the stage."[98] Writing about a year prior to the Sadat initiative, Vatikiotis offered the following generalization about the future of inter-Arab relations:

> In the Arab Middle East, inter-Arab relations them-
> selves remain a labyrinth of intricate and often irre-
> concilable elements. In the past, as a rule, divisions,
> differences, and local conflicts were contained within
> and under an imperial arrangement. Today, in the ab-
> sence of such an arrangement, local states which can
> dispose of wealth can generate more deadly conflict,
> dangerous not only to the region's stability but also to
> that of the rest of the world. Aware of the rivalry be-
> tween the two superpowers, the Arab states today be-
> lieve they can "win" because neither the United States
> nor the USSR can impose its will or pax over them. [99]

Reviewing the inter-Arab scene half a decade later, Vatikiotis noted:

> The epochal shift that occurred in the political and
> strategic balance of the Arab-Israeli conflict is a re-
> sult of Egypt's policy and the not too surprising, in-
> deed anticipated reaction of the Arab states to it. . . .
> The mutual distrust, conflict of interest, and rivalry
> among the Arab states, especially between Iraq and
> Syria, the original leaders of the anti-Egyptian front,
> make it still possible for Egypt to continue her peace
> policy. [100]

Unlike some other analysts (the present author included) Vatikiotis does not believe that the 1980s will see more stability in the Arab countries. On the contrary, he foresees the continued instability of regimes, a trend toward shifting alignments among states, and greater involvement by the superpowers. [101] He elaborated:

> In the Arab Middle East, the competing loci of power
> and rivalry of regional interests will be centered in
> Arabia, Egypt, the Fertile Crescent and North Africa.
> Peripheral conflicts in Africa, the Red Sea, the Eastern

Mediterranean and Southwest Asia will, naturally, affect this competition and rivalry. The pivots of the conflict will be Egypt and the Arab states, Arabia and Iran over the Gulf, Iraq and Iran, Syria and Iraq in the Fertile Crescent (the Palestinians and Jordan included), Algeria and Morocco in North Africa, with Libya fomenting peripheral conflict in Tunisia, Egypt and the Sudan.[102]

Finally, Vatikiotis identifies four features that dominate the perception of regional politics by Arab regimes in the early 1980s:

One is the outcome of the Egyptian-Israeli peace treaty. Another is the long-term impact of events in Iran and the spread of militant religious-populist sedition. A third is the apprehension over the Soviet incursion into Afghanistan. Compounding this is the overall fear that the United States will not or cannot protect the region from the growing Soviet threat.[103]

To these observations and generalizations from the literature can be added several others:

1. Much as in any other system of states, coalitions and alignments[104] in the Arab world tend to shift in such a way as to deny to any single country gains that would make it overly powerful in relation to the status quo.

2. Egypt can make peace without the Arabs, but the Arabs (thus far) cannot make war without Egypt.[105] Egypt fought Israel alone in 1956 and 1969-70; with Syria in 1973; with Syria and Jordan in 1967; and with a grand coalition in 1948-49. The fact remains that no inter-Arab alignment could build a coalition capable of fighting Israel without Egypt as a pivotal participant. Whether the post-Camp David version of an "Eastern Front" will change this state of affairs is very much an open question, particularly in the light of the fragmentation caused by the Iranian-Iraqi war and the continued rivalries between Iraq and Syria, Syria and Jordan, and Syria's involvement in Lebanon. Libya's remoteness merely adds to the difficulties.

3. Nasser was right in arguing, late in his life, that the most effective form of Arab unity is the unity of action. It is a supreme double irony that his successor was able to make this work in war in 1973, but unable to make it work for peace in 1977.

4. It is a myth that Israel is the most important element uniting the Arabs. In fact, if anything, on the practical level ("What is to be done?") Israel divides the Arabs as much as any other factor.

5. It is fallacious to argue that periods of relative calm on the Israeli front breed rivalries, and vice versa. Inter-Arab relations have dynamics of their own and are propelled by a variety of factors, most of which have to do exclusively with the Arabs themselves. Peace with Israel would, in all probability, neither make inter-Arab rivalries disappear nor render them significantly more intense than they have been—but their existence does complicate peace making.

6. One principal reason for inter-Arab instability is the difficulty of establishing any one country as a balancer of power. The Saudis have money and moral authority, but they are weak militarily, small in population, and underdeveloped in manpower. The Iraqis and the Syrians suffer from ethnic fragmentation, endless problems with minorities, a fratricidal feud, and an image of extremism and irresponsibility leading to their isolation. That leaves Egypt, which has become a pariah state in the system, with devastating consequences for the system's stability.

7. Traditional rivalries endure for many years. Changes of regime affect this only marginally. Libya after Qadhafi's revolution has played a substantially different role than in the ancien régime, but this seems to be an exception to the rule. Qassem's Iraq quarreled with Nasser as much as the usurped regime had done, and this seems to be the norm, ideological rhetoric notwithstanding.

8. As time goes on, two main considerations appear to dominate inter-Arab policies. One is the maximization of resources available in the inter-Arab "pool," while maintaining minimal external dependence on donor states. The other is the protection of the state and the regime against penetration by other Arab forces. This consideration is practically supreme. Paradoxically, this is so even with a nonstate actor such as the PLO—an aspect that is fully discussed in Chapter 5.

From all the above, it is evident that inter-Arab relations are entering (indeed, have already entered) a post-qawmiyya phase, in which Arab nationalism will continue to play a role, but more as a cultural context for Arab politics than as a guiding source of unity. Its cultural and psychological attraction will continue to be enormous, but the political units interacting within its framework will no longer attempt to submerge their identities and organizational structures in a pan-state framework. This is more than ever probable in view of "the bureaucratic polity [that] has emerged as the predominant type of political system in the Middle East."[106]

What is a bureaucratic polity? Borthwick explained by way of comparison:

The distinctions between a bureaucratic polity and a totalitarian state are subtle but important. In the latter, the state, through its bureaucracy, attempts to control all aspects of the citizens' life and to have total control over every organization of the society. Every factory, store, restaurant and barbershop is owned and run by the state. The government creates and controls youth outing clubs, workers' cultural clubs, housewives' associations, learned societies for physicists and philosophers, labor unions and political parties. However, in the bureaucratic polity the state controls only the high points of the economy, such as banks, modern industries, and big stores, and the major social and political organizations, such as labor unions, student organizations and political parties. Small shopkeepers, petty entrepreneurs, and small informal social groups are allowed to remain independent. [107]

One may take exception to some of the components of this definition, but unquestionably Borthwick is correct in arguing that the state controls all major focuses of power in the polity; that this is the most widespread type of polity in the Middle East; and that this is not a totalitarian policy, if, one might add, for no better reason than the lack of resources and technology needed to establish and maintain a truly totalitarian regime.

Bureaucratic polities dominated by a state elite (which in itself tends to be dominated by a military that reached power in a risky, extralegal manner) are unlikely to relinquish state power in favor of a transstate polity in which the sharing of power is an agonizing problem yet to be resolved. The case of Syria is instructive: it is the only instance of a state elite voluntarily relinquishing power, and even sovereignty, in favor of the ideal of Arab unity[108] (albeit under most extraordinary circumstances). The elite, however, came to rebel against its exclusion from power and its preemption by the Egyptians, culminating in Syria's secession in 1961 from the United Arab Republic, a traumatic event that was to haunt an entire political generation in the Arab world. [109]

Power-oriented, ambitious, military-dominated state elites[110] are poor candidates for the role of builders of an inter-Arab system that is to be dominated by a single such elite rather than 21. The establishment and institutionalization of the modern Arab state has been such a lengthy and complex undertaking that it is far more likely to endure as the crowning achievement of Arab political development than is the attraction of any pan-state ideology. This is particularly true in view of the increasingly obvious inappropriateness of Egypt as the Arab world's Prussia, especially after the death of Nasser, who at one time had seemed destined to be the Arab world's Bismarck. [111] Arab nationalism today has 21 leaders and, for all practical purposes, that is 20 too many: state elites have defeated the nationalist elite.

What of future efforts toward unity in the name of pan-Arabism? "Arab nationalism is not likely to disappear but its peak in the twentieth century seems to have been passed; other nationalisms have taken its place while the turbulent politics of the Middle East continues."[112]

Sadat, when called to join yet another attempt to create "a federal union,"[113] stated:

> Any union (wahda) would begin with a federation (ittihad) of the united Arab republics, in the sense that each republic with all its bodies . . . would be an independent personality . . . and each republic would be a strong unit (wahda) in itself. . . . From all these strong independent units the federation . . . or a strong state will be built, because [if] each unit within the federation is a strong state . . . then the federation itself or the federated state itself will certainly be a strong state.[114]

This is tantamount to saying that if a viable Arab trans-state unity is sought, first build a strong state in one's own Arab country: something of a reductio ad absurdum of the logic of unity of purpose. Undoubtedly, this particularism is the order of the day.

Even more than Zionism, the ideology of Arab nationalism has virtually no theory of the state.

> Nationalist ideology (and Arab qawmiyya is no exception) is concentrated almost entirely on three things: (a) the exploitation of the "homeland" by the target groups; (b) the vast superiority morally, historically, religiously, etc. of the "homeland" and its proper inhabitants and, (c) this superiority, once the target groups have been destroyed or eliminated, will surface and those who possess it will at last be free to develop to their full capacity (with the assumption that this capacity will be able to solve all the problems).[115]

Among the target groups, the European-type direct colonialism is gone forever; the superpower impingement (direct or indirect) will evidently continue as a tolerable fact of life that can even be manipulated for nationalist purposes; and not only is Israel unlikely to go away, but the largest Arab power, at least, is no longer willing or able to regard the struggle against it as an attractive national goal. What remains is the cultural component; but it has yet to be demonstrated that the great progress in achieving freedom from foreign domination leads to the outbursts of cultural creativity predicted by nationalist ideology.

What is this cultural component, without which "the emperor is naked"? Essentially it comprises the "umbrella" concepts of Arabism (uruba).[116] The prominent Iraqi statesman and ideologue, Abd al-Rahman al-Bazzaz, has offered one explanation: "The Arab nationalism in which we believe is based . . . not on racial appeal but on linguistic, historical, cultural and spiritual ties, and on fundamental vital interests."[117] This is doubtless an elegant and sophisticated formulation, but it has one major flaw: the nature of the connection between the various cultural ties on the one hand and the "vital interests" on the other is not spelled out. Cultural affinities are indeed defined by collective experiences on various levels of human organization, but vital interests are invariably—and exclusively—defined by the predominant form of political organization: here, the contemporary state. The cultural logic is that of the caliphate, and the political logic is that of the mulk. The entire history of modern Arab nationalism vividly demonstrates the enormous gap between the two.

Similar problems are discernible in other definitions. Ideologically, it is customary to attribute much importance to the triple slogan of the Ba'ath, "unity-nationalism-socialism." On the question of nationalism, one major forerunner of the Ba'ath, The National Action League, put forth the following creed:

The Arabs are one nation. . . .
The Arabs have one leader who will make manifest
in his person the possibilities of the Arab nation
which he represents and to which he gives the truest
expression. . . .
Arabism is the national consciousness. . . .
The Arab is master of fate (i.e., his own fate).[118]

Here, at last, there is a link between nationhood, state, and consciousness, in the form of the "one leader." Such a leader did appear, in the person of Nasser (with whom the Ba'ath had a running feud for most of his career), yet he failed to tie the disparate elements of nationhood together in an enduring political way. There have been, indeed, notable achievements of uruba in the past two-and-a-half decades: the revitalization of the Arabic language; an increased awareness of and pride in past accomplishments of Arab civilization; greater respect for the Arabs around the world (though this is undoubtedly also due to their economic prowess). Offsetting all this, however, is the devastation suffered by Arab politics under the powerful impact of the resulting political ideology, which, while specific enough to make every Arab country permeable to incessant outside intervention and subversion in the name of nationalism, was not specific enough to offer a viable alternative such as practical merger into an Arab superstate. Stateness, in Arab nationalist ideology, continued to be the Achilles' heel of the theoretical edifice.

This weakness is best demonstrated by the sophisticated writings of al-Bazzaz, who makes an uncommon effort to penetrate the national experience of Israel (and its relationship to Judaism) in order to learn more about nationalism (and Islam) in the Arab world:

> Israel is a Jewish state, or more precisely "the only
> Jewish state in the world." . . . This point in itself
> would lead us to say that what applies to Israel cannot
> be taken as a criterion because of the differences be-
> tween the nature of Judaism on the one hand and the
> nature of Islam and Christianity on the other. . . .
> if we look at Israel and consider its modern formation,
> it would become clear to us that the religious spirit
> undoubtedly played an active role in the minds and con-
> sciousness of a group of its earlier advocates. . . .
> But the Jews who inhabit Israel today are a mixture of
> races, bloods, colors and languages. Yet they have
> maintained a distinctive identity, not because they are
> the chosen race, or because of their religious belief,
> but because, first and foremost, of their subjugation
> to religious, social and political persecution. [119]

Here again, the cultural, collective experience of nationalism is correctly analyzed. Even the country's language is brought into this framework: "Israel is very careful to make Hebrew the basic element of its nationality."[120] This compares favorably with the enormous importance attached to the Arabic language by practically all theoreticians of Arab nationalism. And al-Bazzaz even gets away from the oft-asserted propaganda claims that Judaism is but a religion, and this is not a sufficient basis for peoplehood or nationhood in Israel. Quite the contrary, al-Bazzaz asserts that

> there are in Israel a group of Jews who do not believe
> in Judaism as a revealed religion; in fact there are

those who do not believe in any religion. . . . on the
other hand there are those who blindly believe in their
race and, like the Nazis, they believe that their nationality is their religion. . . . nevertheless, we consider all these peoples Israelis, culturally and mental-
ly, and consequently nationally. In other words, they
are Israelis from the nationalist point of view, irre-
spective of their religious faith.[121]

Apart from the reference to race, this is not a bad assessment of the commonality of fate that constitutes much of the core of
modern Jewish nationalism. But what al-Bazzaz neglects to analyze
is that which preoccupied Ben-Gurion for so long: the role of the
state in building a framework that alone can enable the people to
realize the cultural values inherent in their collective experience.
The final, necessary step in the transition to the establishment of
a Jewish state, the evolution of political Zionism in the 1930s,[122]
is ignored; the role of the state in the survival of the Jewish people
is disregarded.[123] The weakness of the Zionist theory of the state
is amplified in the weakness of the Arab nationalist theory of the
state.

Not only is the theory of the state weak, but further obstacles
on the road to Arab unity have not been surmounted. For instance,
enormous stress is put on the sound cultural basis for Arab nationalism, but this is something around which social scientists have
developed a legitimate controversy. Some grant the Arab nationalist point of view. For example, Hudson argues that "the hallmarks
of modern Arab identity are, on the ethnic dimension, Arabic language and culture, and on the religious dimension, Islam. On both
dimensions, the inhabitants of the Arab world are overwhelmingly
homogeneous."[124] Yet, he hastens to add:

In emphasizing the ethno-linguistic and religious homo-
geneity of the Arab world (a point so obvious that its
significance is sometimes overlooked), I do not mean
to ignore the existence and political significance of the
non-Arab, non-Muslim, and non-orthodox Muslim
minorities in the Arab world.[125]

This political significance is indeed considerable. Although
no one would deny the primacy of the Arab elements in the cultural
identity of every Arab country, the existence of actually or potentially powerful minorities in the Arab states has played a visible
role in the politics of Arab nationalism and unity. Thus, for instance, the need for national reconciliation with the non-Arab

Southern Sudan was apparently a major factor in the decision of the Sudanese leadership to give up the idea of joining a tripartite federation with Egypt and Libya in the late 1960s and early 1970s.[126] Again, Syria's complex ethnic structure involves it in incessant inter-Arab activity, but the predominant place of the minorities in the ruling Syrian elite makes it suspect in the eyes of other Arab nationalists (as well as in the eyes of its own people).[127] Another example is Iraq, which is ruled by an urban Sunni elite in what is mainly a Shi'ite rural society, a situation exacerbated by an ebbing and flowing Kurdish rebellion,[128] all of which has at times resulted in the virtual isolation of Iraq in inter-Arab affairs. As has been noted, the Palestinian presence in Jordan led to a civil war in 1970–71, which resulted in inter-Arab intervention and culminated in the downfall of the Syrian neo-Ba'ath regime. Again, the ubiquitous ethnosectarian cleavages in Lebanon were a major cause of the 1975–76 civil war, which entailed massive external involvement, climaxing in the intervention of a sizable Syrian military force legitimized by inter-Arab forums as the "Arab Deterrent Force."[129]

It is impossible to ignore the negative impact of these sociological and demographic facts upon the drive to Arab unity: in fact, an entire school of anthropologists and other social scientists depict the emerging picture of pluralism as a "mosaic" in which "people live together by living apart."[130] Even if the metaphor of a mosaic is an exaggeration when applied to the Arab Middle East in its entirety, it is certainly an apt depiction of the scene in several key Arab countries—above all, Iraq and Syria. An Iraqi political sociologist, in attempting to differentiate these latter from Egypt, called them "multiple societies."[131] These two countries have been in the forefront of Arab nationalism in the last generation (in the case of Iraq, even longer). Egypt, which is possibly the most homogeneous Arab country, is no longer willing to lead the drive for Arab unity. Iraq and Syria may be more willing, but multiple societies need a state in order to provide a framework for the positive interplay of social cleavages before they can become leaders of real stature in the region.

In the following pages, data are presented on five key Arab countries in order to demonstrate the pluralistic character of the Arab world.[132]

ETHNIC AND RELIGIOUS MINORITIES
IN EGYPT, IRAQ, JORDAN, LEBANON, SYRIA

The Arab Republic of Egypt

Estimated population (mid-1975): 37,230,000

Community	Size	% of Total Population	Religion	Language	Occupation	Region
Copts	General Estimate 2.5-3 million. (The Coptic Church claims 6 million members)	c.8	mainly Monophysite Christians. Also Orthodox and Uniate	Arabic	civil service, commerce, professionals, artisans	everywhere in Egypt
Greeks	c.15,000 (1970) (numbered 120-150,000 before World War I)	n.a.	Greek Orthodox	Greek	were mainly in commerce, finance. Also artisans, clerks	mainly in Alexandria and Cairo
Jews	c.300 (numbered 65,000 in 1947)		Judaism	Arabic, Ladino Hebrew liturgy	now mainly elderly. were mainly merchants, artisans	mainly in Cairo (formerly in Cairo, Alexandria and other urban centers)
Muslims	n.a.	90	mainly Sunni Muslim	Arabic	all types	everywhere in Egypt
Nubians	several thousand	n.a.	Muslims (are a mixture of Egyptian, African, and Arab elements	have own African language. Also Arabic	peasants, cooks, servants, watchmen	Upper Egypt and urban centers. (Displaced by Aswan High Dam resettled)
Palestinians	33,000 (PLO figures)	n.a.	Sunni Muslim	Arabic	n.a.	n.a.

165

The Republic of Iraq

Estimated population (mid-1975): 11,120,000

Community	Size	% of Total Population	Religion	Language	Occupation	Region
Armenians	23,000 (1965)	n.a.	Orthodox and Uniate Churches	Armenian	n.a.	n.a.
Assyrians (identified with Nestorian Christians)	30-31,000 (1965) (100,000 acc. to Assyrian sources)	n.a.	Uniate Church	Syriac for religious rites, Arabic as spoken language	Mainly professionals, white collar workers	Baghdad
Chaldeans	475,000	n.a.	Uniate Church (branch of Assyrian-Nestorian Church)	Syriac for religious rites, Arabic spoken language	n.a.	Baghdad
Greek Catholics	1,000	n.a.	Follow Byzantine rites	Arabic	n.a.	n.a.
Greek Orthodox	2,000	n.a.	Uniate Church	Arabic	n.a.	n.a.
Jews	c.2,500 (numbered 125,000 in 1947)	n.a.	Judaism	Arabic, Hebrew liturgy	Commerce, Banking crafts	Bagdad

Group	Number		Religion	Language	Occupation	Location
Kurds	Over 2,000,000	18-20	Sunni Muslim	Kurdish	peasants, nomads, mountaineers rough pasture shepherds	(Kurdistan) northern and north-eastern districts
Latin Catholics	2,000	n.a.	Uniate Church	Latin for religious, Arabic as spoken language	n.a.	n.a.
Mandaens (also Sabeans or Sabians)	20,000	n.a.	Religion contains Christian and Muslim elements and borrow-	Arabic as spoken language; ancient Chaldean Aramaic Language in their religious rites	Artisans (mainly silversmiths)	Lower Iraq
Palestinians	14,000 (PLO figure)	n.a.	Sunni Muslim	Arabic	n.a.	n.a.
Protestants	several thousand	n.a.	Several denominations	Arabic	In services, trades, industry	Northern district of Mosul
Yezidis	30,000	n.a.	Religion includes Muslim, Christian and magical elements	Kurdish dialect as spoken language, Arabic in religious rites	n.a.	Jabal Sinjar and North of Masul
Muslims	constitute	50% 40%	Shi'ite Sunni	Arabic Arabic	all types are the dominant group	Everywhere in Iraq

The Hashemite Kingdom of Jordan

Estimated population (mid-1975): 2,690,000

Community	Size	% of Total Population	Religion	Language	Occupation	Region
Bedouin	200,000 (1967)	n.a.	Sunni Muslim	Arabic	Nomads, semi-nomads and settled. Make up bulk of army	117,000 were nomads (1967) Semi-nomads and villagers live in Jordan Valley area
Chechers and Circassians	15-20,000 (1967)	n.a.	Muslims of Caucasian origin Shiite and Sunni respectively	Arabic, also Circassian languages	army, agriculture, government	n.a.
Christians (Include small communities of Armenians and Greeks)	150,000 (1967)	n.a.	Mainly Orthodox also Greek Catholic	Arabic, etc.	n.a.	Amman and East Jerusalem (part of Israel since June 1967)
Muslims	overwhlelming majority		Sunni Muslim	Arabic	all types	everywhere in Jordan
Palestinians	c.643,000 (PLO figure is 900,000)	50-54	Sunni Muslim	Arabic	in government, civil service, trades, professions; laborers servants	Full Jordanian citizens but c.168,000 live in UNRWA camps or tents. 494,000 were registered refugees (1968)

168

Lebanon

Estimated population (mid-1975): 2,870,000

Community	Size	% of Total Population	Religion	Language	Occupation	Region
Armenians	100,000-160,000	6.2 (1932 census)	Monophysite, Orthodox and Uniate Catholic	Armenian	Craftsman, traders, clerical workers	Mainly Beirut
Assyrians	15,000	1 (1932 census)	Nestorian Christian	Syriac for religious rites, Arabic as spoken language	Mainly unskilled laborers	Urban areas
Catholic of Syrian rite	18,000 (1972)	n.a.	Uniate Christian	Arabic, Syriac for religious rites	n.a.	n.a.
Chaldeans	5,957 (1972)	n.a.	Uniate Christian	Arabic as spoken language, Syriac for religious rites	n.a.	n.a.
Druzes	88,000 (1958)	6.3 (1932 census)	Offshoot of Isma'iliyya sect	Arabic	Soldiers and peasants	Mount Lebanon and southeastern districts of Hasbaya and Rashaya
Greek Catholic	183,345 (1972)	6.3 (1932 census)	Uniate Church. Follow Byzantine rite of Catholic Christian Church	Liturgical language is Arabic	Merchants, professionals	Southern and eastern parts of the country. Zahla.

Lebanon (continued)

	Population	Percent (census)	Religion	Language	Occupation	Location
Greek Orthodox	150,000 (1958)	10 (1932)	Greek Orthodox	Arabic	Merchants, traders, etc.	Northern Lebanon, Beirut, Tripoli
Jews	1,000 (1975)		Judaism	Arabic, Hebrew liturgy	Merchants, clerks, artisans	Beirut
Kurds	n.a.	1 (1932 census)	Sunni Muslim	Kurdish Vernacular	Unskilled laborers, porters	Beirut
Maronites	832,636 (1972)	29 (1932 census)	Uniate, Eastern Christian Church	Arabic, French Liturgical language in Syriac	All types	Mount Lebanon, Beirut
Palestinians	150,000 (PLO figure is 240,000)	n.a.	Sunni Muslim (also some Christian denomination)	Arabic		90,000 are refugees in camps and 60,000 live in the rest of Lebanon
Protestants	14,000 (1958)	n.a.	various denominations	Arabic	n.a.	n.a.
Roman	n.a.	1 (1932 census)	Uniate and Catholic Churches	Arabic	n.a.	n.a.
Shi'ites (Mutawalis)	250,000 (1958)	18.2 (1932 census)	Shi'ite Muslim	Arabic	peasants, unskilled laborers	Southern Lebanon "Jabal Amel" and in Coele Syria
Sunnis	286,000 (1958)	20.8 (1932 census)	Sunni Muslim	Arabic	Officials; in trade, crafts, merchants	Tripoli as center

The Syrian Arab Republic

Estimated population (mid-1975): 7,350,000

Community	Size	% of Total Population	Religion	Language	Occupation	Region
'Alawis (Nusseiris) 'Alawites	500-600,000 (1958)	11.5	Islamic sect	Arabic	Military officers, but majority are poor farmers	Mountain of 'Alawites in north-western part of Syria. Also in District of Lataqiyah
Armenians	175,000 (1968) estim. 170,000	n.a.	Monophysite, Orthodox and Uniate Catholic	Armenian	Traders, small-industry, crafts	75% live in Aleppo
Bedouin	n.a.	2-3	Sunni Muslim	Arabic		
Assyrians	15,000 (1968) estim. 30-50,000	n.a.	Nestorian Christians	Syriac	Engage in small-scale agriculture	Khabur
Chaldeans	5,000 (1958)	n.a.	Uniate (Catholic) branch of Assyrian Church	Syriac	n.a.	n.a.
Circassians	20-25,000 (1968)	n.a.	Sunni Muslim	Circassians; Increasingly Arabic speaking	peasants	Southwestern Hawran
Druze	120-150,000 (1968) estim. 200,000	3+	Offshoot of Isma'ilyya sect	Arabic	mountain peasants	Jabal al-Druze Suwayda

The Syrian Arab Republic (continued)

Group	Population	%	Religion	Language	Occupation	Location
Greek Catholics	65,000 (1968)	n.a.	Greek Catholic (follow Byzantine rite)	Greek, Arabic	n.a.	n.a.
Greek Orthodox	200,000 (1968)	n.a.	Greek Orthodox	Syriac liturgy	n.a.	n.a.
Isma'ilis	50,000 (1968)	n.a.	Offshoot of Shi'i Muslims	Arabic	peasants	Hama province; shouth of Salamiya
Jews	3,000 (1968)	n.a.	Judaism	Arabic; Hebrew is liturgical language	Peddlers, shop-keepers, money-chnagers, artisans	Damascus (3,000) Aleppo (1,200) Qamishly (300)
Kurds	400,000 (1968)	7	Sunni Muslim	Kurdish	unskilled laborers, supervisors, foremen (Used as front-line forces in 1973 war. Now on Iraqi border)	northeast border - have been uprooted and deprived of citizenship status and rights
Latins	5,000 (1968)	n.a.	Roman Catholic	Arabic	n.a.	n.a.
Maronites	20,000 (1968)		Eastern Christian Church	Syriac liturgy, Arabic	n.a.	n.a.
Palestinians	138,000 (1975) (PLO figure is 155,000)		Sunni Muslim	Arabic	n.a. some in administration, army	n.a.
Protestants	15,000 (1968)	n.a.	all denominations	Arabic	n.a.	n.a.
Shi'ites (Mutawalis)	15,000 (1968)	n.a.	Shi'ite Muslims	Arabic	n.a.	Aleppo, Homs
Sunnis	4,500,000 (1971) 90% Arabs and 10% Kurds	70	Sunni Muslim	Arabic	all types	majority in all but two provinces

Community	Size	% of Total Population	Religion	Language	Occupation	Region
Syrian Catholics	25,000 (1968)	n.a.	Uniate Church	Syriac and Arabic	n.a.	n.a.
Syrian Orthodox (Jacobites)	70,000 (1938)	n.a.	Monophysite Christians	Syriac and Arabic	n.a.	n.a.
Turcomans	60,000 (1965)	n.a.	Sunni Muslim	Turkic	Semi-nomadic herdsmen and settled agriculturalists	n.a.
Yazidis	3,000 (1968)	n.a.	Offshoot of Islam	Kurdish dialects; use Arabic in religious rites	n.a.	Aleppo, Jazirah

Note: The dates provided in the tables indicate the latest figures available. Others are 1976 estimates. All figures are of necessity approximations, since the Middle East governments concerned do not publish population statistics providing ethnic and religious breakdowns. The last Egyptian census took place in 1947. The last Lebanese census was in 1932. It is generally estimated that Syria's population is 90 percent Muslim and 10 percent Christian.

Abbreviation: n.a., not available.

Source: Middle East Review 9 (Fall 1976): 60-68.

With the evident decline in the fervor of pan-Arabism, the pluralism quantitatively presented here yet again became visible and added to the centrifugal forces in the Arab world. "The Arabs who had once seemed whole—both to themselves and to others—suddenly look as diverse as they had been all along," says Ajami.[133] This diversity, however, is not a mere result of the disenchantment with Arab unity—it is definitely one of its causes as well. The need to think out the role of those who identify (explicitly or tacitly) as non-Arabs in the Arab state is evident.

> The interests of the Arab Muslim middle classes, gov-
> ernment officials, military officers and religious lead-
> ers have been served by the Arab nationalist movement.
> As these levels of the population, long deprived of power,
> have achieved ascendancy, the role of the minorities has
> decreased. Many of the members of the minority groups
> who have remained are willing to accept their national
> identity as Egyptians or Syrians, etc. But they need to
> have their rights as citizens of these states guaranteed
> and they need to have the protection of the law. They
> cannot accept cultural domination as reflected in the
> many Islamic religious references incorporated into
> the national structures of the modern Arab states.
> Their future remains just as uncertain as does the fu-
> ture course and attitudes of the Muslim Arab states in
> which they live.[134]

The feeble theory of the state in Arab nationalism has failed to make much of a contribution to the question, What is the role of the non-Arab in an Arab nationalist state? (One might add that the parallel question, What is the role of the non-Jew in the Jewish state?, is also in need of much further thought in Israel.)[135] Once the fascination with pan-state attractions declines sufficiently, perhaps this pressing need will be attended to.

Inter-Arab relations are now on the eve of a new era: the era of state relations. Will this be a "normal" state system? The attraction of Arab nationalism is not likely to disappear. The solidarity, with 20 other states sharing a common language, heritage, and culture and commanding an immense pool of potential and actual resources, will probably—and naturally—continue. A special relationship with other states of a similar ethnolinguistic background is normal: however, abdication of control over the state and opening the political arena to outside ambitions as a legitimate component of nationalism is not. And indeed, as Albert Hourani observes, "Changes in society and the emergence of new social groups express themselves in political ideologies different in emphasis from the Arab nationalism of the previous elites."[136] This new emphasis is oriented toward the state:

> The need to carry out economic and social development rapidly and by direct intervention of the state, and the concentration of effective force in the hands of the army, will tend towards the formation of governments of military politicians assisted by technocrats, which at least hold out the promise of creating a strong executive power. . . . [As to ideology] there has emerged a wide consensus in favor of a cautious, mixed, empirical type of policy less exposed to the winds of ideology; secularist without a radical break with religion, Arab but not to the extent of sacrificing sovereignty or local interests. [137]

The inter-Arab political scene has always been characterized by tensions between universal, pro-caliphate forces on the one hand and particularistic pro-mulk forces, on the other. At this stage, the latter have triumphed.

> The incongruence between nation loyalty and all-Arab core concerns, on the one hand, and specific state loyalty and specific state interests, on the other, adds additional disharmony to the Arab political scene. Arabism is not intense or exclusive enough to eradicate—at least for the foreseeable future—the state political systems that have developed since World War I. [138]

This political fact of life has been evident for some time; not so its explicit articulation:

> The boundaries of Arab states have been around now for nearly six decades. It is not their existence which is novel, but their power and legitimacy—the power (as much as that power exists in the modern state system) to keep pan-Arab claims at bay and effectively to claim the loyalty of those within. They are no longer as "illusory and permeable" as they used to be. The states that lie within them are less "shy" about asserting their rights, more normal in the claims that they make. [139]

This normalcy by no means implies an end to conflicts, nor even a drastic quantitative reduction in them. In Arab countries— as in the rest of the Islamic world—conflict has always been a way of life, and must not be regarded negatively: "Traditional Islam survived for more than a millenium in a harsh and uncertain environment because it was capable of converting constant tension and conflict into a force for constant political renewal and social survival."[140] The Arab countries, however, have exposed the state to nationalist conflicts that debilitated, subverted, and paralyzed, rather than renewed and revitalized it.

Perhaps the Arab political system will never be entirely "normal," in that it may never be free from special considerations having to do with Arab solidarity. Arab states may never cease regarding one another as something special, to be treated differently than other states, but that is a far cry from the turbulent days of messianic pan-Arabism. The global scene is full of instances in which states maintain special relationships with other states for a host of cultural or ideological reasons. Such special considerations are filtered by, perceived through, and ultimately absorbed in each state's raison d'état: they do not replace it or overwhelm it or paralyze it.

For too long, the Arab nation and the Arab state have devastated each other. It is now becoming an acknowledged fact of life, however, that whether or not the nebulous Arab nation exists, a number of concrete Arab states certainly do. Once the agenda of the inter-Arab system is geared to this reality, both the Arab nation and the Arab states will gain. The intrusion of the unattainable—the utopia of a pan-Arab caliphate—into the realm of the attainable—a mulk, anchored in Arab culture and tempered by Islamic ethics— generated an intolerable reality for more than a generation. That generation and that reality are passing away.

NOTES

1. See G. Ben-Dor, "Nationalism without Sovereignty and Nationalism with Multiple Sovereignties: The Palestinians and inter-Arab Relations," in The Palestinians and the Middle East Conflict: Studies in Their History, Sociology and Politics, ed. G. Ben-Dor (Ramat Gan: Turtledove, 1978); idem, "Inter Arab Relations and the Arab-Israeli Conflict," Jerusalem Journal of International Relations 1 (4) (Summer 1976): 70-76; P. J. Vatikiotis, Conflict in the Middle East (London: Allen and Unwin, 1971); idem, "Inter-Arab Relations," in The Middle East: Oil, Conflict and Hope, ed. A. L. Udovitch (Lexington, Mass.: Heath, 1976); Yair

Evron and Yaacov Bar-Simantov, "Coalitions in the Arab World,"
Jerusalem Journal of International Relations 1 (Summer 1976): 71-
107; Leonard Binder, "The Middle East as a Subordinate International System," World Politics 10 (3) (April 1958): 408-29; idem,
"Transformation in the Middle East Subordinate System After 1967,"
in The U.S.S.R. and the Middle East, ed. Michael Confino and
Shimon Shamir (Jerusalem: Israel University Press, 1972);
Malcolm Kerr, The Arab Cold War, 3d ed. (London: Oxford Uni-
versity Press, 1971); idem, "Persistence of Regional Quarrels,"
in Soviet-American Rivalry in the Middle East, ed. J. C. Hurewitz
(New York: Praeger, 1969); Nadav Safran, From War to War (New
York: Pegasus, 1969); William I. Zartman, "Military Elements in
Regional Unrest," in Soviet-American Rivalry in the Middle East,
ed. J. C. Hurewitz (New York: Praeger, 1972).

2. Fouad Ajami, "The End of Pan-Arabism," Foreign Affairs
57 (2) (Winter 1978-79): 355-73; G. Ben-Dor, "Unity and Disunity in
the Arab World," Monthly Review 9 (September 1973): 3-13 (in
Hebrew).

3. This is best described in Kerr, The Arab Cold War.

4. Quoted in Weekly Media Abstracts, March 11, 1981.

5. Ibid., p. 2.

6. Compare with the data quoted for Professor T. Farah's
research in Ajami, "The End of Pan-Arabism," p. 364.

7. Weekly Media Abstracts, p. 2.

8. Ibid. ("The co-ordination of the research suggests that
some of those referring to the U.S. have had Israel in mind as
well.")

9. Ibid.

10. Ibid., pp. 2-3.

11. Ibid., p. 3.

12. Al-Dustur, December 30, 1980.

13. Ajami, "The End of Pan-Arabism," p. 364.

14. Elias H. Tuma, "The Rich and the Poor in the Middle
East," Middle East Journal 34 (4) (Autumn 1980): 413-37.

15. See the most instructive analysis in John Waterbury,
"Egypt: The Wages of Dependency," in The Middle East: Oil,
Conflict and Hope, ed. A. Udovitch (Lexington, Mass.: Heath,
1976), pp. 291-351.

16. Ibid., p. 291.

17. Arab Press Service, Beirut, January 21-28, 1981.

18. Ibid.

19. Tuma, "The Rich and the Poor in the Middle East."

20. Tuma, quoted in Weekly Media Abstracts, pp. 3-4.

21. Ibid., p. 4.

22. Ibid.

23. Ibid.

24. See, for example, Norman Frohlich and Joe A. Oppenheimer, Modern Political Economy (Englewood Cliffs, N.J.: Prentice-Hall, 1978).

25. Surveyed extensively in Sylvia Haim, Arab Nationalism: An Anthology (Berkeley: University of California Press, 1962).

26. Gad G. Gilbar, "Egypt's Economy: The Challenge of Peace," Jerusalem Quarterly 12 (Summer 1979): 6.

27. Vatikiotis, "Inter-Arab Relations," p. 147.

28. Ibid. See also George Antonius, The Arab Awakening (Beirut: Khayat's, 1961); Zeine M. Zeine, The Struggle for Independence: Western Diplomacy and the Rise and Fall of Faisal's Kingdom in Syria (Beirut: Khayat's, 1960); and Albert Hourani, Arabic Thought in the Liberal Age, 1798-1939 (London: Oxford University Press, 1962).

29. Hisham Sharabi, Nationalism and Revolution in the Arab World (Princeton, N.J.: Van Nostrand, 1964).

30. Vatikiotis, "Inter-Arab Relations," p. 148.

31. See Majid Khadduri, Independent Iraq (London: Oxford University Press, 1960); and Albert Hourani, Syria and Lebanon: A Political Essay (London: Oxford University Press, 1946).

32. Vatikiotis, "Inter-Arab Relations," p. 149.

33. Majid Khadduri, "The Scheme of Fertile Crescent Unity," in The Near East and the Great Powers, ed. Richard M. Frye (Cambridge, Mass.: Harvard University Press, 1957).

34. See M. Khalil, The Arab States and the Arab League (Beirut: 1967); Robert W. McDonald, The League of Arab States (Princeton, N.J.: Princeton University Press, 1968); Hussein A. Hassouna, The League of Arab States and Regional Disputes (Dobbs Ferry, N.Y.: Oceana, 1975).

35. See, for instance, Elizabeth Monroe, Britain's Moment in the Middle East, 1919-1956 (Baltimore, Md.: Johns Hopkins University Press, 1962).

36. Vatikiotis, Conflict in the Middle East; Sharabi, Nationalism and Revolution in the Middle East; and George M. Hadda, Revolutions and Military Rule in the Middle East, 3 vols. (New York: Speller, 1971).

37. This point is developed in detail in G. Ben-Dor, "Inter-Arab Relations and the Arab-Israeli Conflict," and idem, "The Palestinians and Inter-Arab Relations."

38. Fayez Sayegh, Arab Unity: Hope and Fulfillment (Old Greenwich, Conn.: Devin-Adair, 1958); Haim, Arab Nationalism; and Hazem Z. Nuseibeh, The Ideas of Arab Nationalism (Ithaca, N.Y.: Cornell University Press, 1956). See also "Arab Unity," in Yaakov Shimoni and Eviatar Levin, Political Lexicon of the

Middle East in the 20th Century, rev. ed. (Tel Aviv: Shikmona, 1974) (in Hebrew).

39. See Kerr, "Regional Arab Politics," and Vatikiotis, Conflict in the Middle East.

40. Uriel Dann, Iraq under Qassem (New York: Praeger, 1969), and Majid Khadduri, Republican Iraq (London: Oxford University Press, 1969).

41. See A. L. Tibawi, The Modern History of Syria (New York: Oxford University Press, 1969); Patrick Seale, The Struggle for Syria (London: Oxford University Press, 1965); T. Petran, Syria; I. Rabinovich, Syria under the Ba'ath; Kerr, "Hafiz Asad and the Changing Patterns of Syrian Politics"; Ma'oz, Syria under Hafiz al-Asad; and I. Rabinovich, "Full-Circle—Syrian Politics," in Middle East Perspectives: The Next Twenty Years, ed. George S. Wise and Charles Issawi (Princeton, N.J.: Darwin Press, 1981), pp. 129-40.

42. See, for instance, Hurewitz, ed., Soviet-American Rivalry in the Middle East.

43. Kerr, "Regional Arab Politics," p. 61.

44. Of these focuses of tension, the interminable Lebanese civil war has proven to be the most intractable, and is likely to be so for years to come. For the genesis of this quagmire, see John Bulloch, Death of a Country: The Civil War in Lebanon (London: Weidenfeld and Nicolson, 1977) and A. Dawisha, "Syria in Lebanon— Asad's Vietnam?" Foreign Policy 33 (Winter 1978-79): 135-50.

45. See Tuma, "The Rich and the Poor in the Middle East"; Charles Issawi and Mohammed Yeganeh, The Economics of Middle Eastern Oil (New York: Praeger, 1962); George Lenczowski, Oil and State in the Middle East (Ithaca, N.Y.: Cornell University Press, 1960); Stephen H. Longrigg, Oil in the Middle East: Its Discovery and Development, 3d ed. (London: Oxford University Press, 1967); Leonard Mosley, Power Play: Oil in the Middle East (New York: Random House, 1973); Mana Saeed al-Otaiba, OPEC and the Petroleum Industry (New York: Wiley, 1975); Benjamin Shwadran, The Middle East: Oil and the Great Powers, 3d ed. (New York: Wiley, 1974); Robert Stephens, The Arabs' New Frontier (Boulder, Col.: Westview Press, 1976); and Joe Stork, Middle East Oil and the Energy Crisis (New York: Monthly Review Press, 1975).

46. Ajami, "The End of Pan-Arabism," p. 356.

47. Moore, "On Theory and Practice Among Arabs." For an attempt to clarify the ideological terminology related to Arab nationalism and unity, see G. Ben-Dor, "Federalism in the Arab World," in Federalism and Political Integration, ed. Daniel J. Elazar (Ramat Gan: Turtledove, 1979), pp. 193-95.

48. Ajami, "The End of Pan-Arabism," p. 356.

49. See Kerr, "Regional Arab Politics and the Conflict with Israel."

50. Ben-Dor, "Nationalism without Sovereignty and Nationalism with Multiple Sovereignties."

51. Amos Perlmutter, "The Arab Military Elite," World Politics 22 (1970): 291.

52. This was explored as early as September 1957, in Leonard Binder, "Prolegomena to the Comparative Study of Middle East Governments," American Political Science Review 51 (3) (September 1957): 651–68.

53. Numerous sources describe this. See, for example, the relevant chapters in Hadad, Revolutions and Military Rule; Eliezer Beeri, Army Officers in Arab Politics and Society (New York: Praeger, 1969); J. C. Hurewitz, Middle East Politics: The Military Dimension (New York: Praeger, 1969); and the extensive lists of works cited in these three comprehensive surveys.

54. See G. A. Nasser, "The Egyptian Revolution," Foreign Affairs 33 (January 1955): 199–211; and Nasser, The Philosophy of the Revolution.

55. I. W. Zartman, "Military Elements in Regional Unrest," in Soviet-American Rivalry in the Middle East, ed. Hurewitz.

56. Ben-Dor, "Unity and Disunity in the Arab World"; Monte Palmer, "The United Arab Republic: An Assessment of Its Failure," Middle East Journal 20 (Winter 1966): 50–67; Kerr, The Arab Cold War; J. S. F. Parker, "The United Arab Republic," International Affairs 38 (7) (January 1962): 15–28; and Muhammad Hassanayn Haykal, What Happened in Syria (Cairo: 1962) (in Arabic).

57. Zartman, "Military Elements."

58. Kerr, The Arab Cold War.

59. See Ben-Dor, "The National Security Policy of Egypt."

60. This phrase was coined by Malcolm Kerr. See his brilliant analysis in the book of that title.

61. See Haim, "The Ba'ath in Syria"; Rabinovich, Syria under the Ba'ath; and Amos Perlmutter, "From Obscurity to Rule: The Syrian Army and the Ba'ath Party," Western Political Quarterly 22 (4) (December 1969): 827–45.

62. Safran, From War to War.

63. See Aronson, pp. 60–74, and the sources there cited.

64. Ibid., p. 74.

65. Ajami, "The End of Pan-Arabism," p. 357.

66. See the interesting account of this by Heikal in his The Road to Ramadan (London: Collins, 1975). See also the fine analysis in Lawrence Whetten, The Canal War (Cambridge, Mass.: M.I.T. Press, 1974), and the sources cited there.

67. On this, see Whetten's comprehensive analysis.

68. See Ben-Dor, "Civilianization of Military Regimes in the Arab World," in Political Participation and Military Regimes, ed. Henry Bienen (Beverly Hills, Cal.: Sage, 1976).

69. Itamar Rabinovich, Syria under the Ba'ath 1963-1966: The Army Party Symbiosis (Jerusalem: Keter, 1972).

70. This term is explained in detail in Ben-Dor, "Civilianization of Military Regimes."

71. This is meant in the sense of the term as used by Huntington, and elaborated in G. Ben-Dor, "Institutionalization of Political Development: A Conceptual and Theoretical Analysis," Comparative Studies in Society and History 17 (July 1975): 309-56.

72. See Ben-Dor, "Unity and Disunity in the Arab World."

73. See Daniel Dishon, "Inter-Arab Relations, 1967-1973," in Between June and October, ed. Itamar Rabinovich and Haim Shaked (New Brunswick, N.J.: Transaction, 1978).

74. Shwadran, The Middle East: Oil and the Great Powers.

75. Obviously, the more important, furthest removed from the rejectionists, and most adaptable of the two, is Syria. On Syria as the microcosm of inter Arab politics, see Seale, The Struggle for Syria.

76. Raphael Danziger, "Algeria and the Palestinians," in The Palestinians and the Middle East Conflict, ed. G. Ben-Dor, pp. 347-76.

77. Rabinovich, "Full Circle—Syrian Politics in the 1970s."

78. Ajami, "The End of Pan-Arabism," pp. 359-60.

79. Heikal, The Road to Ramadan.

80. On a note of supreme irony, Egypt was to be expelled (or suspended) from the Arab League, the headquarters of which were moved from Cairo to Tunis, whereas in 1965 it had been Egypt that initiated the suspension of Tunisia for proposals that were far short of Sadat's peace initiative.

81. See Ben-Dor, "The National Security Policy of Egypt."

82. See K. K. Ramazani, "The Genesis of the Carter Doctrine," in Middle East Perspective: The Next Twenty Years, ed. Wise and Issawi, pp. 165-80.

83. Zartman, "Military Elements in Regional Unrest," pp. 76-82.

84. Ibid. See also Kerr, "Regional Arab Politics." For somewhat different views, see Safran, From War to War, pp. 76-78, 81-82.

85. Evron and Bar-Simantov, "Coalitions in the Arab World."

86. Ibid., p. 72.

87. Ibid., pp. 72-73.

88. Ibid., p. 85.

89. Ibid., p. 73.

90. Ibid., p. 81.

91. Ibid.

92. Ibid., p. 72.

93. Ibid., p. 88.

94. Ibid.

95. Dishon, "Inter-Arab Relations," pp. 165-67.

96. Ibid., pp. 167-69.

97. Ibid.

98. Ibid.

99. Vatikiotis, "Inter-Arab Relations," pp. 172-73.

100. P. J. Vatikiotis, "Regional Politics," in Middle East Perspectives: The Next Twenty Years, ed. George S. Wise and Charles Issawi (Princeton, N.J.: Darwin, 1981), p. 35.

101. Ibid., p. 49.

102. Ibid.

103. Ibid.

104. See Ch. 11, "Diplomacy and Coalitions," in Deutsch, The Analysis of International Relations.

105. See Ben-Dor, "Inter-Arab Relations and the Arab-Israeli Conflict."

106. Borthwick, Comparative Politics in the Middle East: An Introduction, p. 57. See also, Marvin Zonis, The Political Elite in Iran (Princeton, N.J.: Princeton University Press, 1971); Anouar Abdel Malek, Egypt: Military Society (New York: Random House, 1968); Beeri, Army Officers in Arab Politics and Society; and Albert Hourani, "The Decline of the West in the Middle East," International Affairs 29 (April 1953): 156-86.

107. Borthwick, Comparative Politics in the Middle East: An Introduction, p. 58.

108. See Palmer, "The United Arab Republic: An Assessment of Its Failure," and Gordon Torrey, Syrian Politics and the Military (Columbus: Ohio State University Press, 1958).

109. See Kerr, The Arab Cold War.

110. See Amos Perlmutter, "The Arab Military Elite," World Politics 22 (January 1970): 269-300; G. Ben-Dor, "The Politics of Threat: Military Intervention in the Middle East," Journal of Political and Military Sociology 1 (Spring 1973): 57-69.

111. See Ben-Dor, "Unity and Disunity in the Arab World."

112. "Arab Nationalism Today," Middle East Review 2 (Winter 1978-79): 51.

113. On this, see Ben-Dor, "Federalism in the Arab World," p. 202; Peter K. Bechtold, "New Attempts at Arab Co-operation: The Federation of Arab Republics, 1971-?" Middle East Journal 27 (Spring 1973): 152-72; and Varda Ben-Zvi, "From 'The Tripoli Charter States' to the 'Federation of Arab Republics,'" paper pre-

pared for the Colloquium on the Middle East between 1967 and 1973, Shiloah Center for Middle Eastern and African Studies, Tel Aviv University, December 1974.

114. Al-Ahram, May 26, 1974 (English version from Ben-Zvi, p. 19).

115. Leiden, "Arab Nationalism Today," p. 49.

116. See Haim, Arab Nationalism, "Introduction."

117. Quoted in ibid., p. 164.

118. Haim, The Ba'ath in Syria, p. 134.

119. Al-Bazzaz, This Is Our Nationalism (Cairo: 1963), p. 188 (in Arabic): quoted in Najm A. Bezirgan, "Islam and Arab Nationalism," Middle East Review 1 (Winter 1978-79): 41.

120. Ibid.

121. Quoted in ibid.

122. Cf. Bernard Lewis, Race and Color in Islam (New York: Harper, 1971).

123. Marrus, "Zionism and the Idea of a Jewish State."

124. Hudson, Arab Politics, p. 38.

125. Ibid., p. 39. Most of the literature on minorities is listed in the bibliography in G. Ben-Dor, The Druzes in Israel. Most of the publications appearing since are listed in two special issues of Middle East Review 9, nos. 1 and 2 (Fall 1976 and Winter 1976-77) on "Ethnic and Religious Minorities in the Middle East."

126. See Peter K. Bechtold, Politics in the Sudan (New York: Praeger, 1976).

127. On this, in addition to the aforementioned, see Moshe Ma'oz, New Syria: Political and Social Changes in the Process of Creating a New Community (Tel Aviv: Dvir, 1974) (in Hebrew).

128. Omran Yahya Feili and Arlene R. Fromchuck, "The Kurdish Struggle for Independence," Middle East Review 9 (Fall 1976): 47-58.

129. This force, set up in Riyadh, Saudi Arabia, in October 1976, originally had small additional contingents from other Arab countries, but these have since been pulled out.

130. Carleton Coon, Caravan (New York: Holt, 1951), quoted in Hudson, Arab Politics, p. 59. This notion is a subject of great controversy among social scientists specializing in the Middle East. Hudson himself adds (ibid.): "But useful as this metaphor is, it too is somewhat misleading in that it exaggerates the separateness of communal identities."

131. Al-Bazzaz, "Military Regimes and Political Stability in Egypt, Iraq and Syria."

132. The table was compiled by Joshua Sinai, on the basis of the following sources: Area Handbooks for Arab Republic of Egypt, Iraq, Hashemite Kingdom of Jordan, Lebanon, and Syrian Arab

Republic (1976, 1975, 1969, 1975, and 1971 respectively) (Washington, D.C.: U.S. Government Printing Office); Hayyim J. Cohen, The Jews of the Middle East, 1860-1972 (New Brunswick, N.J.: Transaction, 1973); Michael Curtis et al., eds., The Palestinians, People, History, Politics, prepared under the auspices of the American Academic Association for Peace in the Middle East (New Brunswick, N.J.: Transaction, 1975); Encyclopaedia Judaica, Vol. VI (New York: Macmillan, 1972); Evyatar Levine and Yaacov Shimoni, eds., Political Dictionary of the Middle East in the 20th Century, rev. ed. (New York: Quadrangle, 1974); Monthly Bulletin of Statistics (New York: Quadrangle, 1974); Anne Sinai and Allen Pollack, eds., The Syrian Arab Republic, A Handbook (New York: American Academic Association for Peace in the Middle East, 1976); The Middle East and North Africa, 1975-76, 22d ed. (London: Europa Publications, 1975); The Palestinians, Report No. 24 (London: Minority Rights Group, 1976); The Statesman's Yearbook, 1975-1976 (New York: St. Martin's Press, 1975).

133. Ajami, "The End of Pan-Arabism," p. 365.

134. George Moutafakis, "The Role of Minorities in the Modern Middle Eastern Societies," Middle East Review 9 (Winter 1976-77): 72. Cf. Elie Kedourie, "Nationalism," in The Chatham House Version and Other Middle Eastern Studies (London: Cass, 1970).

135. See Ben-Dor, The Druzes in Israel, pp. 230-44; G. Ben-Dor, "Electoral Politics and Ethnic Polarization," in The Election in Israel—1977, ed. Asher Arian (Jerusalem: Academic Press, 1980), pp. 171-85; Sammy Smooha, Israel: Pluralism and Conflict; Jacob Landau, The Arabs in Israel: A Political Study (New York: Oxford University Press, 1969); and Sammy Smooha and John E. Hoffman, "Some Problems of Arab-Jewish Coexistence in Israel," Middle East Review 9 (Winter 1976-77): 5-15.

136. "Lebanon, Syria, Jordan and Iraq," in The Middle East: Oil, Conflict and Hope, ed. A. L. Udovitch (Lexington, Mass.: Heath, 1976), p. 272.

137. Ibid.

138. Hudson, Arab Politics, p. 55.

139. Ajami, "The End of Pan-Arabism," p. 365.

140. Halpern, The Politics of Social Change in the Middle East and North Africa, p. 10.

5

Stateness and the Arab-Israeli Conflict

There are many factors that make the Arab-Israeli conflict a
unique international problem.[1] Some of these are widely accepted
as facts of life, others are sources of heated scholarly controversy,
but few serious students of the conflict would dispute that much of
the difficulty of its resolution[2] is due to its complex character.
There are several levels of the Arab-Israeli conflict, with the
concomitant problem that contradictions arise between different
types of logic on each level.

> As a Palestinian scholar recently put it, the Arab-
> Israeli conflict derives its peculiar character from
> the enormous tension that exists among four different
> logics in the Arab world: raison d'état (of the various
> Arab states), raison de la nation (Pan-Arabism),
> raison de la révolution (unification and modernization
> achieved by revolutionary methods) and raison de
> status quo.[3]

Although not in complete agreement with this statement, the present
author acknowledges that it contains a good deal of truth. The
argument can also be made that among the four logics, in this
frame of reference it was raison de la nation that complicated the
conflict most, while raison d'état contributes most to the resolution process. Janice Stein has given an apt definition of interstate
conflict as

> the simultaneous pursuit of incompatible objectives by
> governmental actors often, though not necessarily,
> within the context of a potential military option. . . .
> Incompatibility of objectives is frequently complicated
> by misunderstanding and ineffective communication

between the parties to the conflict. This is not to
suggest that conflict is due to misperception; that
is not "real." Often, however, the intensity of the
conflict is increased by the imperfections and limitations of the human perceptual system in a complicated and uncertain environment. War is one phase
within a conflict; the use of military means by governmental actors in the pursuit of incompatible objectives. It is the most intense phase of a conflict
and its dynamic may be different from other phases. [4]

An examination of the Arab-Israeli conflict, however, reveals its incompatibility with this definition. It is not just an interstate conflict; it encompasses much more. Therefore, before known
methods of conflict reduction can be applied, the Arab-Israeli conflict has to be transformed (at least between the parties interested
in, and seeking, conflict reduction) so that it becomes an interstate
conflict. This is what seems to have occurred between Egypt and
Israel, and it is the absence of further transformation that bedevils
the extension and stabilization of the peace process.

What is meant, however, by conflict reduction?

Conflict reduction is much harder to define. Unfortunately, while theorists have devoted a great deal of
attention to defining war, they have spent commen-
surately little time defining peace, the ultimate object of conflict reduction. Peace is not the absence
of conflict; it is rather a change in the rules for
managing conflict. Every social system is characterized by conflict, and very often conflict performs
important and creative functions. The issue is not
the presence or absence of conflict; it is the method
of handling conflict which distinguishes peace from
war. Peace can therefore be defined as "ideal
conflict."

Effective conflict management does not imply
simply a reduction in the intensity of means used by
the participants. Rather, the nature of the conflictual
relationship must be changed so that the parties may
focus constructively on the issues in dispute and
arrive at mutually satisfactory compromises. Nor
is there the expectation that an obvious compromise
always exists and is attainable or that new issues of
conflict will not arise in the future. Indeed, it is
expected that as the parties continue to interact, new

incompatibilities will continue to emerge. When incompatibilities arise, however, both parties agree that they will not resort to coercion to "settle" the issues; moreover, they both agree that they will attempt to settle the issues, rather than leave them in abeyance as a substitute for compromise. The relationship between the belligerents is thereby transformed so that conflict is handled within a context of cooperation. Such a relationship is defined as "peaceful," for there is mutual agreement on the methods of managing conflict.[5]

It is obvious, however, that "peace as ideal conflict" does not simply spring into independent existence where parties are involved in an international conflict. Adversaries must grant each other not only the legitimacy of existence but also the legitimacy of pursuing their own interests (even if these involve mutual incompatibilities); in short, they must regard each other through the prism of raison d'état. To achieve this, they must transform a nonstate conflict into an interstate conflict: a task not very adequately explored in the theoretical literature.

Even so, the psychological perspective, for instance, can give rise to some valuable insights into the problem, especially the "cognitive interaction model of conflict,"[6] which is useful because it explicitly deals with the saliency of stateness in conflict resolution. The starting point of this model states "that there are many international situations in which conflict is generated less by conflicting interests (e.g., scarce resources) than by diverging patterns of understanding (e.g., different epistemologies)."[7]

This point may be rather evident after it is made, but, as has been seen, the theoretical literature, by and large, is oriented toward interstate conflict in which the incompatibilities tend to be the conflicting interests themselves. Yet, when the conflict is cultural (as the Arab-Israeli conflict undoubtedly has been),[8] even a seemingly reasonable compromise on issues of interest as such "is likely to be less than fully satisfactory for either of the players, and is likely to lead to other problems because the basic conflict of understanding has not been dealt with."[9] The problem is one of inability to communicate and thus an inability to define issues, interests, and their possible mutually satisfactory settlement, due to the fact that the adversaries live, think, and speak in incompatible paradigms.[10] This is what will be labeled here a paradigmatic conflict, the resolution of which as such appears to be impossible: prior to conflict resolution, there must first be a transformation that will normalize or routinize the conflict, enabling the gap between the competing paradigms to be bridged. This cannot be done, according to the cognitive interaction model, through the customary arbitration of third parties, for example. Something more conceptual is required. Glenn and his colleagues offer the concept of the "mediating structure," arguing that it is the availability of such structures that determines the applicability of the model to international conflict.

A mediating structure is "a system of ideas—a partial cognitive structure—either actually or potentially shared by the parties to the conflict; the mediating structure affects the self-images of the parties."[11] Three different types of mediating structures are identified: in order of importance, they are institutionalized international bodies, a common culture, and the concept of the sovereign state.[12] In their 1970 assessment, Glenn and his colleagues started out by analyzing the concept of the sovereign state, but found it the least important of the three mediating structures. Yet, in retrospect, it appears that this was in fact the most important mediating structure in the transformation of the Egyptian-Israeli conflict to a nonparadigmatic one and, in foresight, it can be argued that a similar transformation is necessary for the other actors in the conflict also, as a precondition for further progress toward stable peace.

How does the concept of the sovereign state help bridge the cognitive gap? What are its advantages and disadvantages?

> First of all, the main accomplishment of the structure is that it maintains distance between parties likely to come into conflict. This makes a degree of conflict management possible. The very fact that parties appear as reciprocally external within the structure makes the system one to which such models as game theory are often applicable. This, as we have seen in the case of marital conflict, is in itself enough to insure that full emotional resolution of conflict cannot take place. The international structure of sovereign states is found to retain a certain level of tension, as must any competitive system.
>
> The system of sovereign states can also be considered within the context of the cognitive interaction model: it provides all parties with a modicum of similarity of their self-images: countries are states; men are citizens. Here, however, the shortcomings of the structure as a mediator are even more evident: the concept of "legitimate state" is not the same in all cultures, and the common cultural identity derived

from this definition is, by extension (a satisfactory definition by intension is lacking), a shallow one. Thus the structure of the "concert of nations," while it undeniably does play a mediating role, does not take account of the preoccupations pointed out by the cognitive interaction model.[13]

The potential accomplishments are obvious, and need no further explanation. As to the shortcomings, it seems obvious that the other two mediating structures have been even less effective; that "a limited way" of mediating, if it is conceptually significant, still makes a qualitative difference in conflict transformation; and that the concept of state is in fact culturally much less divergent than Glenn and his colleagues suggest. Indeed, the commonality of perception resulting from mutual attitudes of stateness (as can be seen theoretically in Nettl's analysis and can be observed empirically in the Egyptian-Israeli case) is far from shallow. In short, the immense potential inherent in the state is much greater than indicated in the 1970 formulation of the cognitive model.

This underestimation probably has to do with the exaggerated dichotomy (following traditional concepts of Gemeinschaft and Gesellschaft) between nation-state and state-nation:

> A nation-state is a political unit characterized primarily by a community of feeling and tradition shared by its citizens (associative) and only secondarily by the presence of a unifying public administration (abstractive). It is congruent with the sociological concept of Gemeinschaft. . . . The cognitive emphasis in a nation-state is associative.
>
> In the event that considerations of public administration, rather than ethnicity, predominate, the unit is a state-nation. This unit is abstractive in emphasis; many ethnic minorities may share a geographical area and citizenship. The concept of state-nation is congruent with the idea of Gesellschaft. The cognitive emphasis of the state-nation is abstractive.[14]

This seems almost a false dichotomy: not only are there numerous problems in making a distinction of this kind with any degree of accuracy, but the entire point of the state being a mediating structure is that, whatever the type of community contained in its territory, the state as a unit has a logic of its own.

Eventually, peace must be made by statesmen pursuing interests of state, statesmen who may or may not be (perhaps are not likely to be) nationalists pursuing the interests of nation. In a state, if it is a state, the interests and perceptions here falsely identified with "public administration" (is this a differentiated, institutionalized structure of the state?) by definition predominate, even if the "community of feeling and tradition" is very strong. If these two tendencies clash with the increase in stateness, state interests win: they change the patterns of conflict. In this connection, note the assessment in the important article by Ajami:

> The unity forced onto the Arab world by the Arab-Israeli conflict has eroded—perhaps less dramatically than in other areas, but eroded nonetheless. Whatever the future shape of the conflict between the Arab states and Israel, the Sadat diplomacy has dragged the Arabs—with great numbers of them shouting, objecting, feeling violated and betrayed—into the modern game of states. The conflict is no longer about Israel's existence, but about its boundaries; and in inter-Arab affairs, the leading military state has for all appearances rejected the inter-Arab division of labor that assigned it the principal obligation for a pan-Arab cause.[15]

The "modern game of states" in this phase of the conflict has proven to be stronger than ethnic or communal considerations. As might have been expected, raison d'état has triumphed.

This study is in substantial agreement with the school of thought about the nature of peace that accommodates elements both of Fisher's conception of "fractionating" conflict—that is, turning big issues into small ones[16]—and, to a greater extent, Etzioni's idea of "encapsulating" conflict[17]—that is, ruling out military force and legitimizing other modes of conflict. This statement of credo is important not only for the purpose of presenting intellectual credentials, but also for depicting a conceptual image of peace, for the present analysis neither attempts to give specific advice to the policy maker nor tries to describe a utopian state of affairs to be pursued as an ideal. Rather, it makes an effort to put forth a model of peace that seems applicable to the Middle East, in terms of an attainable transformation of the relationships between the political systems in the region. A number of normative prescriptions on the general level can be derived from this model,[18] several of which should be of interest to the policy-making community, at least—but not exclusively—for enriching its own thinking about the issues raised here.

Obviously, the approach advocated is essentially political; that is, it is inherent in the argument presented that the Arab-Israeli conflict is basically a series of incompatibilities involving such eminently political issues as the rights of political communities to exist, the nature of their manifestations, their territorial dimensions, their mutual interaction and interrelationship, the balance of power between them, their ability to mobilize third-party support, and the like. These political incompatibilities are what the conflict is about.[19] Although these issues are undoubtedly greatly influenced by psychological, cultural, economic, and other such exogenous factors, the present approach basically conceives of the conflict as a political system, surrounded by an environment[20] containing many important nonpolitical variables (obviously, linked by a feedback network). And yet, political problems necessitate, above all, political solutions. No good cause is served by conflict analysis that ignores or underemphasizes political incompatibilities, just as little can be explained by political scientists who want to read politics out of political science. No socioeconomic processes or cultural-psychological factors can automatically explain the conduct or transformation of a political conflict.[21] As Rousseau argued, conflict is about politics. And the essence of good politics remains the judicious use of the stick and the carrot—as has been known at least since Machiavelli.[22]

Similarly, one should be on guard against the obviously attractive humanistic fallacies of the romantic approach to peace. Nothing could be more appealing to the mind—and above all, the heart—of the liberal humanist in the Judeo-Christian (or indeed, any other) tradition than the belief that mutual resolutions like "no more war, no more bloodshed" can eventually lead to a utopia in which conflict will wither away. Conflicts do not tend to wither away any more than do states; they can be transformed, reduced, and contained (in very exceptional cases, even resolved) by creative acts of realistic statesmanship. Romantic conceptions of normalization—according to which diplomatic relations, international trade, more intensive movement of people across boundaries, cultural exchanges, and the like are the key to stabilizing peace—seem not only demonstrably false but also outright dangerous, for they divert attention from the essential and make people put their faith in the (politically) trivial. History has shown that most wars have started in "normalized" situations; there is no particular reason to assume that the Arab-Israeli conflict is any more susceptible to this kind of false stabilization than other, no less intensive, conflicts. Thus, while the present author personally identifies strongly with humanistic, antiviolent traditions and firmly believes that the normalization of relations between peoples is a lofty ideal and a

supreme value in its own right, it seems preferable to seek ways
to stabilize peace in the political realm. If this means a return to
realpolitik, so be it. [23]

In attempts over the years to make sense of the complexities
of the Arab-Israeli conflict, this author has worked out a graphic
way of identifying the elements of the conflict. Though developed
independently, some of these ideas are akin to those of the cognitive-
interaction model. [24]

The depth and various levels of Arab hostility toward Israel
throughout the conflict, and some of the issues arising, are depicted in Figure 1 as four concentric circles, each external circle
representing the widening scope of the conflict.

FIGURE 1

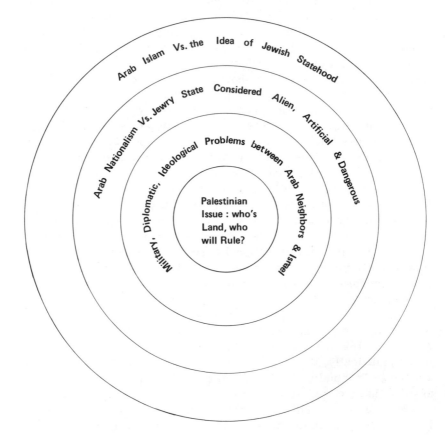

The concomitant expansion of Arab participation in the conflict may also be usefully represented as four widening circles (Figure 2), the expansion being in inverse proportion to the intensity of commitment to the Arab cause against Israel.

FIGURE 2

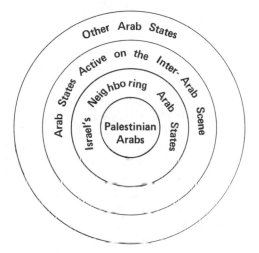

Needless to say, the resulting Arab coalitions are very complex, heterogeneous, and fluid.[25]

Finally, for the sake of symmetry if not historical perspective, the Jewish side in the conflict can also be depicted in circles (Figure 3), expressing a parallel idea.[26]

FIGURE 3

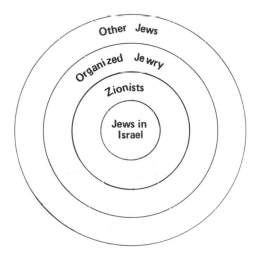

The most important graphic is the first one, which represents the levels of the conflict. Each of these levels, if regarded in relative isolation, would theoretically amount to one particular type of conflict. The inner circle represents the makings of a civil war: two political communities claiming peoplehood struggle for the control of a defined territory. The second circle represents interstate conflict over concrete issues between countries with adjacent territories. The third circle represents ideological conflict of transstate dimensions, theoretically divorced from concrete territorial questions. The fourth circle represents a veritable clash of civilizations—"epistemological conflict."[27] All this adds up to a multidimensional conflict of many elements and many types of logic.[28]

Of course, in the real world of politics these distinctions are very difficult to make, particularly since many actors pursue the conflicts simultaneously. For instance, the Libyan leader, Qadhafi, enthusiastically argues the Palestinian case, supports the Arab confrontation states, presents himself as Nasser's heir in the leadership of pan-Arabism[29] and integrates all this in an ideology of "the Third Theory," embedded in a political doctrine of Islam.[30] Because he pursues the conflict on many levels at once, his hostility to Israel is particularly high. Moreover, since his country has ample financial resources and is remote from Israel, for him the costs of pursuing an ideologically intense conflict are relatively low.[31] Furthermore, since the geographical distance also means that concrete interstate issues between his country and Israel do not really exist, he tends to emphasize either the ideological causes important to him or his commitment to the causes important to others. Since he has nothing concrete at stake, there is nothing concrete to be offered to him in order to induce him to lower the level of hostility. Yet, as long as the Arab world was structured so as to make the raison d'état of the individual states secondary to the raison de la nation arabe (qawmiyya = pan-Arabism), many Arab leaders could not break out of the captivity of the four circles to concentrate on the circle most relevant to them—the second (interstate) circle—because Qadhafi and many Qadhafi-like elements were a primary source to which they were accountable.[32] It was only this military/diplomatic/political arena that contained the potential for the transformation of the paradigmatic conflict to an interstate conflict that would be subject to normal measures and patterns of conflict reduction. The resulting confusion made it very difficult for the Arab countries to develop a practical stand on the Israeli question, something that Kerr in 1972 called a "debilitating liability."[33]

Unfortunately, conflicts have dynamics of their own, and more often than not this dynamic element tends to be escalatory. This has been clearly demonstrated in the Arab-Israeli conflict. Although ideological and civilizational elements have been present from the beginning,[34] one could reasonably argue that, in practice, as long as the conflict was confined to the territory of Palestine/Land of Israel, it was susceptible to such solutions as partition, a binational state, or a federal union. As has already been elaborated, however, a turning point occurred during the 1936-39 Arab Revolt in Palestine,[35] when a pan-Arabization of the conflict occurred and the Palestinians, confronted with a Zionism they could not overcome by themselves, and attracted by the potentially immense strength of the rest of the Arab world, more or less willingly entered upon a historical process that led to increasing abdication of control over their own fate.[36]

This historical process was instrumental in bringing about the tragedy of the Palestinians. As Malcolm Kerr argues,

> Palestinian interests remained in the hands of non-Palestinian Arab regimes whose interests were bound to be somewhat different. . . . The no-war, no-peace policy of the Arab states was a de facto compromise between their own practical interests and those of the Palestinians.[37]

This uneasy compromise still continues: prime examples are the 1974 decision to establish on territories to be evacuated by Israel a "national authority" (sulta wataniyya), and the arguments surrounding possible Palestinian participation in the Geneva Conference.[38] Yet the Palestinians have been unable to escape being the victims of inter-Arab squabbles that hinder a realistic Arab stand on the Palestine-Israel issue.

> The Arab states used the cause of Palestine against each other, but were unable to agree what else to do with it. . . . And despite their inability to render assistance, the Arab states did succeed in preventing the Palestinians from developing institutions of their own, by means of their insistence on sponsoring and exploiting Palestinian organizations for their own competitive purposes.[39]

The result was the appropriation of control by the Arab states over the fate of the Palestinians. It is necessary to add, however, that while the Arab states by this time had a strong enough sense of stateness to exploit this issue for their own purposes, their state interests had not yet developed to the point where the settlement of the conflict (and the restoration of the fate of the Palestinians to their own hands) was perceived as an imperative.

The resulting state of affairs seems best described as "the dialectics of dependence," which has been elsewhere defined in the following terms:

> In the final analysis, Palestinian wataniyya is the last to be frustrated in the Arab world (perhaps the PLO personifies best Palestinian disposition and dependence), and precisely the most adamant advocates of qawmiyya (i.e., Libyan ruler Qadhafi) insist most adamantly that Palestinian wataniyya also be satisfied. This demonstrates most conspicuously the Palestinian dilemma: there is no Palestinian strength without Arab power, but that which gives strength can also curtail and restrict strength. Those who kept the Palestinian issue alive exploited it mercilessly as a political tool for their own purposes. Those who conquered and salvaged the West Bank and the Gaza Strip ostensibly for the Palestinians also kept it away from them. Those who encourage a Palestinian "front of rejection" also make it totally dependent on the parallel "front of rejection" among the Arab states. Fear of political weakness and the temptation of power led to almost total reliance on the Arab states. Almost total reliance on the Arab states curtailed power while creating the opportunity for accomplishments that could not resolve this basic dilemma. This is the meaning of the dialectics of dependence. [40]

Intended to utilize pan-Arab commitments toward the eventual realization of Palestinian statehood, [41] this dialectical process perhaps originated from the very low level of statelike thinking within the Palestinian leadership in the 1930s. [42] Of course, the Palestinians were a stateless community then, but statelike thinking and behavior are not exclusively the reserve of politicians in existing states.

As has already been explained, Zionist political thought had only a very weak dimension of stateness, but the Zionist organizational structure had a strong statelike character: not so its Palestinian counterpart. Moreover, while a Zionist leader like Ben-Gurion quickly adapted to the statelike logic inherent in the concept of partition, after a short initial argument the Palestinian leadership

(and eventually the leadership of the Arab countries) consistently
rejected partition as a basis for statehood. This rejection took
away from them a potential crucial asset: a territorial base upon
which a statelike community could be built.[43] From then on the
Palestinian leaders necessarily became the fellow travelers of
various Arab leaders, pursuing their own interests.[44] The Palestinians' lack of territory rendered their dependence on the Arab
states absolute, but at least the Arab commitment to their cause
during the high tide of messianic pan-Arab nationalism seemed
equally absolute. But while the search for a territorial base continued, with the Palestinian revolution being exported to Jordan and
Lebanon, it became evident that this was the one thing the Arab
states would always deny the Palestinians. Thus, in late 1948
Egypt crushed the "government of All Palestine" in Gaza, with the
approval of the Arab League.[45] For a long time in the general
Arab aspiration of overcoming Zionism (or at least standing up to
it "with honor"), the Palestinians, lacking their own state and
totally in debt to radical Arab nationalism, have sought to be (in a
variety of ideological ways) the catalysts, modernizers, and at
times, radicalizers of the entire Arab world:[46] a role that a great
many Arabs have come to resent.[47]

Thus, the Palestinians and the Arab states held one another
captive: the Palestinians could not pursue their own "state" interests (which were poorly articulated in the first place) because their
only card was their appeal to pan-Arab nationalism, and this nationalism rejected the legitimacy of state interests; for their part, as
Chapter 4 has demonstrated, the Arab countries could not pursue
their state interests vis-à-vis Israel because their entanglement in
pan-Arab nationalism and their commitment to the Palestinians
made this illegitimate. This lack of "normal" Arab politics (that
is, the absence of the interplay of interests of an established state
system) by definition "denormalized" the Arab-Israeli conflict also.
In a conflict, one views, perceives, and defines one's adversary
through one's own self-definition and perception in politics, to a
very significant extent. An abnormal Arab system resulted in an
abnormal Arab-Israeli conflict; the cognitive tensions and contradictions in Arab politics led to an epistemological-paradigmatic
conflict with Israel that precluded progress toward resolving or
settling the conflict.

An escalatory cycle evolved, which fed upon itself and continued almost unabated: the Palestinian issue contributed to radical
pan-Arabism and radical pan-Arabism kept the region in turmoil
and confronted Israel with a transcendental-messianic ideological
zeal. This was the trend for 30 years after the 1936-39 turning
point. The 1967 war and its aftermath signaled that a second

turning point had arrived, and a new shift became discernible.
Whereas in Israel, as has been seen, it shattered existing forms
and shapes of the territorial <u>fait accompli</u> of the state and infused
the entire political community with unprecedented ideological passion, in the Arab world (surprisingly, perhaps, to the superficial
observer), initial hysteria notwithstanding, an opposite trend pre-
dominated. The gap between Palestinian goals and Arab state
interests widened significantly.[48] To the Palestinians it became
evident that reliance on the messianic goals and promises of pan-
Arabism would lead nowhere in the foreseeable future. By 1967,
indeed, it had merely led to a war in which all hopes of Arab unity
and progress were shattered by a defeat that led to the Israeli conquest of even those parts of Palestine that had been in Arab hands.
Moreover, for a while it appeared that with the lack of any real
fighting capacity of the Arab states, the Palestinians would have to
keep alive the armed struggle more or less on their own. They
attracted increased financial support, managed to recruit greatly
expanded manpower, and became the moral visiting card of the
Arab cause. This led, in turn, to attempts to build an organizational structure run by Palestinians, dedicated to the interests of
Palestinians alone.[49] Ajami's analysis is to the point:

> The Palestinians launched the first post-1967 attack
> against pan-Arabism. Given their predicament, their
> economic and political dependence upon the Arab states
> and their lack of a territorial base, theirs had to be a
> different kind of attack. But there was no doubt that
> those who rallied around Yassir Arafat and George
> Habash in the aftermath of the Six Day War had given
> up on pan-Arabism—the first group in the name of
> Palestinian nationalism, the second in the name of
> social revolution. The duel that raged between the
> Palestinians and the Nasserites from early 1968 until
> Nasser's death in 1970 was in essence a fight about the
> independent rights of Palestinian nationalism. If the
> Arab states could not protect themselves against
> Israel, let alone do something for the Palestinians,
> then the latter were to construct their own independent
> politics. In the final analysis, it was Arafat's brand
> of nationalism, with its pledge of non-intervention in
> the internal affairs of Arab countries, that found its
> way into the organized Arab state system, rather than
> George Habash's revolution. Arafat's narrow focus on
> Palestinian nationalism and his avoidance of social and
> ideological issues were in keeping with the new tenor

of Arab politics, and that is why Arafat's course
found a reasonable measure of support in Riyadh:
in his strict Palestinian nationalism there was an
acceptance of reason of state. The acceptance was
not applicable to the two "sanctuaries," Jordan and
Lebanon, hence the two civil wars in which the
Palestinians came to be involved.[50]

Chapter 4 traced the gradual transformation of inter-Arab
relations, between the mid-1960s and mid-1970s, to a more normal
system of inter-Arab politics. This process had its counterpart in
the Arab-Israeli conflict, which was transformed from the paradigmatic to a more normal pattern also. It did not signify a magic
disappearance of previously existing serious problems, nor did it
necessarily mean that future conflict escalation became impossible
or even unlikely. What it did was open up the possibility of "peace
as ideal conflict" between states, even though, as Stein warns,
"the termination of war may be followed by the escalation of conflict as well as by its reduction."[51]

The watershed of the 1970s has not meant the decline of the
problems, but the rise of the state; it has not meant an end to conflicts, but the shifting from one conception of conflict to another,
more flexible, more normal. For instance, in the case of the
Arab-Israeli conflict, the conception of irreconcilable claims of
nationalistic movements for the same territory is simply incon-
gruent with peace, while conflicts over territories, boundaries,
and incremental advantages between states in a more or less normal situation is not. (Therefore, while a conventional analysis of
the Arab-Israeli conflict will point to 1936-39, 1967, and 1977 as
the main turning points of recent decades, in the long run 1970
may turn out to be equally significant.) Even bearing in mind the
proper notes of caution, and even realizing full well that optimistic
analysts of Middle East politics have more often than not been made
to look like fools, by the late 1970s one could have concluded with
ever so cautious optimism, that the dawn of an age of normal states
in the Middle East was at least in sight. Or, as Ajami picturesquely
put it in 1979, "raison d'état, once an alien and illegitimate doctrine, is gaining ground. Slowly and grimly, with a great deal of
anguish and outright violence, a 'normal' state system is becoming
a fact of life."[52] This is even more visible as the 1980s unfold.

Some of that anguish is revealed in the cries of "treason"
with which many Palestinians and their supporters greeted Egypt's
willingness to conclude peace with Israel without first settling
their problem.[53] Of course, however, if there was treason, it
was raison de la nation that was betrayed in favor of raison d'état.

And the Palestinians and the PLO had started taking part in this treason years earlier. Says Ajami:

> The Palestinians, too, have come to see it this way. Whereas it was once heresy to speak of an independent Palestinian state—after all, Palestine was supposed to be part of a larger Arab entity—the Palestinians have come to realize that they too require the normalcy of statehood. Their view has come to converge with the recognition of most Arab states that their own reason of state vis-à-vis Palestinian claims is best served by the Palestinians acquiring their own territory with all the responsibilities such a process usually entails. This explains President Sadat's insistence during the Camp David negotiations on a linkage between an Egyptian settlement and a framework for the West Bank and Gaza Strip, and explains as well Saudi Arabia's cautious response to the summit.[54]

From the very beginnings of the confrontation with Zionism, the Palestinians vacillated between pan-Arabism (qawmiyya) and state nationalism (wataniyya), at times changing their relative weight and emphasis. Eventually, Palestinian nationalism evolved in a situation where it lacked state sovereignty. After 1948, and even more so after 1967, the Palestinian national movement (nationalism without sovereignty)[55] developed an intense and complicated network of interrelations and interdependencies with the inter-Arab version of qawmiyya (nationalism with multiple sovereignties). Although Palestinians and their cause were an enormous influence in the evolution of pan-Arabism, their fortunes vis-à-vis the Arab states have been dismal, and this experience has further eroded their notion of stateness. As Migdal argues,

> They have become a stateless society whose sociopolitical organization has been limited to the rudimentary structures of segmentary lineages. Palestinians tend to resist regarding the institutions of any state, or even of specifically Palestinian movements, as the most effective decision-making units in their lives. Their behavior is oriented, instead, toward an expressive, ideological support of Palestinian organizations and an instrumental view of the institutions of the various states in which they reside. That instrumentalism is expressed in using institutions of the states to further the goals of the units which they do look to for

effective decision-making in their lives—the family and the clan.[56]

When it became clear, however, that neither the clan nor the family on the substate level nor pan-Arabism on the transstate level could satisfy the national aspirations of the Palestinians at a time when all other Arab states pursued de facto their state (watani) interests, the development of Palestinian state nationalism could not be far away. At the same time, the explicit admission of this development could have been most embarrassing; after all, it was only the loyalty to pan-Arabism (qawmiyya) that enabled the Palestinians to rally the Arab states to their cause, and if they now openly abandoned qawmiyya in favor of wataniyya, would that not constitute convenient grounds for Arabs tired of the Palestinian cause to "abandon the ship"? The resulting dilemmas and the mental gymnastics developed to deal with them are best demonstrated by the relevant articles of the Palestinian National Covenant itself.[57]

Article 1

Palestine is the homeland of the Arab Palestinian People; it is an indivisible part of the Arab homeland, and the Palestinian people are an integral part of the Arab nation.

This is simple enough; though it does identify Palestine as the particular homeland of the Palestinian people, they are an Arab people, and the integration of Palestine with the entire Arab nation is emphasized.

Article 10

Commando action constitutes the nucleus of the Palestinian popular liberation war. This requires its escalation, comprehensiveness, and the mobilization of all the Palestinian popular and educational efforts and their organization and involvement in the armed Palestinian revolution. It also requires among the different groupings of the Palestinian people, and between the Palestinian people and the Arab masses so as to secure the continuation of the revolution, its escalation and victory.

This article is really concerned with the mobilization of the Palestinian masses, and their struggle is identified as an explicitly

watani type: that is, concerned with Palestinian interests only. At
the same time, homage is paid to the idea of unity between the
Palestinians and "the Arab masses." Note that figure of speech,
which avoids the term "Arab states."

Article 11

The Palestinians will have three mottoes:
national (wataniyya) unity, national (qawmiyya) mobilization and liberation.

In this article, "liberation" is clear enough. The call for
unity is again on the level of Palestinians, whereas "mobilization,"
in this phrase, refers to the resources of the Arab nation; hence
wataniyya and qawmiyya are simply combined into one slogan. The
apologia comes in the next article, where the necessity to insist on
their wataniyya "at the present stage" is fiercely defended, while
appropriate homage is paid to pan-Arabism.

Article 12

The Palestinian people believe in Arab Unity.
In order to contribute their share towards the attainment of that objective, however, they must, at the
present stage of their struggle, safeguard their
Palestinian identity and develop their consciousness
of that identity, and oppose any plan that may dissolve or impair it.

Presumably, the phrase that indicates opposition to "any plan
that may dissolve or impair" their Palestinian identity is not directed solely against Israel, but also against Arab political forces
that may want to resolve the Palestinian problem in ways that do
not involve the creation of a Palestinian state. In that sense, this
may be considered as already something of a battle cry against
pan-Arabism as a solution to the Palestinian question.

Article 13

Arab unity and the liberation of Palestine are two
complementary objectives, the attainment of either of
which facilitates the attainment of the other. Thus,
Arab unity leads to the liberation of Palestine; the liberation of Palestine leads to Arab unity; and work towards
the realization of one objective proceeds side by side
with work towards the realization of the other.

This is a final affirmation that Palestinian wataniyya and pan-Arab qawmiyya are but two sides of the same coin, that they do not contradict each other, that they facilitate the accomplishing of mutual objectives. How exactly this logic works in practice is not explained. What is reiterated here is an article of faith; the logic is somewhat doubtful.

In this context, it is instructive to examine just how Palestine is defined, after it has been identified as "the homeland of the Arab Palestinian people [and] an indivisible part of the Arab homeland"[58] in Article 1.

In a single, pointed sentence, Article 2 states: "Palestine, with the boundaries it had during the British mandate, is an indivisible territorial unit." This is a most noteworthy phrase for a number of reasons. First, it challenges and rejects all ideas of partition. (Compare this with the earlier analysis of Israeli partition "rejectionists.") Second, since the British in the 1920s created what is now Jordan out of the original mandated territory the ambiguous formulation of Article 2 leaves open the question of Jordan in relation to Palestine. Third, it presumably soothes the fears of conservative Arab forces concerning possible Palestinian challenges to the territorial status quo in the rest of the Arab world. Finally,—astoundingly for a radical, revolutionary, anti-imperialist movement—it sanctifies—in fact defines—the homeland in terms of boundaries created by a colonial power. There is not even a reference to the pan-Arab tenet that inter-Arab boundaries are artificial and should be abolished in favor of a united Arab entity. Not only are the boundaries of Palestine sanctified, but the legitimacy of the British mandate is retrospectively recognized!

While the rejection of partition merely reiterates an age-old policy of the Palestinian nonstatelike leadership,[59] it can be said that good sense is shown in the implication that, although created by the colonial powers, the present order in the Middle East (as elsewhere in the postcolonial world) should constitute the basis for the territorial status quo.

Mental gymnastics aside, any thorough examination of the evolution of Palestinian nationalist thought[60] clearly demonstrates that vis-à-vis pan-Arab ideals, at least, the notion of Palestinian state interests has become progressively stronger; in fact, by the late 1970s it came to dominate in the Palestinian mind the traditional pan-Arab orientation. To this extent, the ideals of pan-Arabism have been betrayed not just by the Egyptians but also by the Palestinians; but there is nothing more natural than the evolution of the logic of concrete stateness at the expense of unattainable transstate ideals. Even so, while Palestinian political thinking has become more state-oriented (that is, more political), it often still expresses itself vis-à-vis the relationship with Israel in terms of a total societal confrontation (that is, encompassing all the concentric circles of the model), lacking altogether those elements increasingly evident in the policies of the Arab states in general and of Egypt in particular. Note the argument in one of the Fatah movement's publications:

> The liberation action is not only the removal of an armed imperialist base, but, more important—it is the destruction of a society. [Our] armed violence will be expressed in many ways. In addition to the destruction of the military force of the Zionist occupying state, it will also be turned toward the destruction of the means of life of Zionist society in all their forms—industrial, agricultural, and financial. The armed violence must seek to destroy the military, political, economic, financial, and ideological institutions of the Zionist occupying state, so as to prevent all possibility of the growth of a new Zionist society. The aim of the Palestine liberation war is not only to inflict a military defeat but also to destroy the Zionist character of the occupied land, whether it is human or social.[61]

This is a classic description of the aims of a party to a paradigmatic conflict. In this sense, if this particular pamphlet is any indication, while the Palestinian leadership has made great progress by adopting a statelike posture in inter-Arab affairs, on the question of Israel it seems to be a political phase or two behind the leadership of the Arab states. This ought not to be particularly surprising: the lack of a state should, and does, make a difference in the evolution of political patterns of thought and behavior. Elsewhere[62] an attempt has been made to present a detailed analysis of the role and patterns of the Palestinians in inter-Arab politics, in six stages up to the mid-1970s, and it was found that in most instances the Palestinians did, indeed, tend to follow a political pattern that had characterized the Arab states one stage (and at times even two stages) previously. There was clearly a political gap between the Arab state and this salient Arab nonstate actor. "This gap, which shows how the patterns of Palestinian political competition become distorted in terms of time compared to the sovereign Arab states, may be referred to in theoretical terms as a 'sovereignty lag.'"[63] Perhaps "stateness lag" would be a better term, as an addition to Nettl's conceptual framework.

Of course, a "chicken-and-egg" argument may be made on this point: the Palestinians lack a state, thus their thinking is not statelike; give them a state, and their thinking will change. Perhaps this argument does not lack sound logic, but a great many interim attempts (for example, Sadat's challenge to the Palestinians to establish a government in exile,[64] surreptitious American and Israeli efforts to negotiate with PLO-affiliated leaders, and, above all, the evidence of history) should be regarded as at least as important as a speculative assumption based on a dubious logic. In this context, one may well speculate (since the chicken-and-egg approach is itself speculative) what course the annals of the Palestinians and the Arab-Israeli conflict would have taken, had a Palestinian equivalent of a postulative-cognitive Ben-Gurion also grasped the logic of stateness inherent in partition, and had such a leader in 1937 managed to rally the badly factionalized Palestinian political elite behind the idea of a Palestinian state in a partitioned Palestine. Perhaps such a Palestinian Ben-Gurion could have helped to set in motion a train of events that would have resulted in the creation of an Arab state in three-fourths of Western Palestine with no wars and no refugees?[65] Along the same lines, one may well ask what fortunes would have awaited the Palestinians— and their neighbors—had the Palestinians not rejected the 1947 U.N. partition plan, which clearly would have been the statelike thing to do. A Palestinian state could have been created in 46 percent of Western (mandatory?) Palestine, again without wars or refugees, without the Palestinians having to grant a Jewish state full legitimacy at the time. These things, as one knows, did not happen. This in itself is not a decisive argument, but it does show that unstatelike thinking results in a failure to seize opportunities that statelike thinking would be quick to grasp (as was amply demonstrated in Ben-Gurion's case).

It is not the intention here to offer solutions to the Palestinian problem,[66] but it is clear to all concerned[67] that if a stable, peaceful relationship is to develop between Arabs and Israelis, the Palestinian problem (whether considered the heart of the conflict or merely a symptom) must be settled, for "the Palestinians . . . are real people, with a real problem, the solution of which is long overdue."[68] Real people will find solutions to real political problems in some statelike framework, whether independently, federated with Israel, Jordan, both, or in some other way.[69] All this requires a comprehensive peace settlement, which must be negotiated; for realistic negotiations, one must have a statelike political logic. On that score, Palestinian history has been far from encouraging, for levels of stateness can be attained without a state, as is demonstrated by the Zionist experience.

Changes do occur, however, in the Arab-Israeli conflict, and sometimes they are so rapid as to leave even the best-informed minds adrift. Note the case of Dr. Boutros Boutros-Ghali who, as acting foreign minister and minister of state for external affairs in Egypt, accompanied Sadat to Jerusalem and was instrumental in negotiating the Egyptian-Israeli peace treaty. Although his writings after the October War were among the harbingers of a new Egyptian attitude evolving toward Israel,[70] as late as 1976 he wrote:

> No formula for peace is of the slightest value if it is not sanctioned by the community of Arab states. Any attempt, therefore, to obtain interim agreements through bilateral arrangements made with separate Arab states can do nothing more than serve the aspirations of certain American or Israeli circles. In reality, such an attempt has no chance of success, for no Arab state can possibly allow itself to betray its own sense of being Arab.[71]

Yet within a couple of years, Ghali, guided by raison d'état, was to assist in the negotiating of just such an interim agreement, a treaty that conformed almost exactly to the formula so emphatically rejected above, while obviously still following a raison de la nation.

The escalatory cycle has been broken. The circles of the conflict no longer necessarily reinforce, or feed upon, one another. The evolution of stateness by necessity has transferred the emphasis to the domain of the second circle, the only one in which substantial conflict reduction has indeed been possible.[72] This is not a unilinear development; reversals are possible. Statelike evolution is not a deterministic process. Furthermore, even a relatively normal system of states is not a utopia. As Ajami warns,

> In a world of states we cannot be sanguine about saying that a state system has been normalized. . . . Counter-elites and young officers may rebel; not in the name of pan-Arabism, but because they have a better cure for the ailment of the state. And in a situation of that kind, "betrayal" of obligations to other states could be a convenient justification for a political game that remains dangerous and deadly.[73]

It is clear that for the time being, at least, the tide has turned. It cannot be a coincidence that the most statelike Arab country, Egypt, has been the first to make peace with Israel (while the least ideologically hostile Arab country, Lebanon, is also one of the least statelike and has thus been unable to contribute to the peace process).[74] This also creates a situation in which Israel's actions make more difference than ever before. In earlier stages of the conflict, Israeli actions could be (and were) easily and frequently misperceived because of the paradigmatic nature of the conflict.[75] Now that stateness as a mediating structure between Israel and at least some of the Arab states is finally very much in existence, the more statelike Israel is, the more it can contribute to the progress of the peace process.[76]

What kind of stable peace can one realistically expect to emerge from the next, more statelike, stage of the Arab-Israeli conflict?[77] By and large, as has been noted, modern conflict theory states that "peace" does not necessarily mean "conflict resolution" or "conflict termination."[78] It does mean conflict reduction and a substantial transformation in the patterns of conflict management. The Arab-Israeli conflict is a set of interactions constituting a subsystem of the Middle East regional political system. If this were otherwise, and if the Egyptian-Israeli bilateral relationship could be detached from the regional system as a whole, the problems would be altogether different. This, however, is decidedly not the case. A stable peace between Israel and Egypt is inconceivable in a dramatically unstable environment that threatens each of the two as well as their fledgling peaceful bilateral relationship. Stable peace is attainable only in a relatively stable region. Since the Middle East region as a whole has been characterized by endless conflicts from time immemorial,[79] the idea of stable peace necessitates a regionwide realignment of forces and a transformation of political relationships. (One hesitates to use the grandiose term "new regional order," which may have undesirable connotations.) Thus, stabilizing peace between Egypt and Israel is a tall order that must be analyzed in a regionwide context; alternatively formulated, one may go so far as to argue that the term "stable peace between Egypt and Israel" is almost meaningless while the Middle East as a whole stays as it is.

As argued before, peace—and, therefore, stable peace—does not necessitate the ending of conflict. A stable peace in the present context does not, therefore, mean the end of the Arab-Israeli conflict. In the foreseeable future—in almost any conceivable scenario—many major incompatibilities between Israel and the Arab states will continue to exist. They can be dealt with, however, in a variety of ways consistent with peaceful relations between states. Similarly, relative stabilization of the region will not do away with most of the conflicts in inter-Arab relations, inside the Arab countries, between the Arabs and non-Arabs, and the like. (The linkages between these conflicts and the Arab-Israeli conflict have been discussed in Chapter 4.)[80]

On the other hand, in order to accomplish a minimal degree of stability, peace should exclude one extreme type of conflict: in Kissingerian terms, the "revisionist conflict."[81] By this is meant the exclusion of incompatibilities that revolve around the right of the actors to exist and to interact, which incompatibilities, by their very nature, challenge any institutionalized set of rules of the regional political "game." This does not mean the suppression of all radical forces as such; in fact, it only means also harnessing radical forces into a system of interaction in which the idea of legitimate participation is well accepted—a system that allows for radical action as long as it threatens neither the existence of the actors nor the accepted modes for conducting conflict between them. Furthermore, it is important to emphasize that stable peace means dynamic peace. Indeed, just as peace must allow for collaboration as well as conflict, it must also allow for change as well as continuity.[82] Stability is not identical with continuity; indeed, there is nothing more dangerous to stability than equating it with freezing the status quo at a given point in time. In the Middle East no such peace can endure for long. Conceivably, it could have endured only on one condition, or, rather, according to one (highly unlikely) scenario: the unambiguous, permanent division of the Middle East into clear spheres of influence by the superpowers, creating a new "iron curtain reality." For many reasons, however, which are both obvious and irrelevant in this present study, such a state of affairs in the foreseeable future is highly improbable.[83]

There have been many revisionist forces in the Middle East. The most important of these (notwithstanding its image as a status quo power) has been Israel itself, albeit reluctantly. Its right of existence challenged and its legitimacy denied, it has built up immense (in regional terms) military clout and a special relationship with the world's greatest power and has developed many other crucially important political resources—without, however, having been allowed to play a role in its surroundings remotely proportionate to, or commensurate with, its potential, capabilities, and resources. Thus, one of the key powers in the region has been forced into virtual isolation, causing a major distortion of the configuration of power in the area. Out of this position of substantial isolation, Israel has still managed to make its weight felt in its immediate vicinity on a number of occasions. There is certainly more than a grain of truth to the argument that Israel's might contributed quite decisively on more than one occasion to the continued existence of pro-Western regimes in Jordan and Lebanon. (There is much less truth in the argument concerning Israel's power of deterrence vis-à-vis the major Arab powers.[84] This complex question, however, is not really pertinent to this discussion.)

On the other hand, it can be argued fairly persuasively that these occasions merely heightened the sense of Israel's revisionism (the term obviously used in a special, very broad sense),[85] for its acts protected the weak, minor Arab powers (with whom Israel could not make peace anyway, precisely because of their weakness) from the strong, major Arab powers (with whom peace would have to be made, if it were to be made at all), thus distorting even further the more or less natural outcome of power struggles in the Arab world. This helped Israel to create at least a partial cordon sanitaire in case of war; but to a considerable extent it also distorted a reasonable balance of power in the region. In the absence of peace, this was tolerable. If peace comes, it will cease to be so, for stable peace must rest on the manifestation of the balance of power, not on its distortion.[86] Stable peace can endure only if Israel is allowed to play a regional role commensurate with its resources and potential. These should suffice for an important role as one major power among several in the region; they do not suffice to dominate the region, nor are they adequate, it seems, to play the key role as the holder of the regional balance (an intriguing idea suggested by Nissan Oren).[87] Israel's weight could be made to count in a variety of ways, although obviously not in every case. The nature of the inter Arab system, for example, is such that in some instances its permeability to outside intervention (or even participation) is restricted, even reduced almost to zero, while in other cases the Arab states want to settle their affairs exclusively on their own. There is no point in forcing them to abandon this stance in issue areas of crucial importance and of a specifically Arab character, if these do not involve Israel's interests.

On the other hand, in an era of stable peace Israel must have access to cooperation, alliances, and coalition with as many potential partners as possible, in order to secure its interests and protect its security—and this must include the key Arab states. For this to be effective, first of all Israel should be allowed to play a relatively free role as a regional power, and this concession must be made by the major Arab powers, in addition to Egypt. This would be at the core of the true political meaning of "normalization."[88] (If such a concession were made, it would to some extent blur the often-made distinction between negative and positive peace.)[89] Almost equally important, however, in this case, is that Israel play a flexible role on a relatively nonideological basis (by which is meant low selectivity in choosing partners for alliances, not abandoning one's own values).[90] This involves making choices on the basis of desirable interests such as regional stability, neutralizing revisionist influences, restricting the emergence of a single dominant factor, and other such important pragmatic considerations. Within this framework, while refraining from cynical policies involving "selling" allies and partners "down the river," there will be a need to reassess Israel's traditional policy toward Jordan (indeed, it is already high time such a reassessment was made) and Lebanon. Such a reassessment will not mean assisting in the destruction of these minor powers (indeed, this would amount to unacceptable revisionism), but giving them a role their abilities allow them to play, while possibly enlarging the regional stakes to be played for by the major Arab and other regional powers.[91]

The Egyptian-Israeli peace treaty has a great significance in this respect also. It may well turn out to be the turning point on the road of Israel's quest for legitimacy as a partner in the regional system (normalization!). There is no certainty at all that this will be the case; in fact, the present, almost surprisingly unified and vehement Arab rejection of Egypt's way[92] precludes, for the time being, the acceptance of Israel as such a partner. It is clear, however, that the present state of affairs can only be transitory. The Arabs cannot for long go on excluding both Israel and Egypt (the two mightiest military powers in the area, the latter until recently the leader of the Arab world),[93] from the regional system. Egypt cannot for long consider a partnership with Israel (an alliance of "outcasts" and "pariahs," however mighty) an alternative to a major role in the Middle East if the leadership of the Arab world is lost (which may or may not be the case). Israel may be satisfied in seeing its strongest potential enemy temporarily isolated in the Arab world, but its leadership must surely realize that this will not lead to stable peace; in fact, it may jeopardize peace in the medium or long run.

The logical ideal for Egypt is to have both peace with Israel and a leading role in the region. If this is indeed the Egyptians' desire (and it seems to be so), then they must seek a way for Israel to become a legitimate partner in the region, thus removing the stigma from the Egyptian-Israeli leadership. The question, however, is not just how to accomplish this, but what is the price that Israel will have to pay: and how to persuade it to pay that price?

The price will undoubtedly have to do with the Palestinian question. True, a good case could be made for the next step in the peace process being taken in the direction of Syria, veritably a key country in the present equation.[94] From the Israeli point of view, a settlement on the future of the Golan Heights would not be nearly as painful as a settlement on the future of the Palestinians will undoubtedly be, while the benefits of Syria joining the peace process would be immense and, in fact, might make a decisive difference. On the other hand, it is not likely that Syria will join in, even on the most generous terms for itself, unless a broader arrangement is involved, one that includes at least a provision for settling the Palestinian question. Indeed, this appears to be true for the other major Arab countries as well; to an extent even the Egyptian case is not very different. Although the Egyptian-Israeli treaty is theoretically supposed to stand on its own feet, legally, if no movement is made on the Palestinian issue, and if the question is unresolved after five years, with Egypt still isolated in the Arab world, the future for a stable peace will look bleak, regardless of the legal arguments involved. The political linkage is easy to see, and the subject here is definitely politics.

Much ink has been spilt over the alleged centrality of the Palestinian question in the Arab-Israeli conflict, and on the complex interrelationship between the Palestinian politics and the inter-Arab system.[95] A great deal of the argument is really not very relevant: conflicts evolve dynamically and change their character, and even if it is proved that historically the Palestinian issue was the one that initiated the conflict, because of the dynamics of the conflict it by no means follows that it is the heart of the problem today. Therefore, it is advisable to abandon this centrality argument and to look at the salient considerations as they are at present. First, the autonomy plan agreed upon by Egypt and Israel is an elegant way of agreeing to disagree, postponing consideration of the fundamental components of the Palestinian question for a few years[96] until the Egyptian-Israeli peace changes the situation for the better, forming a new reality in which the resolution of the question may become easier ("creative ambiguity"?!). Second, peace is and will remain unstable until some other major Arab powers join in the process, one way or another. Third, these apparently will not join unless more concessions are made by Israel concerning an independent Palestinian entity; on this point, as discussed more generally earlier, Sadat apparently made a major miscalculation.[97] Finally, the Arab countries insist on the resolution of the Palestinian question, not because of the power of the Palestinians but because the commitment to this cause seems to be well entrenched in the Arab world on both the elite and popular levels, notwithstanding the cynical abuse of the Palestinian issue by the Arabs on numerous occasions. The fact is that an irresistible force (the Arab commitment to a Palestinian state) has met an immovable object (Israel's refusal to agree to such a state). The question is whether one of them will yield, and if so, which. Lacking a positive answer, the question also arises whether, in such a polarized situation, a middle way can be found—not that middle ways are always desirable.

The context of the question should always be kept in mind. The Arab states have, more or less voluntarily, given the Palestinians a semi-veto-power over the possibility of a comprehensive Arab-Israeli peace.[98] They could abrogate this obligation, but they seem absolutely unwilling or unable to do so, especially since their case has been given a good hearing by public opinion around the world. From the Israeli point of view, there seems to be very little that Israel can do to persuade the Arabs to radically change their minds on this issue. If the issue is to be resolved, there are really no good choices for Israel: every solution will mean painful concessions, worrisome uncertainties, risks, problems, emotional turmoil. The choice will be merely between bad and worse.[99] Yet, political reality is a powerful constraint; a settlement with the Palestinians as such (or with Jordan, for that matter) was not worth serious Israeli concessions, but peace with Egypt was apparently worth some substantial concessions. Stabilizing peace in a comprehensive, regional context may be worth truly major concessions.

It is possible that against this background the admission of the Palestinians as a legitimate actor in the system—thus preempting the major source of revisionism[100]—is a reasonable price for Israel to pay, if, in return, its own legitimate position in the system is enhanced to the point where stable peace is a realistic possibility. This admission by Israel will probably involve Jordan, and the links of the Palestinians with Jordan will have to be given concrete political expression (which may in practice take one of a variety of forms),[101] if the move is to be a realistic one. But even in this case, the present form of Israeli political control in the West Bank (and the Gaza Strip) in all probability will not endure. At least, that is what looks likely at this stage, although—because all such analyses should neither transgress the rules of viability nor presume that viable limits remain static—the parameters of what is politically viable change, especially in fluid periods of political history such as the one that has followed Sadat's visit to Jerusalem.

One eminently reasonable option to the problem of the territories would be a federal solution—the classic example of the politics of eating one's cake and having it too. There are dozens of possible variations on this theme—easily available and thoroughly explored in the publications of the Jerusalem Institute for Federal Studies[102]—several of which appear to be equitable and mutually profitable and seem reasonably safe from the security point of view. By definition, however, all federal solutions revolve around shared sovereignty, and thus any federal solution—to some extent symmetrical, to some extent reflecting the asymmetry inevitably inherent in the resources of the partners—must fall short of total Palestinian sovereignty. It is difficult to determine, particularly in the lack of adequate empirical research, to what extent this would be acceptable to the Palestinians, and especially to the key Arab states involved.

This possibility, however, in itself depends on the further evolution of stateness among the parties concerned. Federations or, rather, successful federations are not born of weakness, are not the result of a need to cover the lack of viability of the states concerned. Rather, federalism seems to hold out a greater prospect of success where the states concerned are reasonably well developed. As Valerie Earl argues, "where statehood in any but the most formal or legalistic sense scarcely exists, a discussion of federalism seems highly irrelevant, and a federal system a venture beyond the reach of leaders who must struggle to stay in power and to begin to feed their people."[103] Experiments with federalism in the Arab world to date have not been encouraging.[104] Nevertheless, the increase in the level of stateness that has opened up the possibility of an Arab-Israeli peace may also eventually create the possibility of utilizing a federal approach to the Palestinian problem to promote the peace process. This may be a relatively unlikely solution, however, and possible alternatives have to be seriously considered also.

Again, there is genuine uncertainty about future political viabilities. In this particular case, it is the difficult question of satisfying a complex, fragmented nationalism evolved during the dynamics of an acute conflict. Much depends on how nationalism in general will fare in the Middle East in the next few years, when the Palestinian question will be dealt with. In the context of Arab nationalism, Palestinian nationalism is one of the last major claims that have not yet been satisfied.

Disregarding for the moment the complex interrelationship between the all-Arab qawmiyya and the Palestinian wataniyya,[105] it is suggested that at present the age of nationalism in the Middle East (which has been so dominant in regional politics in the past generation or two) is at its peak, has perhaps even surpassed its peak.[106] That is, the complex, turbulent, and at times violent historical process of transforming imperial provinces, badly fragmented multiple societies, and religiously/ethnically based communities into territorially based states oriented to a dominant center, has not yet been completed, although it has gone a long way toward successful completion—surprisingly rapidly and decisively in the past decade in particular. (It must be said, however, that many reputable scholars dispute this argument.) Federal solutions that may not have been viable at the peak of nationalism may become viable when that peak is surpassed and stateness is on the rise. A major actor in a regional system may be rejected as belonging to another, illegitimate trend claiming national rights at the peak of nationalism, but may be accepted—with or without renouncing or abandoning the argument about the legitimacy of its national aspirations—as a legitimate partner when that peak is surpassed. What has to be done to stabilize peace can be accomplished much more easily when nationalist fervor at least partially subsides, due to the successful institutionalization of the state. If the analysis (or, rather, diagnosis) here presented is wrong, perhaps stable peace will not be attainable at all until the dawn of a regional postnationalist age.

A postnationalist age is of necessity an age of stateness. That the mediating structure of stateness has been instrumental in getting the Egyptians and the Israelis as far along the road to stable peace as they are is itself not only a remarkable accomplishment but also a sign that the postnationalist era has already partially arrived. Yet, inside both Egypt and Israel, as well as other countries involved in the Arab-Israeli conflict, eras of enormous ideological tension such as the age of nationalism do not come to an end without a great deal of anguish, as Ajami puts it. Moreover, in all the countries concerned, the nationalist era is still fighting a rearguard action, as it were. It will not go away without a spirited fight: the battle for peace will continue to be fought between the forces of nationalism and stateness. In the Arab-Israeli conflict it is clear that nations have brought about wars, and states, peace. The ongoing battle between raison de la nation and raison d'état, if not exactly synonymous with, is critically interdependent with the battle between the forces of conflict exacerbation and war on the one hand and conflict reduction and peace on the other.

The fallacy that weak Arab states are "good for Israel" has never been more evident, if it is accepted that Israel's own interest lies above all in peaceful coexistence with its neighbors. Weak Arab states may or may not be able to do well on the battlefield, but they are likely to get involved in wars against Israel anyway. Strong Arab states may potentially pose a more serious challenge to Israel on the battlefield, but they are much less likely to get there in the first place, because for them balance of power, raison d'état, and conflict as competition by nonviolent means with other states pursuing their interests are more meaningful concepts of statecraft than are weak counterparts permeated with the logic of nationalism and revolution (which in a strong state do not capture it but are contained by it).

Stable peace, then, can be achieved only under certain specific conditions (which may not prevail) after making some cruel trade-offs in priorities (which may not be made), which themselves require a great deal of creative statesmanship (which may not materialize). Exogenous factors, particularly of global dimensions, might change the environment in a decisive way. Thus, there is no certainty that the type of stable peace here conceptualized—or indeed, any other stable type of peace—will endure. If, however, the crucial variables dealt with in this book (and, above all, stateness as the key conceptual variable) develop more or less in the way anticipated, a relatively stable peace is attainable. This stable peace will not be an ideal peace.[107] It will not lead to general disarmament, total reconciliation, or termination of conflict. On the contrary, this will be a peace embedded in fluid interaction and lively conflicts, but within institutionalized bounds and rules. True, in the "game of states" (a phrase that seems preferable to "game of nations," which Miles Copeland coined in a somewhat different context) rules may break down, relations may deteriorate, and the always delicate balance of power may even collapse. There is no guarantee that this will not happen in the Middle East. On the other hand, there is at least an equally good chance that the game and its rules <u>will</u> endure (especially when no actor has a strong motivation or a strong capacity to challenge them) and that eventually the habitual legitimate interaction of the actors will lead to improved human relations (not the other way around!).

If peace is <u>not</u> stabilized, a situation will remain in which the Arabs, motivated largely by ideological hostility but also lured by the strong statistical asymmetry of potential resources in their favor, will "gang up" on Israel. In such a situation, Israel would perhaps have to preempt, once more, or even to "deconventionalize"[108] the arms race to maintain a balance; in any case, the dangers of war would be quite immediate. All this may lead to an imposed settlement, a return to the era of interim settlements, a "balance of terror" sustaining a fragile negative peace, or simply an uneasy biding of time—"waiting for Godot," but armed to the teeth. None of these possible developments seems very attractive. True, when discussing the kind of (relatively) stable peace here analyzed, one should keep in mind that it guarantees no absolute security (indeed, there is no absolute security), nor is there any certainty that it will work; but, to paraphrase Churchill, the main argument in its favor is that all other likely alternatives appear to be worse.

To the romantic humanist who believes that peace is made between peoples and not just governments, this may not be good enough. The facts show, however, that the same Egyptian masses that were whipped into a frenzy of anti-Israeli hostility in 1967 and 1973 were the same masses that cheered for peace with Israel in 1977; what changed was the leadership's perception. Egypt's leaders reached the conclusion (via state logic!) that <u>raison d'état</u> necessitated peace with Israel. In the wake of that conclusion, often citing in their speeches passages from Islamic literature that had previously been used to create anti-Israeli (and at times simply anti-Jewish) hysteria, they managed to get the masses out on the streets demonstrating for peace. Fortunately—or unfortunately, depending on one's point of view—the romantic components of the people's ideology proved to be susceptible to manipulation by the state elite. From another point of view, the state elite in Egypt (and Israel) to a significant extent succeeded in harnessing popular emotion to changing (even outright contradictory) goals of state diplomacy. The people, in this case, did not in fact "vote with their feet," as Lenin would have it, against war. The politicans (who, in this case, were statesmen in the most literal sense of this frequently misused term) "voted" with their minds: by their reasoning, the costs made the continuation of intense conflict a bad bargain for their states. As John Dewey once wryly observed, "sometimes men do not decide their controversies, but get over them."[109]

Deutsch persuasively argues that

> actual conflicts among states often resemble mixtures
> of fights, games and debates, with this or that element
> predominating in the combination at different times
> and places. The art of statesmen, governments and
> responsible citizens then consists in managing these
> international conflicts so as to keep them within
> tolerable bounds; to safeguard as far as practicable
> the current national interests while these interests
> continue to evolve and change; to gain time and strength;
> and to ensure the national survival.[110]

Nations "fight"; states conduct "games and debates."[111] Nations confront each other mostly in paradigmatic conflict; states are more frequently able to routinize and normalize conflict. Of course, even in such cases, conflicts do not just disappear; political reality does not become a stasis. The function of a state system is not to worship the status quo or to suppress all conflict. The function of the system, as George F. Kennan puts it, is

> not to inhibit [the] process of change by imposing a
> legal straight jacket upon it but rather to facilitate it;

to ease its transition, to temper the asperities to which
it often leads, to isolate and moderate the conflict to
which it gives rise, and to see that these conflicts do
not assume forms too unsettling for international life
in general.[112]

This can be done only by states. To return to Ibn Khaldun's
terms, it may be said that an Arab world caught up in the mystique
of the caliphate cannot tolerate the reality of the mulk. Only when
the caliphate is recognized for what it is—a dream, a utopia, a fig-
ment of the imagination—can the Arabs live with the reality and
logic of the mulk. And only when the Arabs learn to accept the fact
that they live in mulks will they learn to tolerate what the logic of
the caliphate, however, forever rejects: a Jewish mulk.

NOTES

1. Fifteen (!) factors have been identified and described elsewhere. See G. Ben-Dor, "Conflict Reduction Through Negative
Peace: Exploring the Future of the Arab-Israeli Conflict," in Termination of Wars, ed. Nissan Oren (Jerusalem: Leonard Davis
Institute for International Affairs, Hebrew University, forthcoming).
2. On forms of conflict resolution, management, reduction,
and termination, see Juergen Dedring, Recent Advances in Peace
and Conflict Research: A Critical Survey (Beverly Hills and London:
Sage, 1970) (with its most extensive bibliography); and Janice Gross
Stein, "War Termination and Conflict Reduction or, How Wars
Should End," in Jerusalem Journal of International Affairs 1 (Fall
1975): 1-27, and the sources cited there. Numerous relevant items
are listed in G. Ben-Dor, "Conflict Reduction Through Negative
Peace," in The Palestinians and the Middle East Conflict: Studies
in Their History, Sociology and Politics, ed. Gabriel Ben-Dor
(Ramat Gan: Turtledove, 1978). Yet another general survey of the
literature is to be found in Avner Yaniv, "Conflict Theory and the
Arab-Israeli Conflict," Jerusalem Journal of International Relations
3 (Fall 1977): 71-95.
3. Shlomo Aronson, "David Ben-Gurion: Israel's Democratic
Bismarck and His Heirs, 1949-1967," in idem, Conflict and Bargaining in the Middle East (Baltimore, Md.: Johns Hopkins University Press, 1978), p. 361.
4. Stein, p. 15.
5. Stein, pp. 15-16. The term "ideal conflict" is taken from
Kenneth E. Boulding, "Toward a Theory of Peace," in International
Conflict and Behavioral Science, ed. Roger Fisher (New York:
Basic Books, 1964), pp. 70-88.

6. Edmund S. Glenn et al., "A Cognitive Interaction Model to Analyze Culture Conflict in International Relations," Journal of Conflict Resolution 14 (1) (March 1970): 35-48.

7. Ibid., p. 36.

8. On its cultural/attitudinal aspects see, for instance, Y. Harkabi, Arab Attitudes to Israel (Jerusalem: Keter, 1972) and the provocative work by Gil Carl AlRoy, Behind the Middle East Conflict: The Real Impasse between Arab and Jew (New York: Putnam, 1974). On the resulting problems, see G. Ben-Dor, "Miscommunication and Fallacies in the Arab-Israeli Conflict," in Images and Reality in World Politics, ed. Nissan Oren (Jerusalem: Leonard Davis Institute for International Affairs, Hebrew University, forthcoming).

9. Glenn et al., "A Cognitive Interaction Model," p. 35.

10. As defined in Thomas Kuhn, The Structure of Scientific Revolutions (Chicago: University of Chicago Press, 1968).

11. Glenn et al., "A Cognitive Interaction Model," p. 37.

12. Ibid., pp. 38-39.

13. Ibid., p. 38.

14. Ibid., p. 45.

15. Fouad Ajami, "The End of Pan-Arabism," Foreign Affairs 57 (27) (Winter 1978-79): 355-73.

16. Roger Fisher, "Fractionating Conflict," in International Conflict and Behavioral Science, ed. Roger Fisher (New York: Free Press, 1964), pp. 91-109.

17. Amitai Etzioni, "On Self-Encapsulating Conflicts," Journal of Conflict Resolutions 8 (3) (September 1964): 242-55.

18. "We may think of models as serving, more or less imperfectly, four distinct functions: the organizing, the heuristic, the productive and the measuring." From Karl W. Deutsch, The Nerves of Government: Models of Political Communication and Control (New York: Free Press, 1966), p. 8. Explanatory functions in this view are treated as special cases of the organizing function.

19. For innumerable examples, see the comprehensive survey edited by John Norton Moore, The Arab-Israeli Conflict, 3 vols. (Princeton, N.J.: Princeton University Press, 1974).

20. See Ch. 1, "Peace and Conflict Systems," in Dedring, Recent Advances in Peace and Conflict Research, pp. 33-53.

21. The present author thinks, therefore, that in 1977 Sadat was either wrong, misunderstood, or inarticulate in saying that "70% of the conflict is psychological," unless he meant that incompatible logics created what he termed a "psychological" gap between the parties.

22. And, in some ways, as has been seen, even earlier, at least since Ibn Khaldun.

23. Variations on the theme of the "romantic" approach to peace can be found in parts of the "human relations" approach as well. See Dedring, passim.

24. Surprisingly, there is a similar formulation in the work of a well-known Egyptian author and journalist whose earlier writings were harbingers of changes to come in Egyptian attitudes to Israel. See Mohammed Sid-Ahmed, "Is an Egyptian-Israeli Peace Treaty Conducive to an Overall Middle East Peace?" Center for International and Strategic Affairs, University of California, Los Angeles, Working Paper No. 24, May 1980, p. 5.

The three models of the Arab-Israeli conflict described in this chapter are discussed in detail in G. Ben-Dor, "Conflict Reduction Through Negative Peace," and idem, "Nationalism without Sovereignty and Nationalism with Multiple Sovereignties: The Palestinians and Inter-Arab Relations," The Palestinians and the Middle East Conflict: Studies in Their History, Sociology and Politics, ed. G. Ben-Dor (Ramat Gan: Turtledove, 1978).

25. See G. Ben-Dor, "Inter-Arab Relations and the Arab-Israeli Conflict," Jerusalem Journal of International Relations 1 (Summer 1976): 70-96; Yair Evron and Yaacov Bar Simantov, "Coalitions in the Arab World," Jerusalem Journal of International Relations 1 (Winter 1975): 71-107; P. J. Vatikiotis, "Regional Politics," in Middle East Perspectives: The Next Twenty Years, ed. George S. Wise and Charles Issawi (Princeton, N.J.: Darwin 1981); and Malcolm H. Kerr, "Regional Arab Politics and the Conflict with Israel," in Political Dynamics in the Middle East, ed. Paul Y. Hammond and Sidney S. Alexander (New York: Elsevier, 1972), pp. 31-68.

26. Needless to say, a comprehensive representation of the conflict would have to include still broader circles of external actors. The primary concern here, however, is with Arabs and Israelis, and it is only their participation in the conflict that the circles are designed to help analyze.

27. Glenn et al., "A Cognitive Interaction Model," p. 36.

28. P. J. Vatikiotis, Conflict in the Middle East (London: Allen and Unwin, 1971).

29. See Ajami, "The End of Pan-Arabism," p. 363.

30. Elie Kedourie, "Religion and Secular Nationalism in the Arab World," in The Middle East: Oil, Conflict and Hope, ed. A. L. Udovitch (Lexington, Mass.: Heath, 1976), p. 190.

31. See G. Ben-Dor, "Inter-Arab Relations and the Arab-Israeli Conflict," pp. 87-91.

32. See Ajami, "The End of Pan-Arabism"; G. Ben-Dor, "The 1970s: A Decade of Change in Arab Politics," in Changing Patterns of International Politics, ed. Nissan Oren (Jerusalem:

Leonard Davis Institute for International Relations, Hebrew University, forthcoming); and Kerr, "Regional Arab Politics and the Conflict with Israel."

Ajami's essay is extremely important, but he may be slightly overstating his case. The present author prefers "the decline of Pan-Arabism" to "the end of Pan-Arabism," as was argued, along lines similar to Ajami's, in G. Ben-Dor, "Civilianization of Military Regimes in the Arab World," Armed Forces and Society 1 (May 1975): 317-27.

33. Kerr, "Regional Arab Politics," pp. 54-55, 56-60.

34. See Neville Mandel, The Arabs and Zionism Before World War I (Berkeley and Los Angeles: University of California Press, 1976).

35. Numerous sources discuss this. Possibly the best of them is Yehoshua Porat, The Palestinian Arab Nationalist Movement, Vol. 2 (London: Cass, 1977). See also Ann Mosely Lesch, "The Palestine Arab Nationalist Movement Under the Mandate," in William B. Quandt, Fuad Jabber, and A. M. Lesch, The Politics of Palestinian Nationalism (Berkeley: University of California Press, 1973); and numerous Arabic, Hebrew, and English items in David Bukay's bibliography, in The Palestinians and the Middle East Conflict: Studies in their History, Sociology and Politics, ed. G. Ben-Dor (Ramat Gan: Turtledove, 1978).

36. See Y. Amitai, "The Arab States and the Palestine War, 1945-1948: From Political Involvement to Military Intervention," University of Haifa Jewish-Arab Center, Institute of Middle Eastern Studies, Occasional Papers on the Middle East, No. 5, April 1976 (in Hebrew); and Meir Pail, "The Appropriation of the Political Sovereignty over Palestine by the Arab States, in the Period of the 'War of Independence' (1947-1949) . . ." in Hatzionut, ed. Daniel Carpi (Tel Aviv: Hakibbutz Hemeuhad, 1973), pp. 439-89 (in Hebrew).

37. Kerr, "Regional Arab Politics," p. 63, and "Conflict with Israel" in Political Dynamics in the Middle East, ed. P. Y. Hammond and S. S. Alexander (New York: Elsevier, 1972).

38. Yehoshafat Harkabi, Palestinians and Israel (Jerusalem: Keter, 1974), Ch. 17.

39. Kerr, "Regional Arab Politics," pp. 62-63.

40. G. Ben-Dor, "Nationalism without Sovereignty and Nationalism with Multiple Sovereignties," p. 152. PLA refers to the Palestine Liberation Army, composed of units integrated with (and thus controlled by) the armies of several Arab states (Egypt, Jordan, Syria, and Iraq).

41. See Dan Schueftan, "The Palestinians, The Arab States and the Arab Commitment to the 'Cause of Palestine' as Factors in the Palestinian Dimension of the Arab-Israeli Conflict," in The

Palestinians and the Middle East Conflict: Studies in their History, Sociology and Politics, ed. G. Ben-Dor (Ramat Gan: Turtledove, 1978).

42. See Yehoshua Porat, "The Palestinian-Arab Nationalist Movement," in The Palestinians: People, History, Politics, ed. Michael Curtis et al. (New Brunswick, N.J.: Transaction, 1975) and the sources previously cited. For an Arab perspective, see Naji Alush, The Arab Resistance in Palestine, 1914-1948 (Beirut: 1968) (in Arabic).

43. This has indeed caused the Palestinians endless difficulties. For the problems involved in developing a credible strategy under such circumstances, see: Akram Dairi and Major Haytham Ayoubi, Towards a New Arab Strategy (Beirut: 1969) (in Arabic); Abu Hamman, The Resistance from the Military Standpoint (Beirut: 1971) (in Arabic); and Shawqi Khairallah, The Road to Jerusalem (Beirut: 1973) (in Arabic); cf. the analysis of the earlier period of Naji Alush, The Arab Resistance in Palestine 1914-1948 (in Arabic).

44. This is brought out in an instructive, though highly apologetic, manner in the memoirs of Ahmad Shuqeiry, Forty Years of Life on the Arab and International Scene (Beirut: 1972), and On the Road to Defeat with the Arab Kings and Presidents (Beirut: 1972) (both in Arabic).

45. Pail, "The Appropriation of the Political Sovereignty over Palestine."

46. See, for instance, Gerard Chaliend, La Résistance Palestinienne (Paris: Editions du Seuill, 1970); Abu Zughod in Shuun Filastiniyya, No. 11 (1972); Y. Harkabi, The Problems of the Palestinians (Jerusalem: Ministry of Foreign Affairs, no date), pp. 15-16.

47. Some Palestinians also raised doubts on this point. See, for instance, Alias Murgus, The Palestinian Resistance and the Present Situation (Beirut: 1971) (in Arabic); also Gerard Chaliend, "Le Double Combat du FPLP," Le Monde Diplomatique, July 1970; and Fuad Jabber, "The Arab Regimes and the Palestinian Revolution," Journal of Palestine Studies 2 (2) (Winter 1973): 79-101.

48. See Kerr, "Regional Arab Politics."

49. See G. Ben-Dor, "The Institutionalization of Palestinian Nationalism 1967-1973," in From June to October, ed. I. Rabinovich and H. Shaked (New Brunswick, N.J.: Transaction, 1978) and the sources there cited.

50. Ajami, "The End of Pan-Arabism," p. 360.

51. Stein, "War Termination and Conflict Reduction," pp. 17-18.

52. Ajami, "The End of Pan-Arabism," p. 356.

53. Properly (and legally) speaking, the Egyptians insisted at Camp David on two peace treaties. Although not legally connected, the general framework relating to the Palestinian question was signed first, at the insistence of the Egyptians. For the texts, see Middle East Focus 2 (July 1979): 20-29.

54. Ajami, "The End of Pan-Arabism," p. 37.

55. See G. Ben-Dor, "Nationalism without Sovereignty and Nationalism with Multiple Sovereigntics"; Joel S. Migdal, "State and Society in a Society without a State," in The Palestinians and the Middle East Conflict, pp. 377-402.

56. Migdal, "State and Society in a Society without a State," pp. 396-97. See also, Palestinian Society and Politics, ed. J. S. Migdal (Princeton, N.J.: Princeton University Press, 1980); Shaul Mishal, "Conflictual Pressures and Co-operative Interests: Observations on West Bank-Amman Political Relations, 1949-1967," ibid.; and Palestinian Arab Politics, ed. Moshe Ma'oz (Jerusalem: Jerusalem Academic Press, 1975).

57. Harkabi, Palestinians and Israel, pp. 51, 57-60.

58. Ibid., p. 51. See also Hisham Sharabi, Palestine and Israel: The Lethal Dilemma (New York: Pegasus, 1969).

59. See Eliezer Beeri, "The Emergence of Palestinian Arab Leadership," in The Palestinians and the Middle East Conflict; Studies in their History, Sociology and Politics, ed. G. Ben-Dor (Ramat Gan: Turtledove, 1978); and Y. Porat, "The Political Organization of the Palestinian Arabs under the British Mandate," in Palestinian Arab Politics, ed. Moshe Ma'oz (Jerusalem: Jerusalem Academic Press, 1975). For some of Arafat's views, see Filastin al-Thawra, January 1, 1973.

60. In addition to the aforementioned sources, in preparing this chapter use has been made of radio broadcasts (such as the Voice of Fatah-Cairo and the Voice of the PLO-Damascus), the articles, surveys, and chronologies of the Journal of Palestine Studies (published since 1972 in Beirut jointly by the Institute of Palestine Studies and Kuwait University), the Amman publication al-Fatah, and the following Beirut periodicals, newspapers and agencies (all affiliated with or oriented toward various Palestinian organizations): Shuun Filastiniyya, Filastin al-Thawra, al-Hadaf, al-Muharrer, al-Huriyya, and Wafa (news agency).

On the military aspects of Palestinian nationalist ideology, see, for instance, Akram Dairi and Major Haytham Ayoubi, Towards a New Arab Strategy (Beirut: 1969) (in Arabic); Abu Hamman, The Resistance from the Military Standpoint (Beirut: 1971) (in Arabic); and Shawqi Khairrallah, The Road to Jerusalem (Beirut: 1973) (in Arabic).

61. "The Liberation of the Occupied Lands and the Struggle Against Soviet Imperialism," Tahrir al-Aqtar al-Muhtala wa-Uslub al-Kifah dhid al-Istiimar al-Mubashar (Revolutionary Studies and Experiments, Dirasat wa-Tajarib Thawriyya, No. 8; Beirut, no date), pp. 16-17. For a further explanation of this, see G. Ben-Dor, "The Strategy of Terrorism in the Arab-Israeli Conflict: The Case of the Palestinian Guerrillas," in International Violence: Terrorism, Surprise, Control, ed. Yair Evron (Jerusalem: Leonard Davis Institute for International Relations, Hebrew University, 1979), pp. 126-65.

62. G. Ben-Dor, "Nationalism without Sovereignty and Nationalism with Multiple Sovereignties," pp. 152-56.

63. Ibid., p. 155.

64. On such attempts, and a systematic assessment of possible solutions to the Palestinian problems, see G. Ben-Dor, "The Palestinians and the Future of Middle East Politics: A Tentative Exploration of Some Alternative Scenarios," in Middle East Perspectives: The Next Twenty Years, ed. George S. Wise and Charles Issawi (Princeton, N.J.: Darwin, 1981), pp. 147-63.

65. On the dispersion of the Palestinians in the wake of the war, see Nabil Shabath, "High Level Palestinian Manpower," Journal of Palestine Studies 1 (2) (Winter 1972): 81-95; and Ibrahim Abu Lughod, "Educating a Community in Exile: The Palestinian Experience," Journal of Palestine Studies 2 (3) (Spring 1973): 94-111.

66. For some of the author's views on this point, see G. Ben-Dor, "The Palestinians and the Future of Middle East Politics."

67. See, for instance, Section A of "The Framework for Peace in the Middle East," Camp David Accords, ibid., p. 147.

68. Bernard Lewis, "The Palestinians and the P.L.O.: A Historical Approach," Commentary 59 (1) (January 1975) (quoted in ibid., p. 147), pp. 32-48.

69. These are surveyed and assessed in G. Ben-Dor, "The Palestinians and the Future of Middle East Politics."

70. In 1974-75, looking for some "peaceful" voices in the Arab world, one would have noted that the leading Arab military commentator Haytham al-Ayoubi, for instance, admitted, while advocating a continuing Arab strategy of attrition and "non-peace," that no decisive victory was possible for either side. "The Future Arab Strategy," in Palestinians in Confrontation, ed. Yoram Nimrod (Givat Haviva: 1975) (in Hebrew), p. 12. The unwinnability of future wars led other Arab intellectuals to think along new lines also; see, for example, Fuad Jabber, "Not by War Alone: Curbing the Arab-Israel Arms Race," Middle East Journal 28 (3) (Summer 1974): 233-247. Boutros-Ghali, however, the leading Egyptian journalist and political scientist, thought in terms of a cold war, and patterns

of (hostile) coexistence: "A Prediction of Possibilities After Peace," in Arabia and Israel, ed. Immanuel Sivan (Jerusalem: Truman Institute, 1974), p. 81 (in Hebrew).

71. Boutros Boutros-Ghali, "The Arab Response to the Challenge of Israel," in The Middle East: Oil, Conflict and Hope, ed. A. L. Udovitch (Lexington, Mass.: Heath, 1976). An Israeli equivalent, of sorts, would be Moshe Dayan, who in 1973 preferred "Sharm el-Sheikh without peace to peace without Sharm el-Sheikh," but in 1978 had to go and explain to the settlers there why he had signed a peace treaty based on exactly the opposite logic!

72. A careful examination of Sadat's speeches, for instance, shows that his earlier ideological attitudes do not differ substantially from those of most other Arab politicians where Israel and the Jews are concerned. What is likely to have caused his transformation is not ideology, but his conversion to raison d'état. See George Carposi, A Man of Peace: Anwar Sadat (New York: Manor Books, 1977); Paul Eidelberg, Sadat's Strategy (Montreal: Dawn, 1979); Raphael Israeli, The Public Diary of President Sadat, 3 vols. (Leiden: Brill, 1978); and, of course, Sadat's autobiography, In Search of Identity. Consult also Shimon Shamir, Egypt under Sadat: The Search for a New Orientation (Tel Aviv: Dvir, 1978) (in Hebrew) and the sources there extensively cited.

73. Ajami, "The End of Pan-Arabism," p. 373.

74. Michael C. Hudson, The Precarious Republic: Political Modernization in Lebanon (New York: Random House, 1968); idem, "The Palestinian Factor in the Lebanese Civil War," Middle East Journal 32 (Summer 1978): 261-78.

75. See G. Ben-Dor, "Miscommunication and Fallacies in the Arab-Israeli Conflict," in Images and Reality in World Politics, ed. Nissan Oren (Jerusalem: Leonard Davis Institute of International Relations, Hebrew University, forthcoming).

76. See the passionate argument by the senior Israeli analyst of the conflict, Yehoshafat Harkabi, in Winds of Change in the Arab-Israeli Conflict (Tel Aviv: Dvir, 1978) (in Hebrew).

77. Much of the remainder of this chapter is a variation of the arguments made first in G. Ben-Dor, "Stabilizing Peace in the Middle East: Israel, the Palestinians and the Arab States," International Spectator 33 (December 1979): 778-83.

78. Dedring, Recent Advances in Peace and Conflict Research, pp. 117-213. See also Michael I. Handel, "War Termination—A Critical Survey," Jerusalem Papers on Peace Problems, No. 24, Leonard Davis Institute for International Relations (Hebrew University, Jerusalem, 1978).

79. See G. Ben-Dor, "Political Culture Approach to Middle East Politics," International Journal of Middle East Studies 8 (1)

(January 1977): 43-63; P. J. Vatikiotis, Conflict in the Middle East; Leonard Binder, "The Middle East as a Subordinate System," World Politics 10 (3) (April 1958): 408-29; Malcolm H. Kerr, "Persistence of Regional Quarrels," in Soviet-American Rivalry in the Middle East, ed. J. C. Hurewitz (New York: Praeger, 1969), pp. 228-41.

80. One such attempt at exploring this subject was made in G. Ben-Dor, "Inter-Arab Relations and the Arab-Israeli Conflict," which also lists most major works in this field.

81. This approximates (but is not identical to) some "paradigmatic" conflicts.

82. Halpern, "The Revolution of Modernization in National and International Society," Revolution (NOMOS 8) (New York: Atherton Press, 1966). These ideas from Halpern's paradigm are discussed in great detail in G. Ben-Dor, The Druzes in Israel, pp. 3-33.

83. Cf. William B. Quandt, Decade of Decisions: American Policy Toward the Arab-Israeli Conflict (Berkeley and Los Angeles: University of California Press, 1977); Bernard Reich, Quest for Peace: U.S.-Israel Relations and the Arab-Israeli Conflict (New Brunswick, N.J.: Transaction, 1977); and Nadav Safran, Israel: The Embattled Ally (Cambridge, Mass.: Bellknap Press, 1978).

84. On this, in addition to the aforementioned sources, see also Dan Horowitz, "The Israeli Concept of National Security and the Prospects for Peace in the Middle East," in Dynamics of a Conflict: A Re-examination of the Middle East Conflict, ed. Gabriel Sheffer (New York: Humanities Press, 1976), pp. 235-75.

85. Compare with Henry A. Kissinger's original formulation in A World Restored (New York: Grosset and Dunlap, 1964).

86. Needless to say, the entire concept of balance of power makes sense only in a region of states; it may be totally inapplicable to relations between nations, as such.

87. Public lecture, the Leonard Davis Institute for International Relations, the Hebrew University, Jerusalem, July 1978. There is an analogy here, of course, with Britain in the European state system in the nineteenth century.

88. Unfortunately, this term is all too often misunderstood in both Egypt and Israel, and in any case lacks the necessary political depth.

89. This is a crucially important theoretical point in peace studies. See Dedring, Recent Advances in Peace and Conflict Research, pp. 20-22; and Johan Galtung, "Violence, Peace and Peace Research," Journal of Peace Research 3 (1969): 167-91.

90. This point needs special emphasis, because it is particularly open to misinterpretation.

91. The genesis of such a process may one day be discernible in the still untold story of the Syrian-Israeli-Lebanese triangle of 1976.

92. Cf. Amos Perlmutter, "A New Rejectionism," Foreign Policy (34) (Spring 1979): 165-81.

93. See the data in G. Ben-Dor, "The National Security Policy of Egypt: Forces, Doctrines and Political Strategies," in The National Security Policies of the Emerging Nations, ed. Edward Kolodziej and Robert Harkavy (Lexington, Mass.: Heath, 1981).

94. This is argued in detail in G. Ben-Dor, "Inter-Arab Relations and the Arab-Israeli Conflict."

95. See G. Ben-Dor, "Nationalism without Sovereignty and Nationalism with Multiple Sovereignties," and the sources there cited.

96. Aryeh Shalev, The Autonomy: Problems and Possible Solutions, CSS Papers No. 8 (Tel Aviv: Center for Strategic Studies, Tel Aviv University, January 1980).

97. See Shai Feldman, "Peacemaking in the Middle East: The Next Step," Foreign Affairs 59 (Spring 1981): 756-81.

98. See G. Ben-Dor, "The Institutionalization of Palestinian Nationalism."

99. The choices are systematically analyzed in Feldman, "Peacemaking in the Middle East."

100. Thus settling the question of stateness for the Palestinians.

101. Feldman, "Peacemaking in the Middle East"; G. Ben-Dor, "The Palestinians and the Future of Middle East Politics"; Eugene V. Rostow, "Palestinian Self-Determination: Possible Futures for the Unallocated Territories of the Palestine Mandate," Yale Studies in World Order 5 (1979): 147-72.

102. Several of these are contained in Self Rule/Shared Rule: Federal Solutions to the Middle East Conflict, ed. Daniel J. Elazar (Ramat Gan: Turtledove, 1979). See also Les Cahiers du Féderalisme 5 (Janvier-Mars 1979), "Proche Orient: fédéralisation au gerre mondiale."

103. Valerie Earle, Federalism: Infinite Variety in Theory and Practice (Ithaca, N.Y.: Cornell University Press, 1958), p. 212.

104. See G. Ben-Dor, "Federalism in the Arab World," in Federalism and Political Integration, ed. Daniel J. Elazar (Ramat Gan: Turtledove, 1979). For Sadat's views on this see al-Ahram, May 26, 1974.

105. Explored in G. Ben-Dor, "Nationalism without Sovereignty and Nationalism with Multiple Sovereignties."

106. That is, losing its primacy to stateness.

107. "Ideal peace," of course, is a term entirely different in meaning from Boulding's "Peace as ideal conflict."

108. As distinct from simply "going nuclear." For an elaboration of this concept see the discussion in G. Ben-Dor, "Conflict Reduction Through Negative Peace."

109. Quoted in Karl W. Deutsch, The Analysis of International Relations (Englewood Cliffs, N.J.: Prentice-Hall, 1968), p. 132.

110. Ibid.

111. These terms do not necessarily have the everyday meaning associated with them. See Ch. 2, "How Conflicts Arise Among States," in ibid., pp. 112-32. (Note, for instance, "fight-type conflict processes tend to be automatic and mindless," p. 113; a "very different type of conflict resembles games in which each player maintains rational control over his own moves, though not necessarily over their outcome," p. 114; and, "debates are conflicts in which adversaries are changing each other's motives, values or cognitive images of reality," p. 130).

112. Quoted in G. Ben-Dor, "Stabilizing Peace in the Middle East," p. 1.

6
Stateness and the Future of Middle East Politics

The study of Middle East politics is a notoriously slippery field. Max Weber's classic observation on the nature of politics—"Politics is a strong and slow boring of hard boards. It takes both passion and perspective"[1]—seems to take on added strength and significance in the Middle East context. Passion has been found in overabundance in the region; but in talking about a perspective for the future, it is as well to keep in mind that "We do not know where currently observed changes may lead in the long run; hence we must keep the possibility of alternative developments conceptually open."[2] As usual, Middle East politics is in transition; hence one must be on guard against the "fallacy of retrospective determinism," since the future is "genuinely uncertain."[3] Indeed, it is as well to be on guard against any kind of determinism.

This is more an effort in forecasting some probable future trends than an attempt at a prediction with any degree of determinism. The difference between a prediction and a forecast should always be borne in mind:

> A prediction usually dispenses probabilistic interpretation; a forecast is always conceived within a certain probability range. A prediction is generally made in terms of a point or event; a forecast is made in terms of alternatives. A prediction focuses upon one outcome; a forecast involves contingencies. The composite distinction between predicting and forecasting—in terms of probability, contingent outcomes, and specification of alternatives—lies at the core of existing approaches to the future.[4]

This uncertainty, of course, is not unique to the Middle East. Every area of the world has its "perhapses." Rokkan has this to say in the very last paragraph of an authoritative book on the European state: "One last perhaps, then: perhaps, as is so often the case, we only begin to understand this momentous process—the formation of national states—when it begins to lose its universal significance. Perhaps, unknowing, we are writing obituaries for the state."[5] This is decidedly a European perhaps. Whether or not it is time to look beyond the nation-state or just beyond the state in Europe is highly debatable; but there is no question that a current obituary of the state in the Middle East would be premature. Perhaps Europeans, who have had a state system for some time, should start looking beyond it, but for those who live in the Middle East the state is the thing to look to.

Why this tendency to start writing obituaries for the state in Europe? There are manifold trends at work throughout European and global politics and economics, which raise questions:

> Remember the definition of a state as an organization, controlling the principal means of coercion within a given territory, which is differentiated from other organizations operating in the same territory, autonomous, centralized and formally coordinated. If there is something to the trends we have described, they threaten almost every single one of these defining features of the state: the monopoly of coercion, the exclusiveness of control within the territory, the autonomy, the centralization, the formal coordination; even the differentiation from other organizations begins to fall away in such compacts as the European Common Market.[6]

It seems very premature, however, to look for these trends in the Middle East. Several European countries have struggled with the challenge of state building since the fourteenth century[7] and, having been remarkably successful, they may be about to undergo a transition to the next stage, whatever that may be. The countries of the Middle East, on the other hand, have been on the road to stateness for only a few decades, and it is only now that success is in sight: there is a significant time lag here that cannot, and must not, be disregarded.

This conspicuous time lag, of course, has not escaped the attention of theoreticians. Thus, Rokkan speaks of a "general movement toward a worldwide state system," which to some extent includes the following "blocks of events":

> (1) the formation of a few early national states amid a great variety of other political structures in Europe;

(2) the mapping of most of Europe into distinct national
states through wars, alliances, and a great variety of
other maneuvers; (3) the extension of political and economic domination from the European base to much of
the rest of the world, notably through the creation of
client states and colonies; (4) the formation—through
rebellion and through international agreement—of formally autonomous states corresponding approximately
to the clients and colonies; (5) the extension of this
state system to the entire world. [8]

Anticipating objections to his calling these distinguishable phases,
Rokkan falls back on a "main rhythm that has three beats":

(1) the formation and consolidation of the first great
national states in commercial and military competition with each other, accompanied by their economic
penetration of the remainder of Europe and of important parts of the world outside of Europe: roughly
1500 to 1700; (2) the regrouping of the remainder of
Europe into a system of states, accompanied by the
extension of European political control into most of
the non-European world, save those portions already
dominated by substantial political organizations (e.g.,
China and Japan): roughly 1650 to 1850; (3) the extension of the state system to the rest of the world both
through the acquisition of formal independence by colonies and clients, and through the incorporation of existing powers like China and Japan into the system:
roughly 1800 to 1950. [9]

One might add that there is a fourth "beat," or perhaps a profound aftereffect of the third "beat": the formal extension of the
state system to the postcolonial world has had to be accompanied
by a lengthy, complex, and painful indigenous political process in
which a structural and behavioral dimension of stateness has
emerged: the formal "shell" of the state has had to be filled with
an indigenously created political content. In the Middle East, however, this process has been very condensed and intense.

The globalization of the state system raises huge question
marks after statements like "no more Europes" and "there is nothing to learn from the European experience." [10] Rokkan's schema,
for one, indicates otherwise.

If this scheme is correct, the study of European state-
making has at least one point of relevance to the

politics of the contemporary world: Europeans played
the major part in creating the contemporary international state system, and presumably left the imprints
of their peculiar political institutions on it. It is probably even true . . . that a state which has adopted
western forms of organization will have an easier time
in the international system; after all, the system grew
up in conjunction with these forms. [11]

This is evidently true. But there is much more to the impact of
Europe on Middle East stateness: the European powers exported
the institutional structure of the state (which was bequeathed to the
local elites after independence as an "overdeveloped" structure compared with other existing social institutions); they extended around
the world an international system that sanctified the territorial
status quo and granted the elites, through control of the state machinery, access to enormous resources. At the same time, they
also exported their own radical-style mass politics, enmeshed in
social and national ideologies. In Europe, these developments had
been slow and gradual and had had a certain natural rhythm. In the
Middle East, all were basically alien: the idea of the territorial
state was as new and strange as was the idea of nationalism to those
accustomed to the Islamic universalism of the Ottoman Empire. The
simultaneous arrival of these dialectically related, enormously ex-
plosive, political trends generated critical situations in Middle East
politics. But they all came from Europe. As Tilly admits, "The
European state-makers constructed, then imposed, strong national
governments before mass politics began. In new states, the two
processes tend to occur together. That is the 'cumulation of crises'
already anticipated by the experiences of Germany and Italy."[12]

This is undoubtedly correct. The Europeans created the genesis of the Middle East state and they also inspired the genesis of
Middle East nationalism. The resulting havoc could have been anticipated. So, too, could the eventual outcome: the triumph of the
state, but only after a lengthy period of tension, conflict, and violence. Both the time elements and the particular contents of nationalism in the Middle East were significantly different from the European experience; not so, however, the actual key components of the
process. Indeed, the emerging Middle East state bears an almost
uncanny resemblance to its European antecedent of centuries ago.
Compare the features certain to be found in contemporary states all
over the region to the following description:

The structure which became dominant in Europe after
1500, the national state, differed from . . . alternative

possibilities in several significant ways: (1) it controlled a well-defined, continuous territory; (2) it was relatively centralized; (3) it was differentiated from other organizations; (4) it reinforced its claims through a tendency to acquire a monopoly over the concentrated means of physical coercion within its territory. So, in a sense, explaining how the national state won out amounts to accounting for territorial consolidation, centralization, differentiation of the instruments of government from other sorts of organization, and monopolization (plus concentration) of the means of coercion. [13]

It was in the specific sphere of the means of coercion that European governmental technology was absorbed most successfully in the Middle East. [14] This added an extra dimension of intensity to the conflicts arising with such rapidity between states and nations in the formative years of the Middle East regional political system; and this is again a feature that bears an astonishing resemblance to the evolution of the state system in the Europe of yesteryear:

It is also precisely at this point that Finer brings out most sharply another argument . . .: that state-makers were actually building an interlocking system of states; general wars became the principal means by which the realignments of the participants and their boundaries occurred, the principal moments at which multiple changes of membership and alliance occurred, as well as principal occasions on which the relations between rulers and ruled changed rapidly. [15]

This is true with regard to the Middle East in the last generation or so, with one exception: by the time the Middle East states entered the "game," boundaries were much harder to change, for they were now fixed by the European-originated global system:[16]

The second international process which my analysis has so far neglected is the crystallization of a system of states acknowledging, and to some extent guaranteeing each other's existence. Perhaps the Treaty of Westphalia (1648), at the close of the Thirty Years' War, first made it clear that all of Europe was divided into distinct and sovereign states, whose boundaries were defined by international agreement. Over the next three hundred years the Europeans and their

descendants managed to impose that state system on
the entire world. The recent wave of decolonization
has almost completed the mapping of the globe into
that system. [17]

It may be necessary, at this point, to remember that, theoretically speaking, this is not a unilinear, irreversible process.
The building of states is a challenge to which practically all countries are called, but to which not all succeed in answering (historically speaking):

Most of the European efforts to build states failed.
The enormous majority of the political units which
were around to bid for autonomy and strength in 1500
disappeared in the next few centuries, smashed or absorbed by other states-in-the-making. The substantial
majority of the units which got so far as to acquire a
recognizable existence as states during those centuries
still disappeared. [18]

Here the comparison between earlier historical developments
in Europe, on the one hand, and in the Middle East in the twentieth
century, on the other, does indeed break down. The nature of the
global system and its Middle East substructure is such that states
no longer "disappear," for disrupting the territorial status quo due
to state building might create havoc with international stability.
Yet countries still may—and do—fail in state building. The cost of
failure, however, is not disappearance, but incoherent, uncontrol-
lable conflict. The extreme case in the Middle East is undoubtedly
Lebanon: its failures and weaknesses in state building have turned
it into a dumping ground for revolutionary and ideological forces
that the stateness of other countries is unable to tolerate any longer
within their own boundaries. But even this process is not irreversible; the price of failure is no longer absolute.
Another divergence from the European experience—as might
be anticipated—has to do with the factors that seem to explain why
certain countries succeed in state building and survive, whereas
others do not. Not only is survival easier these days, as has been
seen, but success (which may not be easier) is probably related to
different factors than those found to be applicable in Europe centuries ago. This is an entirely natural divergence, due to the differences in the concrete conditions that appear over time and space.
On this score, indeed, the comparison with Europe yields limited
results.

The most general conditions in the European experience that appear to predict survival and state making, according to Tilly, are

> (1) the availability of extractable resources; (2) a rela-
> tively protected position in time and space; (3) a con-
> tinuous supply of political entrepreneurs; (4) success
> in war; (5) homogeneity (and homogenization) of the sub-
> ject population; (6) strong coalitions of the central power
> with major segments of the landed elite. A high stand-
> ing on one of the factors can make up for low standing
> on another. [19]

Obviously, the concrete sociopolitical structure of the Middle East is in fact so different that the specifics here mentioned have but a limited applicability. Even so,

> some features of state-building processes, and of the
> circumstances which accompanies them in Europe,
> also deserve inquiry. First, specialized organization
> works. If the "task at hand" is well defined and con-
> sists of manipulating the outside world, the ruler who
> builds a special-purpose organization and keeps it sup-
> plied with resources tends to have the advantage over
> his rivals. [20]

This description is applicable to a host of cases in the history of Middle East state making also.

The early efforts of the 1950s to derive sweeping universal conclusions on political development became so exaggerated and bizarre as to give way to a counterswing of the pendulum, whereby arguments emphasizing the uniqueness of the non-Western experience led to the "no more Europes" approach, an exaggeration in the opposite direction. Perhaps in due time the dialectics of intellectual history will lead to a return to a sensible attitude: that, whereas some questions are hardly amenable to universal comparisons, others virtually necessitate a comparative perspective. Questions such as the role of religion in politics[21] and the fundamental differences between, on the one hand, Islam and Judaism, and on the other, all Christian churches, present such unique characteristics as to justify every caution against hasty comparisons. At the same time, the phenomenon of the state, and the emergence of the state system as the linchpin of regional politics, are phenomena that, being exported from Europe, did not, by any stretch of the imagination, lose enough of their generic characteristics to make comparisons useless or meaningless.

A final point to be derived from the European experience is the high cost of state building. As Tilly observes, the authors of his book "explicitly . . . agree that the building of states in Western Europe cost tremendously in death, suffering, loss of rights, and unwilling surrender of land, goods, or labor. Implicitly, they agree that the process could not have occurred without great costs."[22] This is a point of enormous moral and ethical significance, which, however, is difficult for the social scientist or the historian to handle: "we do not agree so completely on the minimum costs it would have taken, on how much the actual costs exceeded the minimum, and for what reasons, or on the extent to which the benefits outweighed the costs; all these judgements contain large moral and larger speculative components."[23]

State building, then, for all the elegance of the scientific term, exacted a horrendous human cost. Why was this so? For Tilly,

> The fundamental reason for the high cost of European state-building was its beginning in midst of a decentralized, largely peasant social structure. Building differentiated, autonomous, centralized organizations with effective control of territories entailed eliminating or subordinating thousands of semiautonomous authorities. If our analysis of armed forces is correct, most of the enormous cost of military activity—by far the largest single cost of state-making—sprang from the effort to reduce rivals inside and outside the territory. Building states also entailed extracting the resources for their operation from several million rural communities. If our analyses of taxation and food supply are correct, European states could not have acquired much more power than they had at the beginning of the seventeenth century without collaborating in the destruction of the landed peasantry. In any case, they did collaborate.
>
> Most of the European population resisted each phase of the creation of strong states. Our analyses of taxation, of food supply, and (less directly) of policing show that the resistance was often concerted, determined, violent, and threatening to the holders of power. The prevalence of tax rebellions, food riots, movements against conscription, and related forms of protest during the great periods of state-making help gauge the amount of coercion it took to bring people under the state's effective control.[24]

This is a grim story, indeed. It becomes even grimmer when one considers that the most important structure requiring the resources obtained through such massive coercion was the military machine.

> The formation of standing armies provided the largest
> single incentive to extraction and the largest single
> means of state coercion over the long run of European
> state-making. Recurrently we find a chain of causation
> running from (1) change or expansion in land armies to
> (2) new efforts to extract resources from the subject
> population to (3) the development of new bureaucracies
> and administrative innovations to (4) resistance from
> the subject population to (5) renewed coercion to (6)
> durable increases in the bulk or extractiveness of the
> state.[25]

Again, this European experience of centuries ago bears an eerie resemblance to the process that has unfolded in the Middle East in recent decades. The coercive, extractive, and penetrative capacities of the state have been enormously enhanced, and a huge proportion of the extracted resources has been invested in armies and security forces, some of which have been utilized for conducting war, some for interstate subversion, and some for internal manipulation. By and large (particularly in the cases of the Arab countries and Iran), this process has entailed massive centralization and repression. From the very beginnings of the nineteenth century, imperial attempts at state building in the Ottoman Empire, Egypt, and elsewhere in the area meant increased tyranny and oppression, creating a distressingly negative process of political socialization. In the beginning, at least, the strength of the state and oppression by the state machinery went hand in hand.

This unholy alliance is reason enough for a humanistic social scientist to treat the state in the Middle East with more than a grain of suspicion. To this very day, state machineries in most Middle Eastern countries appear to be particularly unsavory, inhuman, oppressive mechanisms with little concern for humane values. The heavy-handed secret police system is ubiquitous in most states, sometimes having more undercover agents at an opposition meeting, rally, or demonstration than any opposing organization. Even where overwhelming state power is adorned with socialist rhetoric, this tends to be state socialism (frequently called by cynics in the Arab world—with a grain of truth—"police socialism"). Khomeini's state—Islamic republic—has not shown much imagination or creativity, but the number of "hanging judges," firing squads, and "monkey trials" in the country has proliferated, creating a truly depraved condition. In General Zia's Pakistan, massive repression, pure and simple, is the order of the day—not to mention the debilitating effect the enormous concentration of resources in the hands of the state has on the initiative, enterprise, and creativity of any individual or group in the bureaucratic polity. Is, then, stateness still to be applauded, or is it to be condemned, in the name of universal values ?

Technically speaking, the answer is "neither." Social scientists may thus merely identify the trend to an increasing level of stateness, draw a few probable conclusions for the future, and then rest their case. But that is not good enough. The ultimate goal of social and political inquiry is the search for "the good life" (or, at least, the institutional preconditions thereof), and no amount of argument along lines of scientific objectivity should absolve the analyst from making at least some general observations about the relationship between the phenomena studied and the values that make such study worthwhile—which, indeed, make it possible in the first place. [26]

This question deserves a thorough discussion on both the empirical and the theoretical levels. At the empirical level, one may note that a higher level of stateness has been accompanied by a gradual civilianization of military regimes. [27] A careful examination of this phenomenon indicates that the two processes (the strengthening of stateness and the gradual but substantial introduction of civilian elements into the ruling elite) are intimately intertwined. Above all, the most statelike Arab country, Egypt, having once been among the prototypes of civilian regimes in the postcolonial world, has become one of the pioneers of the postmilitary regime in the Third World. [28]

Even more significant is the adoption in Egypt of the so-called Open Door Policy (infitah)[29] in the mid-1970s. This is a drastic reorientation of Egypt's policy away from that of the étatistic years of the Nasser regime. This new policy involved the reduction of the role of the state sector in the economy, the liberalization of controls, the encouraging of a greater role for market forces in economic activity, and attracting foreign and private domestic investment. In domestic politics, the policy is now to tolerate (and positively encourage) a semicompetitive party system, to eliminate many restrictions on freedom of speech and organization, and to assign a greater role to press, parliament, elections, and parties vis-à-vis the gigantic state bureaucracy. Globally, infitah gives rise to the attempt to intensify the relationship with likely sources of foreign investment—all the better if they are likely to approve the new policies on other grounds, as well—namely, the United

States, Japan, and Western Europe. Regionally, infitah has necessitated (and indeed has already brought about) a drastic reduction in regional conflict in general and the so costly Arab-Israeli conflict in particular, so that attention and energy may be directed toward the mounting domestic socioeconomic problems.

This policy may eventually fail, for the magnitude of the domestic challenge is simply staggering and the resources are relatively meager. And failure may be very costly indeed; even a partial failure may bring about dramatic reversals. But this is not the point. What the policy of infitah amounts to is an effort to transform Egypt into a more open society, one in which pluralism and individual human rights will have a much greater measure of legitimacy and protection. The diverse elements of infitah complement each other, for the new orientation has a certain coherent logic. That success is far from assured and that many previous changes of policy have taken place in Egypt is true beyond argument. But the very fact that the most statelike Arab country has begun to evolve from one characterized by an <u>étatist</u>, nationalist, authoritarian, military, one-party regime to something approximating a semiopen society, more pluralistic, more civilianized, less oppressive, is most significant.

Having more or less successfully completed its state building (at least in relation to the rest of the Arab world), Egypt was able to experiment with a more open society. It would be no exaggeration to argue (1) that no such experiments would have been attempted had state building been unsuccessful, since successful state building is a necessary—although insufficient—condition for such experiments; (2) that Arab countries still facing serious challenges to stateness are very unlikely to experiment with more open societies; (3) that the likelihood of such experiments will increase, should their level of stateness continue to rise substantially; and (4) that this pattern, with all due respect to differences in timing and cultural specifics, does not diverge from the European pattern, but rather is reinforced by it. If all this is true, stateness and a future more humane pattern of politics are far from being contradictions.

At the opposite end of the scale of stateness from Egypt, in the Arab world, stands Lebanon. The weakness and the underdevelopment of the Lebanese state[30] have generated a veritable tragedy in that country. The fury entailed in the clashes among social and nationalist forces (both domestic and imported) cannot be controlled by the machinery of the feeble state. The Lebanese political arena has become a theater for ambitious men, movements, and countries from all over the Middle East, creating havoc in the country. The human and material costs of the incessant devastation are staggering. True, the Lebanese citizen, living in a weak state, has been relatively free from state oppression, but the price paid for this has been nothing less than total civil bankruptcy. Instead of being oppressed by their own state, the citizens of Lebanon are threatened by private militias, Syrian soldiers, Palestinian commandos, Israeli airplanes. The casualties of Lebanon's disorder—a direct result of a virtual absence of stateness—have been far in excess of any imaginable figure attributable to the kind of repression experienced elsewhere in the Arab world. The casualties of nonstateness—not only Lebanon since 1975 but also Jordan, 1970-71, and Yemen, 1962-67— far outweigh the casualties of stateness. What real meaning does the lack of state oppression have in a country like Lebanon when life, movement, and property are always threatened (and frequently are taken) by myriad social, nationalist, and foreign forces that take advantage of the virtual abdication of the Lebanese state?

Individual human values are a fragile commodity. They can be threatened from many directions. Too much state authority is evidently dangerous, but so is too little. If the case of Lebanon is any indication, in the Arab Middle East too little stateness is the more dangerous. Human values have very little meaning in the lack of political order,[31] and political order in the Middle East means an order of states.

A second empirically observable danger to freedom and the proverbial pursuit of happiness in the Middle East has been ubiquitous regional conflict. Seemingly endless wars between various countries have claimed numerous casualties, have taken up the best years of the lives of millions of young people, have brought about (and at times seemingly legitimized) further restrictions on individual rights, freedoms, and sociopolitical pluralism. For years the struggle against Israel was the reason (excuse?) that made the curtailment of freedom necessary in Egypt (along with other, domestic considerations). Even in democratic Israel, at times military government of minorities, emergency legislation (inherited from the British mandatory regime), and stiff censorship laws related to security matters (which latter, in a conflict of this magnitude, may mean just about anything) have been tolerated in the name of conflict with the Arabs. The cemeteries all over Israel, Egypt, Jordan, Syria, Lebanon, Yemen, and other countries of this much troubled region are full of the graves of tens of thousands of human beings slain in the frequent wars pursued in the name of national ideals. The cost paid by individual Israelis and Arabs in human, material, psychological, and civic terms for the acts of violence perpetrated in the "hot" stages of both the Arab-Israeli conflict and various inter-Arab rivalries has been staggeringly high. As stateness has increased and has brought about very substantial conflict reduction in both the Arab-Israeli and the inter-Arab systems, the human cost has also been drastically reduced.

At no point was state oppression a match for the staggering costs of violent conflict. As nothing has been so instrumental in conflict reduction as raison d'état, and as raison d'état prevails only in countries with a relatively high level of stateness, perhaps the costs involved in state building in the Middle East can be evaluated only in comparison with the costs implied by the alternative: an absence of stateness, allowing social and nationalist forces to run amok. And again, a passing reference to Europe may be in order[32]: human values and rights have probably never enjoyed a higher measure of protection for any length of time than in Western Europe since the Second World War, in a set of states integrated into the global political system via alliances based on a balance of terror. The balance of terror is indeed frightening, but the state logic involved has been instrumental in bringing to Western Europeans unprecedented freedom and opportunity to realize individual values. All this has come about not as a result of some latter-day poststate utopia, but in the age of the state—the state in a postnationalist age.

The postnationalist age in Western Europe is very much in evidence. It does not mean that nationalism is over, finished, gone. It does not even mean that ethnic problems are resolved (obviously, in several Western European countries this is in fact far from being the case). It does mean that the states in existence are accepted as the actors in the system, whether or not they are congruent with nationalist ideals; that ethnic incompatibilities do not bring their existence into question; and that nationality questions are not allowed to threaten them. In a most profound sense, state and nation are disconnected. Even though the Western European countries are by and large based on relatively homogeneous national cultures (which give the countries their particular variations of the European way of life), this identity of state and nation is neither absolute nor even particularly salient. The Western European states exist in their present forms and boundaries due to the outcome of the Second World War and the ensuing global agreement on the virtual partition of Europe. The corollary is that nationalist claims do not—and cannot—overlap boundaries. They cannot fragment, create, overthrow, or merge states. States do not allow themselves to be used as the tools of nationalist forces. The Europeans know how their state system came into being and are reconciled to their inability to change this. The truth contained in statements such as "There is one German nation, but there are two German states" is at the heart of Western European politics today. It is in this sense that Western Europe is already in a postnationalist age; for the time being, at least, the Western European states have triumphed over their nations.[33]

In the Middle East things are far more complex. While the Western Europeans seem to have found a fairly stable postwar political order, the Middle East is still in search of a post-Ottoman regional order. Even in the late Ottoman period the moribund, decentralized, and feeble machinery of the empire barely managed to hold its diverse components together in an uneasy peace. The "fleeting moment" of Europe in the Middle East introduced more destabilizing factors than anything resembling an imperial peace. And it is the uneasy, indeed antagonistic, relationship between states and nations since independence that has exacerbated disorder more than anything else.

In the Middle East context, there is (ostensibly) a single Arab nation, but 21 Arab states; there is (ostensibly) one Jewish nation, but most of it is outside the Jewish state. While there is (ostensibly) one Iranian nation, it is barely held together in the face of strong centrifugal ethnic forces, and its present regime is immersed in transcendental, messianic Islamic ideology, while pursuing a war in the name of the Iranian nation over territory claimed by Iraqi Arab nationalists. The commitment to the idea of one Arab nation overwhelmed the Arab states for a generation and more. The commitment to the idea that the Jewish state must coincide with the historical Land of Israel possessed by the Jewish nation has bedeviled Israeli statecraft for half a generation. The idea that Islam is a viable political alternative to the Iranian state has generated a chaotic Iranian revolution that continues to devour its own sons. Unlike Europe, there is yet to be accomplished a generation of stability in the Middle East in which the state truly succeeds in harnessing nationalism, cutting it down to a size containable within the state. As has been seen, however, the hopeful signs in this direction have multiplied to an unprecedented extent in the past decade or so.

Clement Henry Moore suggested in 1970 the term "colonial dialectic," which "assumes a constructive confrontation, one of 'identity of opposition' between master and slave (colonizer and colonized)."[34] But it would seem that the real colonial dialectic in the Middle East is different, and that its essence lies in the tensions and contradictions between state and nation.[35] The European colonial powers, both via direct rule and indirect cultural penetration, exported to the Middle East the most modern governmental technology available in the form of the state apparatus. This governmental technology has a logic of its own, which, however, is not easily exportable. The Europeans exported instead the logic of nationalism, taken from their own radical style of politics, which was soon to pass its peak (though not before it had created one of the greatest devastations in the history of mankind). The peoples in the Middle

East inherited, therefore, the <u>structure</u> of the state and the <u>idea</u> of the nation: this is the heritage that generated the colonial dialectic and the ensuing grim struggle between the two poles.

One sociologist concerned with acculturation, Levy, has observed that "in every single instance in which there has been contact between the members of relatively modernized and relatively non-modernized societies . . . the structures of the relatively non-modernized society have begun to change in the direction of the structures of the relatively modernized society."[36] This is obviously true in the case of the Middle East. The most powerful—and thus most attractive—modern structure is the state. This was indeed understood by the ruling elites in the Middle East, quick to grasp the immense potential inherent in the power of the state and to take advantage of the fact that the structure of the state is a transferable commodity. But Levy spoke <u>only</u> of structure. While the state is indeed such a structure, it is also much more than that; it has behavioral and attitudinal attributes, and these are not easily transferred or exported. There resulted a paradox: the state is easily exportable as a structure, but stateness as a logic is difficult to transfer. Similarly, nations as structures are also difficult to export, but the logic of nationalism is easily transferred.

The Middle East ended up with the powerful instrument of the state, but instead of this instrument being tempered by its own logic, it was inflamed with the passion of nationalism, itself reinforced by social radicalism and revolutionary ideals derived from totalistic (though not necessarily totalitarian) religious systems. This contradiction has had to be worked out gradually, slowly, progressively. The ensuing process has been grim, painful, and violent. Yet, where signs of resolving this contradiction are perceptible in the Arab world, as in Egypt, for example, the concomitant political changes augur well in terms of a more hospitable climate for human values and liberties. In Turkey, too, the threat to these values emanates not so much from the state (which here seems to have resolved its contradictions with nationalism long before the Arab countries), but from political elements and forces that argue the logic of (mostly imported) social, revolutionary, and religious ideologies, a logic that questions the traditional <u>raison d'état</u>. The danger is reinforced by the unequal distribution of stateness in Turkey in general and the center-periphery gap in particular.[37]

Empirically, then, there is ample evidence that in most of the Middle East the gravest sources of danger to human values, rights, and liberties have stemmed not from excessive state power, but from social radicalism, political disorder resulting from a low level of stateness, and violent conflict due to nationalism insufficiently controlled by <u>raison d'état</u>.

Having concluded that, at least in the Middle East, stateness may indeed be conducive to maximizing human values at this stage, one may raise an additional theoretical question: in an age of increasing international interdependence, when transstate activity is ever on the increase in the Western world in the era of multinational corporations, satellite communications, and the European Economic Community, is it not rather old-fashioned to continue to look to the territorial state as the fundamental political unit within which the human potential is realized? Does it not make more sense for the postcolonial countries to take a shortcut, so to speak, and to combine the emphasis on individual rights and needs on the one hand with large efficient, viable transstate institutions on the other? Why bother with building numerous small and fragile Arab (or African) states? Why not proceed straight to an Arab (or African) Economic Community, or even a more integrated version thereof?

The answer is simply that such a shortcut is not possible. The evidence from all around the globe indicates that common traits such as language, religion, and tradition are less decisive for transstate integration than is a minimal threshold of stateness. Assuming that the age of forcible integration into empires is a bygone era,[38] human beings must first learn to live in states before they can proceed to live (and to live humanely) in polities beyond the state. Thus, while the Latin American republics share a common religion, a common language (with the exception of Brazil), a colonial heritage, and even a fear of the huge colossus to the north, a Latin American superstate is nowhere in sight; nor is an even modest version of the European Economic Community.

Similarly, African and Arab countries, respectively, have a good many cultural and ideological characteristics in common. In the Arab case, in particular, common language, cultural heritage, religion, and other traditions[39] appear—on the surface at least—to constitute an especially powerful and solid framework for politics beyond the single state. Yet, as has been seen, the political facts patently contradict this superficial appearance: not only is Arab unity a more remote utopia than ever, but even an Arab version of the EEC has so far been well beyond reach. Oddly enough—if the observer remains at the superficial level—it has been Europe, separated by a multitude of languages and the historical Catholic/Protestant cleavage, and torn by centuries of strife and by two world wars, that has gone at least as far as creating a functioning economic association with some political features (although this is, of course, still a very far cry from the end of the Western European state, reports concerning the death of which, to paraphrase Mark Twain, have been greatly exaggerated). One might argue that this is due to a historical process that is simply farther along in Europe, following an early start, and/or to a higher level of modernization. It seems, however, that in this process, too, in conflict reduction, the state is perhaps the most important conceptual variable. The higher level of stateness in Western Europe compared with the Third World may explain better than any other single factor (though there may be a multitude of other relevant ones) why the Europeans are farther along the way to a transstate framework (even though the European state is here for a long time to come). Stateness seems to be a prerequisite for transstateness.[40] Countries cannot cooperate in transstate frameworks before they have learned to operate a state. The logic of transstateness cannot be grasped until the logic of stateness itself is thoroughly assimilated. If one wants to protect human values and rights in the Middle East, to reduce and contain conflicts, and to establish political order in the area, then there will have to be a region of states; the shortcut seems impossible, both on theoretical and empirical grounds.

It is well to look to a future beyond the state, for what really matters, from the humanistic point of view, is the individual in interaction with other individuals, not political power as such. But, precisely because society is ultimately more important than the state, stateness has to be settled first. "Seek ye the political kingdom" first—not because it matters more, but because, in the lack of political order, no normal social development is possible. The state cannot replace society, but it must protect society. In the lack of political order, social and individual values are meaningless; they cannot be realized, nor can they be protected from assault, violence, and chaos.

In the past, theories of institutionalization were influential in the thinking related to political order.[41] According to this line of thought, political order was most likely to be created by political parties. The extent of the need of reorientation is brought out by a reexamination of a blunt concluding sentence in the seminal article by Huntington, which first presented the idea of institutionalization as the key to political order: "If it is a choice between a party and a personality, choose the party: better the Ba'ath than Nasser."[42] If the choice is between a party and a personality, the former may indeed be the more sensible choice, but the phrase "better the Ba'ath than Nasser" rings hollow, even false. Of course, one now has the wisdom of hindsight in making a judgment, but there can be little question that post-Nasser Egypt enjoys a much greater extent of political order (and openness) than Ba'athist Syria or Iraq. "Better the Ba'ath than Nasser" assumes that the Ba'ath is indeed an institutionalized party in the proper sense of the term, and that Nasser's role was in fact that of "a personality." The truth is that

the Ba'ath (in both the Iraqi and the Syrian versions) has been
seized and factionalized along numerous regional, ethnic, and personal, as well as ideological, lines, and while its existence as a
bona fide party functioning in more than one Arab country cannot be
questioned, its level of institutionalization and its contribution to
political order have been less than Huntington indicates. Also, the
reference to Nasser ruling as a personality ignores his role as a
"functional Pharaoh" running a central apparatus built around the
majesty of the Egyptian state, even though this was done in a patrimonial manner.[43] If the outcome is a stronger Egyptian state on
the one hand, opting for a more open society, and weaker Iraqi and
Syrian states on the other, more conflict-oriented and less prone
to open their societies, then surely "better Nasser than the Ba'ath."
Better still is "Sadat rather than the Ba'ath." Again, this is all
with the wisdom of hindsight, but the point is crucially important.
The theory of political development has overemphasized the party
and has underemphasized the state. This is true even of Nettl's
formulation, insofar as it deals with the Third World.[44] It is time
to change these research priorities.

Like it or not, the future shape of Middle East politics is
likely to take the form of a region of states. Conflict will not go
away; it will be conducted among states (hopefully tempered by reasons of state) and inside states (hopefully contained and restrained
within them). As for nonstate actors, the decline of pan-state ideologies vis-à-vis the state will accelerate and/or the ideologies will be
absorbed within the political structure of the state. As for a nonstate actor, such as the PLO, it wants to rule a state; it wants to do
so at the expense of another state; and its main strength (and its
main weakness, also) derives from the support it is able to mobilize from other states. Palestinian statehood eventually will have
to be settled, and will be settled, by states.

Though conflict is to continue, will there be a reconciliation
between nations and peoples ? No one can tell. The European experience indicates that if there is a reconciliation, it will follow
peace made by states, and not the other way round. The French
and German peoples were reconciled when the French and German
states made peace and entered an alliance; it would be absurd to
say that the peoples forced (or even encouraged) their governments
to make that peace. Similarly, the Egyptian and Israeli peoples did
not demand that their governments make peace. But when raison
d'état motivates statesmen to peacemaking, the road to reconciliation between peoples, and perhaps nations, is open. All the evidence indicates, however, that such breakthroughs are made by
states rather than by nations. Those who want peace should look to
a postnationalist era rather than to the demise of the state.

The best argument, then, for a back-to-the-state approach is simply that the state is a fact of life as a dominant actor in the regional scene for a long time to come, and those who have to live with this fact of life had better make sure that it is a "state with a human face." What are the chances for such a state? And what are the forces that will perhaps engrave such a face on the state?

In discussing these crucial questions, one needs to go back for a moment and recall why the state was supposed to have lost its human face in the first instance. As pointed out previously, Cassirer, lamenting the depraved condition of the state, attributed this condition to the fact that after Machiavelli the political world, the realm of the state, "lost its connection not only with religion or metaphysics but also with the other forms of man's ethical and cultural life."[45] This may or may not be a misreading of Machiavelli, but it is certainly a misreading of the tragedy of the modern state. The state is an instrument; it is the most powerful structural instrument human organization has ever possessed. As such, it is susceptible to abuse and misuse, to corruption and perversion. Need one speak further about the possibility of the perversion of the state in the century of Stalin and of Hitler, the century of the concentration camp and the gas chamber? The causes of the perversion of the state are as diverse as human nature. The argument that the depraved condition is due to the disconnection of the state from human ethics, religion, and culture is simply not adequately supported by the historical evidence. While it is true that power for its own sake, when possessed by a state, produces depraved conditions, far worse conditions have been created by the violent clash of human cultural, religious, and ethical systems, untempered, unrestrained, and uncontrolled by states. Worst of all is the rampage of a state infused with the ideals of the nation or of a social system, which it executes with a missionary zeal. The real extreme perversions of the state (fascism and totalitarianism) have been generated not by a disconnection from cultural, religious, and metaphysical systems, but rather by too close a connection between the state and such systems, when the terrifying power of the modern state has been absolutely dedicated and totally mobilized in pursuit of the goals of such systems. A German state seeking power for its own sake is bad; worse is a German state propagating the ambitious goals of the German nation; worst is a German state infused with the messianic mission of national socialism. The Nazi version of the depraved condition (probably the worst such example in history) was the perversion of the state by metaphysics penetrating the state. Far from being "lost," the connection was too close.

As to the postcolonial state in the Third World, no amount of cynical abuse of state power could have led to what metaphysical zeal produced in Cambodia. In murdering between one-fifth and one-sixth of the population and literally enslaving most of the rest, the Khmer Rouge regime perpetrated a quasigenocidal campaign of coercion and repression, in the name of an ideology dedicated to the establishment of a certain social system. This is the real depraved condition. The connection of the state with metaphysical and other cultural and social systems has produced all too many such perversions.

Yet, needless to say, such cultural and social systems of thought are at the very heart of civilization—but then, so is the state. The same human imperatives that create society and social systems of thought also naturally produce the political association, the state. As Ibn Khaldun put it, "Human civilization certainly needs political government by which its affairs are arranged in proper order";[46] and (following Aristotle), "human association is necessary; the philosophers express this in saying: 'man is a citizen by nature.' This means that association is indispensable; it is civilization. . . ."[47] Thus, the depraved condition can be overcome only by studying (and eventually perhaps reforming) the state in its proper context. As the state is the only human institution that makes civilization possible, the science of the state must be, as it was for Ibn Khaldun, the science of humanity.[48] What does this mean in concrete, contemporary terms?

There are many paths to civilization and many contemporary variations thereof. These variations are expressed in nationalist, social, and cultural systems of great diversity. It has already been argued in some detail that when these systems overwhelm the state, infuse it with their zeal, and replace its logic with their own, disaster is likely to occur; but this does not mean, by any stretch of the imagination, that the state functions in a cultural vacuum. Rulers of states ultimately rule over people; these people are organized (sometimes by the state, often prior to its coming into being) into social and cultural systems and have their own beliefs, tenets, values, habits, and customs. While a state has no business (except at horrendous human and political cost) to take up the mission of propagating, imposing, and exporting these goals, values, and traditions, neither should it interfere internally with the pursuit of happiness for individuals and groups according to the dictates of the system they believe in. Stateness means that the state elite should be properly concerned with looking after the welfare of the citizens, not that it should define for them what that welfare is nor how they should pursue their happiness. Stateness is not identical with étatisme. By definition, for a political structure to be statelike it must remain autonomous, at least to the extent of not being captured by social forces, but this autonomy cuts both ways: the state should

not attempt to overwhelm the other structures that are also entitled
to their autonomy.

Terrible political consequences flow from the subversion of
the logic of state by social, religious, and national logics in the
proper realm of the state—peace and war, security and law, welfare and the well-being of the citizens. Terrible moral consequences flow from the intrusion of the logic of state into the proper
realms of other social systems, for state logic cannot define the
meaning of group connections, human values, and metaphysical relations. The saliency of the state does not mean preemption by the
state of all spheres of human activity, but a dogged defense of the
right to conduct its affairs in its proper realm according to its own
logic; if this is prevented, other spheres of civilization will also be
unable to function. But the autonomy must be mutual. Just as the
state cannot subjugate its logic and interests, other structures must
not give up their values and logic in their own proper spheres. Each
is supreme in its own kingdom, so to speak; obsequiousness in the
face of others only breeds contempt. Note Nasser's account of his
experience with some Egyptian intellectuals in 1955:

> I remember visiting once one of our universities where
> I called the professors together and sat with them in
> order to benefit from their scholastic experience.
> Many of them spoke before me and at great length. It
> was unfortunate that none of them advanced any ideas,
> instead each confined himself to advancing himself to
> me, pointing out his unique fitness for making miracles.
> Each of them kept glancing at me with the look of one
> who preferred me to all the treasures of earth and
> heaven. [49]

Nasser's contempt is obvious and justified. Rather than proudly asserting their roles, ideas, values, and preferences in their own
realms, the intellectuals evidently wanted to flatter their way into
the realm of state, where different values and a different logic reign
supreme. A statesman must not be guided in questions of state and
war by intellectuals pursuing their abstract reasoning; an intellectual, seeking truth, must be guided not by reasons of state but by
the logic and truth of science, which is a distinctly different paradigm. [50]

Indeed, the state (and state rule) is a complex phenomenon.
It is based on power and is guided by considerations of power, but
it is anchored in a much more complicated environment.

> The theory of the ruling class tends to present society
> as divided into two strata, rulers and ruled, few and

many. We have also seen that there are few and many, but a definition of our rule and of ruling processes brings us far afield from the simplicity of concepts envisaged by Mosca and Pareto. The only conclusion we can formulate at this point is that the varieties of rule are endless—and the demands which enter into them are endless. What seemed so simple or so logical, even to investigators of but a few years ago, is far more complex than was imagined by the first scholars who visualized the problem. For such problems are not merely historical, as Tocqueville and Taine believed, though they are, inter alia, historical: they are not purely constitutional, though they are also constitutional; they are not simply sociological within the meanings embraced by Pareto and Mannheim, though they are sociological. They are also, as Durkheim and de Grazia saw, moral and philosophical problems; they are problems of culture as well, when the term is used in the vague, endless and rationalizing meaning employed by Elliot. [51]

The universe of a ruling state elite has at least two dimensions. Better put, members of a state elite live simultaneously in more than one world. Their primary responsibility (the other face of power) is to the state, its interests, reason, and logic. In this particular world, they probably have more in common with statesmen in other countries than with their own people outside the realm of state, for stateness has universal features of its own. At the same time, in their "other world," statesmen must protect the well-being of the society in their states. Ultimately, the security and prosperity within the state must yield fruits for society. The state must allow society to evolve, change, and develop; for this, favorable external conditions must be secured and sufficient resources provided. But, again, the logic of state and the logic of society are separate; both must be allowed as much free play as possible. On this both Nasser and Ben-Gurion were somewhat ambivalent. Nasser, for example, observed: "We live in a society that has not yet taken form. It is still fluid and agitated and has not yet settled down or taken a stabilized shape."[52] This being the case, he went on to conclude:

Our people are now like a caravan which seeks to follow a certain route, but the route is long, and the diversions to be encountered are many. Thieves and highwaymen may hold it up, and the mirage mislead it

from the true way. The caravan, as a result, might
be dispersed. Groups might go astray one way or the
other, and individuals scatter in different directions.

This, then, is our role, the situation being what
it is—to gather together the scattered and stray parts
and help them take one way, the right way. When this
is done, when dangers are allayed, the caravan is left
then to proceed in peace and security along the proper
way.

This is our role, and I cannot conceive it to be
otherwise. [53]

This role, however, can indeed be conceived otherwise. The
role of the state (and in fulfilling this role, state logic should yield
to nothing) is to protect the caravan against thieves and highwaymen,
to allay the dangers, to make sure the caravan may safely proceed;
the goal must indeed be for the caravan to be "left to proceed in
peace and security along the proper way." But the proper way is
not for the state to map. The state must only provide an arena in
which a controlled interplay of social and cultural forces eventually
works out—through social dialectics—what the proper way is. The
task of the state is big enough of itself, and must not be expanded
to include the deciding of proper ways. The state is a product of
society; it must protect society; it must enable social conflict and
evolution to follow their natural course. The state cannot substitute for society, just as society (or nation) cannot substitute for the
state. Nasser goes on to an extreme when he refers to a social
"mission with which Fate has entrusted us."[54]

Similarly, in listening to Ben-Gurion in 1969 bemoaning that
Israel "is not a nation, not yet. . . . It cannot be considered a nation until the Negev and Galilee are settled; until millions of Jews
immigrate to Israel; and until moral standards necessary to the
ethical practice of politics and the high values of Zionism are sustained,"[55] one must guard against an almost mystical blurring of
the boundary between state and society. A Jewish state can help
settle the Negev and Galilee only up to a point; it can help facilitate
the immigration of millions of Jews to Israel, but only to a limited
extent. The intrusion of the state into the realm of ethics would be
altogether inappropriate; moral standards and high values cannot be
"manufactured" by the state at all, but must derive from the authentic tradition of the people. The Israeli state cannot allow historical
and national traditions to subvert its raison d'état in settling the
question of realistic boundaries; Jewish historical and national traditions cannot allow the state (any state—even a Jewish one) to dictate to them moral standards or ethical values. To reiterate the
argument: stateness is not étatisme.

To be sure, the state may play an educating role in times of rapid social change. In fact, the Ben-Gurionist conception of the state as an educational institution[56] is a proper one, if not pushed to a logical, Platonic extreme. The state, its institutions, and its challenges are excellent frameworks for allowing Jews to realize the values that conditions in the diaspora denied them. But the Jewish state cannot and should not make Jews wish to realize any particular set of values that are not part of authentic Jewish tradition, any more than Nasser's state could or should have set the correct course for the caravan of Egyptian society. Up to a point, the postcolonial state as educator amidst social change is a useful and reasonable option; beyond that point, the dangers of étatisme, totalitarianism, and other perversions of the state loom large.

A country does not live by raison d'état alone; such a life would be very poor indeed. But that part of its political structure that belongs properly to the realm of state should be guided by reasons of state. Other possibilities are worse. It is bad enough that one needs to concede so much strength to a structure that is basically coercive, centralized, and extractive. Mixing the logic of this structure with that of other systems, however, merely creates more confusion and political incoherence.

How does this argument fit with the observation that both Islam and Judaism are totalistic civilizations that demand the allegiance of the faithful in all spheres of human activity, and that the formal separation of state and church is practicable in neither? The contradiction is more apparent than real. Political communities will continue in the future to be defined in the Middle East according to religious criteria, among others. Ruling elites in states will continue to claim allegiance to Islam and Judaism, and constitutional/ juridical decisions will be greatly influenced by religious heritage. This need not directly impinge on raison d'état.

Yet raison d'état can never be absolute. Statesmanship derives in part from the political realm, in which stateness indeed has many universal features, shared by state elites (and other statelike political participants) practically everywhere. The drive for power and the management of the power-state dictate a logic and morality of their own. At the same time, those who run the state and periodically have to define what raison d'état actually means live in a given culture and society and are the products of concrete and specific social and intellectual conditions. How do these political and cultural spheres merge in statecraft?

A clue to the answer—as to so many others—is to be found in the profound thought of Ibn Khaldun. Ibn Khaldun realized that the type of state he lived in was a power-state (mulk), and that in a power-state (and every state in the Middle East today conforms to

the mulk in Ibn Khaldun's typology) the interest of the state over-
rides any other consideration. The interests of the state are paramount, because in order to discharge the responsibility of the ruler
for the state, its safety, order, and welfare, that ruler must have
sufficient power. [57] Thus far, Ibn Khaldun and Machiavelli are in
agreement, but since the former is constrained beyond this point by
an extra, Islamic, dimension to the theory of the state, Machiavelli
would go much further than Ibn Khaldun, who held to Muslim ethics.
As Rosenthal puts it,

> Necessità, political necessity in the interests of the
> state, demanded by "Reason of State," made Machia-
> velli condone morally reprehensible actions, such as
> violence, treason, breach of faith and even murder.
> For Ibn Khaldun these are evil and bound to recoil not
> only on the perpetrators but on the state as a whole;
> they must prove injurious in the end. Machiavelli
> recognizes that they are bad, but he deems them use-
> ful for the state, and for that reason justifiable. [58]

It is inevitable that statesmen have to face such dilemmas
throughout their careers. The proper role of religion (and, indeed, any other cultural system concerned with ethics) in resolving these dilemmas is the one assigned by Ibn Khaldun. No consideration derived from religion can override the paramount interest
of the state, but when the question is, What means are to be used?
in order to realize these interests, not everything is permissible.
The theorist of raison d'état holds to Muslim ethics, and morally
reprehensible extreme acts are not acceptable. Such acts are not
only reprehensible from the ethical point of view, but they must
also prove injurious, in the long run, because statecraft is not conducted in a moral or social vacuum; an Islamic state cannot pursue
its interests in ways that are non-Islamic or anti-Islamic. The responsibility of looking after the well-being of the community cannot
be properly discharged in ways that blatantly contradict the dearest
values, values that constitute the very moral fiber of the community.
    The thin dividing line here between what is permissible and
what is forbidden in the name of raison d'état is also an intricate
one. Ibn Khaldun himself was apparently troubled by the specifics
involved, but he held steadfastly to the principle that raison d'état
cannot permit that which Muslim ethics forbids. Note, however,
the implicit logic of the argument: it is not a situation where raison
d'état demands one thing, and Islamic ethics another; it is not as if
rulers were tempted to do something that may have proved to be
good for the community but were prevented from doing so by the

prohibitions of Islam. In the long run, such a contradiction cannot exist; whatever is forbidden by Muslim ethics not only cannot be good for the community—the well-being of which the state must safeguard—but, in fact, must prove to be injurious. This is the basis of the proper role of religious and cultural ethics in the state. Thus, not only is there a necessity for a series of ethical constraints on raison d'état, but, in fact, the very definition of raison d'état must carry—in addition to the universal components derived from the political culture of power as a generic phenomenon—a moral dimension derived from the values of the community in which the state is anchored. There is much truth in the universalization of Ibn Khaldun's thesis: the raison d'état of an Islamic state cannot be defined in ways that necessitate utilizing means contradicting the teachings of Islam. Equally, the raison d'état of a Jewish state cannot be defined in ways that necessitate means reprehensible to Judaism. The same should apply to other ethical constructs such as Christianity and socialism.

Careful attention must be paid, however, to the logic of Ibn Khaldun's argument and its implications. What is argued and implied is not that Islam should define the raison d'état of the power-state. Nor is there an argument that the reasons of state must give way to the reasons of religion, morality, or any other system. What is argued and implied is that a golden path must be found in which raison d'état reigns supreme, but is tempered and refined by Islamic ethics. Islam does not invade, subvert, overwhelm, or capture the state; it accepts its supremacy (in its proper sphere) so long as the logic of state takes into consideration the ethical constraints of Islam. This does not mean that Islam (or Judaism) can define boundaries and decide questions of systems of taxation, administrative practices, diplomacy, alliances, and other matters of statecraft. These must be defined and decided by the state (which is ultimately responsible for looking after the safety and well-being of its citizens—Muslims, Jews, or Christians); but when the decisions are made, and definitions formulated, statesmen must not forget that they are Muslims or Jews, that the state is but an instrument for the benefit of the communities of which they are integral parts, and that while their autonomy extends very far indeed, it does not extend so far as to violate the ethics of the community. The universality of power is complemented by the particularism of morality. Machiavelli's dilemma, "Can a Christian prince be a prince while remaining Christian?" is resolved by Ibn Khaldun: yes, a prince can remain Christian (or Jewish, or Muslim). True, he cannot run a state on the basis of Christianity, Judaism, or Islam. In his pursuit of the interest of the state, Christianity, Judaism, or Islam cannot tell him what to do, but they can tell him what not to do. Their ethics cannot dictate <u>raison d'état</u>, but they can restrict the means employed to pursue <u>raison d'état</u>. In this (perhaps limited, but nonetheless very significant) sense, the prince is still a Christian (or Muslim or Jew). This is not to say that society merely restrains the state, nor that the relationship is simply dialectical. While the negative impact of restraint is more visible, immediate, and frequent, at the same time there is also a positive, if less salient, input of social values to the state. With this dual contribution the nation (or religion, or culture) not only circumscribes the state, but also enriches it, without assaulting its integrity.

Even this positive aspect of society's contribution can, however, pervert the role of the state, if taken to an extreme. Hannah Arendt laments: "Nationalism is essentially the expression of this perversion of the state into an instrument of the nation and the identification of the citizen with the member of the nation."[59] Indeed, this perversion of the state by the nation (or religion) is dangerous and must be avoided. But this need not create a depraved condition in which the state loses connection with ethics altogether.

The connection with ethics (of the kind propagated by Ibn Khaldun) must stem from the nature of the community. The community in a state tends to be a nation. The case of the Middle East supplies at least partial evidence to support Nettl's contention that "if the entry of the third world onto the stage of modern socioscientific consciousness has had one immediate result (or should have had), it is the snapping of the link between state and nation. What were awkward exceptions before . . . have now become almost a rule of non-nation-states."[60] On the other hand, states without political communities tend to be empty shells. There is at least a partial truth in Carl Friedrich's generalization that "such is the dialectic of the political that the state seeks, and must seek, to foster the growth of a nation, indeed must posit its potential coming into being."[61] If this is true, and if the ethical constraints on <u>raison d'état</u> stem from the morality of such communities, it is better to have such communities based on an authentic historical experience rather than on a mindless imitation of Western norms or on a synthetic fabrication by the state, which is often devoid of either authenticity or morality.

This point is argued <u>in extremis</u> by Professor Y. Leibowitz who, in an unduly harsh critique of modern-day Israel, cries out:

> The character of Israeli society and of its statehood
> have been decided by the fact that 3 million human be-
> ings of Jewish origin define themselves in Israel as a
> new people without history and without tradition, with-
> out ideology or values. All this is lacking because this
> people is made up of Jews who in the great majority (or

at least their elites) break the link with the essential
content of the historic Jewish people, namely with
Judaism. . . . It is not a Jewish people which builds
a state for itself, but a state which builds a people for
itself. Therefore, the only collective national content,
the only collective value, is the State. . . . The national content does not express itself except as a
patriotic nationalism which becomes the "religion" of
this [new] people. . . . Israeli society, detached
from Judaism, cannot fill its own national framework
except with content taken from the West. . . . But
Western culture cannot appear in the Israeli context
except as an imitation, often as a caricature of itself.
It does not show the best but the worst aspects of
Western culture, such as the permanent search for
the pleasures of an ever-rising standard of self-
fulfilling material life; such as an extremist form of
humanism, paralyzed in its social sensitivity, bestial-
ized by entertainment, sport, eroticism and pornog-
raphy; such as a fanatic enthusiasm and reverence for
military heroism. [62]

Brutal words, indeed. If they seem but a more sophisticated
variation of Khomeini's critique of the Shah's Iran, [63] this is no coincidence. It is the revolt of the man of tradition against what
Segre calls cultural "self-colonization," [64] which means (in the
case of the Jews) "ideological dependence upon alien culture, the
sterilization of its own, and the massive switch of Jewish brains
from fields of interest and research connected with Judaism to those
of the Gentile world." [65] This is a very complex process common
to most of the Third World:

The reason is to be found not only in the psychological
dilemma of the love/hate relationship which charac-
terizes the victim/victimizer situation but in the very
nature of Europe's colonization of the world, an historical phenomenon which "was neither a chain of crimes
nor a chain of beneficence; it was the birth of the modern world itself." In consequence, dependent peoples,
including the Jews, demanded—despite all ideological
resistance—more and not less Europeanization. It is,
after all, one of the characteristics of the modern
world that all groups with any kind of common political
self-consciousness tend to be politically independent,
even if their "nationhood" is an accident of very recent
history. [66]

Such self-colonization, it might be argued, is inevitable in the sphere of stateness. The modern world is a world of states; entry to the modern world necessitates stateness. The immense potential of the state as an instrument of power has proven to possess an irresistible appeal. Nor is the real problem the self-colonization of the state. The state may be a positive instrument for many worthwhile goals and is, after all, merely an instrumental structure. The real problem is the cultural content of the community in which the state is embedded. What is needed is probably an intellectual liberation movement leading to cultural nationalism in a political "kingdom of stateness." But if an impressive range of critics, from Leibowitz to Khomeini, find the present state of affairs deplorable, they have themselves (and their like-minded colleagues) to blame, at least as much as anyone else.

"Political science starts with a state and examines how it affects society, while political sociology starts with a society and examines how it affects the state, i.e., the formal institution for the distribution and exercise of power," according to Bendix and Lipset's definition.[67] Following this terminological distinction, both Islamic and Zionist thought in recent decades have produced a modicum of political sociology and even less in the way of political science. Despite the decades of the political revival of Islam and a preoccupation with the Jewish state in the Zionist movement, not much is known about the Islamic state or the Jewish state (not to mention the near-total bankruptcy of Arab nationalist ideology, which has no real theory of the state, either).

If Marxists today have the intellectual courage to admit that "it nevertheless remains true that the Marxist theory of the state is underdeveloped and . . . there remains much work to be done,"[68] Muslims and Jews could perhaps exercise at least a similar degree of self-criticism and confess that they do not really possess an adequate insight into what an Islamic or a Jewish state should be like. Having unavoidably and unequivocally adopted the state as the form of the political framework in which they must live in the foreseeable future, it remains for Jews and Muslims to work out what specifically Jewish or Islamic version of the state is to be realized in the real world of politics. Leibowitz is right in castigating the mindless emulation of Western forms of life in the Jewish state,[69] and is equally correct—as well as challenging, provocative, and stimulating—in making the distinction between a Jewish state and a state of Jews. But while his critique of the latter is persuasive, his passionate argument for the former is not. All he has to offer for a Jewish state is a return to obeying the cumulative body of traditional Jewish laws (the <u>Halakha</u>): something that the large majority of Israeli Jews are obviously not willing to do. The entire concept of fusing the state (which knows no Judaism) and Judaism (which knows no state) escapes Leibowitz—or, perhaps more correctly, it is denied by him. As Segre has observed,

> For Leibowitz there is no Jewish philosophy or ethics,
> or specifically Jewish political or social idea. . . .
> "The only specifically Jewish creation that actively ap-
> peared in history is the Halakha, that is, the attempt
> to organize the rules of human life against a background
> of law, the aim of which is the service of God."[70]

If there is no Jewish political idea of the state, there ought to be one; otherwise the question of the Jewish state will never be resolved. The return to the Halakha (a system born in a lack of stateness) is not acceptable to most Israeli Jews, while just another state that happens to be populated by Jews is inadequate, as Ben-Gurion used to say:

> Only by being a model nation of which every Jew,
> wherever he is, can be proud, shall we preserve the
> love of the Jewish people and its loyalty to Israel.
> Our status in the world, too, will not be determined
> by our material wealth or by our military valour, but
> by the radiance of our achievement, our culture, our
> society—and only by virtue of these will we acquire
> the friendship of the nations.[71]

But this statement, too, remains on the level of vague generality. It is all very well to say that the Jewish state cannot be like others, but must have a specifically Jewish character, whether as a model society or a community of the Halakha. As the state is a concrete, modern structure, how is fusion with the values of Judaism to be accomplished? What is there in the Jewish political tradition that is pertinent to building a contemporary state? How does a Jewish state differ from other states? What does a large non-Jewish minority do in a state that is dedicated to Jewish values? How are Israeli Jews who want neither to return to the rigor of the Halakha nor to be "better" than other peoples, but simply to enjoy a measure of security and prosperity attainable in the Western countries, to be persuaded to be a model nation? The basic question needs to be asked again and again: how does the Zionist enterprise make the transition from a state of Jews to a Jewish state?

Substitute "Muslim" for "Jew," "Islam" for "Judaism" in the above formulation, and there is an almost uncanny similarity to the concept of the Islamic state. There have been many states of Mus-

lims, but where is the Muslim state? Khomeini's critique of the
Shah's regime bears an astonishing resemblance to Leibowitz's
outburst against modern Israel: less systematic, more mythical,
less sophisticated; but equally clear, blunt, and brutal. The alternative offered (the Islamic republic) is a Muslim version of the
return to the Halakha, and is currently being violently implemented,
at enormous human cost. The state is given but little serious
thought and analysis, and it is evident that Khomeini's revolutionaries do not really know what to do with it.

The fact is that despite frenzied Zionist and Islamic political
activity, neither Zionism in Israel, nor Islam in the Arab countries
and Iran (not to mention Turkey), has developed a political science,
a science of state (which, to Ibn Khaldun, was the science of civilization and humanity). For Israeli, Arab, and Iranian political
thinkers, there is no more significant challenge than to delve into
the very depths of this concept and to generate some creative and
viable options. For this, however, they need a respite from the
incessant violence that has plagued the Middle East for so long.
The state—with all its unresolved problems—may be on the way to
creating such a respite, however partial, if only for reasons of its
own.

The Arab-American scholar, Edward N. Said, is clearly
right when he says of the Middle East:

> To this huge mound of imponderables it has been cus-
> tomary to bring political analysis armed mainly with
> ideological cliches of a frightening simplicity. Rarely
> have the concepts of justice, realism and compassion
> played any role in attempts to think about the Middle
> East. In the end, it is the most basic human instru-
> ment that will bring peace, and certainly that instru-
> ment is not a fighter plane or a rifle butt. This in-
> strument is self-conscious, rational struggle con-
> ducted in the interests of human community. [72]

In the Middle East, the human community is organized in
states that in following their self-conscious, rational interests have
already achieved a partial (though admittedly fragile and vulnerable)
peace. It is to be hoped (for it is yet unproven) that such a pursuit
of their interests will broaden and stabilize peace. In any case,
the state as the basic form of political organization will be a fact
of life for a long time to come. It is up to the peoples of the Middle
East in general, and the intellectuals among them in particular, to
see to it that theirs are states with authentic human faces.

NOTES

1. Max Weber, "Politics as a Vocation," in From Max Weber: Essays in Sociology, ed. H. H. Gerth and C. Wright Mills (New York: Oxford University Press, 1946), p. 128.

2. Reinhard Bendix, Nation-Building and Citizenship (New York: Wiley, 1964), p. 13.

3. Ibid.

4. Nazli Choucri, "Forecasting International Relations: Problems and Prospects," International Interactions 1 (2) (1974): 63-86, quoted in Raymond Cohen and Saul Friedlander, "A Taxonomy of Short-Term Forecasting Problems in International Relations," Hebrew University of Jerusalem, 1975, p. 3. Mimeographed.

5. Stein Rokkan, "Dimensions of State Formation and Nation Building: A Possible Paradigm for Research on Variations within Europe," in The Formation of National States in Western Europe, ed. Charles Tilly (Princeton, N.J.: Princeton University Press, 1975), p. 638.

6. Ibid.

7. Joseph Strayer, On the Medieval Origins of the Modern State (Princeton, N.J.: Princeton University Press, 1970); and idem, Medieval Statecraft and the Perspectives of History (Princeton, N.J.: Princeton University Press, 1971).

8. Rokkan, "Dimensions of State Formation," p. 637.

9. Ibid.

10. Charles Tilly, "Reflections on the History of European State-Making," in The Formation of National States in Western Europe, ed. Charles Tilly (Princeton, N.J.: Princeton University Press, 1975), pp. 81-82.

11. Rokkan, "Dimensions of State Formation," pp. 637-38.

12. Tilly, "Reflections," p. 69.

13. Ibid., p. 27. Even Tilly's comments on fragmentation and the dominance of the state (pp. 28-29) have a distinctly contemporary ring in Middle East politics, as do Strayer's comments on the mosaic versus unitary regnum in relation to stateness. (Strayer, Medieval Statecraft, pp. 346-47.)

14. Cf. Samuel E. Finer, "State- and Nation-Building in Europe: The Role of the Military," in The Formation of National States in Western Europe, ed. Charles Tilly (Princeton, N.J.: Princeton University Press, 1975), pp. 84-163.

15. Tilly, "Reflections," p. 52.

16. Even the most statelike Arab country, Egypt, has had a good part of its frontier system determined by European manipulation. See Gabriel R. Warburg, "The Sinai Peninsula Borders, 1906-47," Journal of Contemporary History 14 (4) (October 1979): 677-92.

17. Tilly, "Reflections," p. 45.

18. Ibid., p. 38.

19. Ibid., p. 40.

20. Ibid., p. 29.

21. See Donald Eugene Smith, Religion and Political Development (Boston: Little, Brown, 1970).

22. Tilly, "Reflections," p. 71.

23. Ibid.

24. Ibid.

25. Ibid., p. 73.

26. See W. G. Runciman, Social Science and Political Theory (Cambridge: Cambridge University Press, 1965), especially Ch. 8, pp. 156-75.

27. See Gabriel Ben-Dor, "Military Regimes in the Arab World: Prospects and Patterns of Civilianization," Armed Forces and Society 1 (May 1975): 317-27.

28. This is discussed in detail in G. Ben-Dor, "The National Security Policy of Egypt," in Security Policies of Developing Countries, ed. Edward A. Kolodziej and Robert E. Harkavy (Lexington, Mass.: Heath, 1982).

29. See Waterbury, "Egypt: The Wages of Dependence"; Anwar al-Sadat, "The October Paper," al-Ahram, May 1, 1974; Gad Gilbar, "Egypt's Economy: The Challenge of Peace," Jerusalem Quarterly 12 (Summer 1979): 6-20; Haim Barkai, "Egypt's Economic Constraints," Jerusalem Quarterly 14 (Winter 1980): 122-44.

30. See Michael C. Hudson, The Precarious Republic (New York: Random House, 1968).

31. See Samuel P. Huntington, Political Order in Changing Societies (New Haven, Conn.: Yale University Press, 1968), especially Ch. 1.

32. See Anthony D. Smith, Nationalism in the Twentieth Century (London: Martin Robertson, 1979); and Karl W. Deutsch, Tides Among Nations (New York: Free Press, 1979).

33. Needless to say, any but the most determinist social scientist will admit that this is a result of concrete political conditions in Europe that may significantly change in time. Thus, this is not an irreversible process.

34. Clement Henry Moore, Politics in North Africa (Boston: Little, Brown, 1970), p. 34.

35. See Benjamin Akzin, State and Nation (London: Hutchinson University Library, 1964).

36. Marion J. Levy, Jr., Modernization and the Structure of Societies (Princeton, N.J.: Princeton University Press, 1960), pp. 743-44. For a thorough critique of this approach, see C. S. Whitaker, Jr., "A Dysrhythmic Process of Political Change," World Politics 19 (2) (January 1967): 190-217.

37. See Serif Mardin, "Center-Periphery Relations: A Key to Turkish Politics?" in Post-Traditional Societies, ed. S. N. Eisenstadt (New York: Norton, 1972).

38. See Rupert Emerson, From Empire to Nation: The Rise to Self-Assertion of Asian and African States (Cambridge, Mass.: Harvard University Press, 1960).

39. See G. Ben-Dor, "Unity and Disunity in the Arab World," Monthly Review 9 (September 1973): 3-13 (in Hebrew) for an elaboration of these characteristics and their relative lack of political efficacy.

40. There is a broad variety of approaches to this question. A huge literature is cited in Juergen Dedring, Recent Advances in Peace and Conflict Research: A Critical Survey (Beverly Hills and London: Sage, 1976), pp. 84-98; and in Karl W. Deutsch, The Analysis of International Relations (Englewood Cliffs, N.J.: Prentice-Hall, 1968), pp. 198-276. See also Daniel Elazar, ed., Self-Rule/Shared Rule: Federal Solutions to the Middle East Conflict (Ramat Gan: Turtledove, 1979). The latter volume contains many pertinent comments on the case of the Middle East.

41. See Huntington, Political Order in Changing Societies, and the critique in G. Ben-Dor, "Institutionalization and Political Development: A Conceptual and Theoretical Analysis," Comparative Studies in Society and History 18 (3) (1975): 309-56.

42. Samuel P. Huntington, "Political Development and Political Decay," World Politics 17 (3) (April 1965): 430-86.

43. Machiavelli, "States must be founded or reformed by a powerful individual." The Discourses (New York: Modern Library, 1950), p. 138.

44. J. P. Nettl, "The State as a Conceptual Variable," World Politics 20 (July 1968): 559-92.

45. Ernst Cassirer, The Myth of the State (Garden City, N.Y.: Doubleday, 1955), p. 140.

46. Ibn Khaldun, quoted in Erwin I. J. Rosenthal, Political Thought in Medieval Islam: An Introductory Outline (Cambridge: Cambridge University Press, 1958), p. 93.

47. Quoted in ibid., p. 86.

48. Ibid., pp. 84-85. See also Muhsin Mahdi, Ibn Khaldun's Philosophy of History (London: Allen and Unwin, 1957).

49. Gamal Abdel Nasser, The Philosophy of the Revolution (Cairo: no publisher, no date), p. 37.

50. See Kuhn, The Structure of Scientific Revolutions (Chicago: University of Chicago Press, 1968).

51. Renzo Sereno, The Rulers (New York: Harper, 1962), p. 176.

52. Nasser, The Philosophy of the Revolution, p. 68.

53. Ibid., p. 71.

54. Ibid., p. 73.

55. Quoted in Amos Perlmutter, "Redemption, Colonialization and Partition"; "The Political Strategy and Struggle of Yishuv in Palestine, 1917-1947," in Israel: The Partitioned State and Its Challenges, 1917-1980. One of a series of papers given at the Lehrman Institute in New York, 1979-80.

56. A parallel to Ben-Gurion's reeducation of the Jewish masses would be the Egyptian emphasis on creating "the new Egyptian man." See Hamed Ammar, On Building Human Beings: Studies in Cultural Change and Educational Thought (Beirut: 1964) (in Arabic); and Nissim Rejwan, "Culture and Personality: Building the New Egyptian Man," The New Middle East 41 (February 1972): 16-18.

57. Rosenthal, Political Thought in Medieval Islam, p. 107.

58. Ibid.

59. Hannah Arendt, The Origins of Totalitarianism (New York: Harcourt, Brace, Jovanovich, 1973), p. 231.

60. Nettl, "The State as a Conceptual Variable," p. 560.

61. Carl I. Friedrich, Man and His Government (New York: McGraw-Hill, 1963), p. 551.

62. Letter to the Editor, Haaretz, May 27, 1975. (English version from Dan V. Segre, A Crisis of Identity: Israel and Zionism (New York: Oxford University Press, 1980).

63. See Ayatollah Ruhollah Khomeini, Islamic Government (no publishers, no date).

64. Segre, A Crisis of Identity, pp. 8-9.

65. Ibid., p. 8.

66. Ibid., p. 9. The reference in the quote is to Rupert Emerson, "The Passing of the European Order," Encounter 9 (November 1957), quoted in Emerson, From Empire to Nation, p. 84. See also Albert Memmi, The Colonizer and the Colonized (Boston: Beacon Press, 1965); and Frantz Fanon, The Wretched of the Earth (New York: Grove Press, 1968).

67. Reinhard Bendix and Seymour Martin Lipset, "Political Sociology: An Essay and Bibliography," Current Sociology 6 (2) (1957): 79-99.

68. Leo Panitch, "The Role and Nature of the Canadian State," in The Canadian State: Political Economy and Political Power, ed. Leo Panitch (Toronto and Buffalo: University of Toronto Press, 1979), pp. 6-7.

69. For an elaboration, see G. Ben-Dor, "Crisis in Israeli Society," Middle East Focus 4 (May 1981): 19-23.

70. Segre, A Crisis of Identity, p. 95.

71. David Ben-Gurion, speech at the Jerusalem Ideological
Conference, 1958, published in Forum for the Problems of Zionism,
Jewry and the State of Israel 4 (Spring 1959): 121; quoted in Segre,
A Crisis of Identity, p. 94.

72. Edward N. Said, New York Times, November 19, 1979
(quoted in Amos Perlmutter, "The Second Partitioned State," in
Israel: The Partitioned State and Its Challenges, 1917-1980, one
of a series of papers given at the Lehrman Institute in New York,
1979-80, pp. 60-61). Said argues in the remainder of what he says
in defense of the Palestinian cause, which does not affect the basic
thesis. It must be acknowledged, however, that the present author's
argument applies to a somewhat different context.

About the Author

GABRIEL BEN-DOR is Professor of Political Science and Deputy Rector at the University of Haifa, Israel, where he has taught Political Science and Middle Eastern Studies since 1972. He was chairman of the Department of Political Science and Director of the Institute of Middle Eastern Studies at that institution. In 1979-81 he was visiting Professor of Political Science and International Affairs at Carleton University in Ottawa, Canada.

Dr. Ben-Dor is the author of The Druzes in Israel: A Political Study, editor and co-author of The Palestinians and the Middle East Conflict, co-editor and co-author of Political Participation in Turkey. He has published numerous articles in scholarly journals in the fields of Middle East Politics, The Arab-Israeli Conflict, Political Development, and the Study of Military Regimes.

Dr. Ben-Dor holds a B.A. from Hamline University, St. Paul, Minnesota and an M.A. and Ph.D. from Princeton University, Princeton, New Jersey.